AF787018

National perspectives on a multipolar order

MANCHESTER
1824
Manchester University Press

National perspectives on a multipolar order

Interrogating the global power transition

Edited by

Benjamin Zala

Manchester University Press

Copyright © Manchester University Press 2021

While copyright in the volume as a whole is vested in Manchester University Press, copyright in individual chapters belongs to their respective authors, and no chapter may be reproduced wholly or in part without the express permission in writing of both author and publisher.

Published by Manchester University Press
Altrincham Street, Manchester M1 7JA

www.manchesteruniversitypress.co.uk

British Library Cataloguing-in-Publication Data
A catalogue record for this book is available from the British Library

ISBN 978 1 5261 5937 3 hardback

First published 2021

The publisher has no responsibility for the persistence or accuracy of URLs for any external or third-party internet websites referred to in this book, and does not guarantee that any content on such websites is, or will remain, accurate or appropriate.

Typeset
by New Best-set Typesetters Ltd

Contents

List of figures — *page* vi
List of contributors — vii
Acknowledgements — viii
List of abbreviations — ix

Introduction: The utility and limits of polarity analysis – Benjamin Zala — 1

Part I: Rising and re-emerging powers

1 'Mirror, mirror on the wall': China and the concept of multipolarity in the post-Cold War era – Nicholas Khoo and Zhang Qingmin — 21
2 India: Seeking multipolarity, favouring multilateralism, pursuing multialignment – Ian Hall — 42
3 Brazil: Pursuing a multipolar mirage? – Luis L. Schenoni — 65
4 Multipolarity in Russia: A philosophical and practical understanding – Elena Chebankova — 94

Part II: The unipole and its allies

5 Does the United States face a multipolar future? Washington's response through the lens of technology – James Johnson — 121
6 Japan and the dangers of multipolarisation – H. D. P. Envall — 144
7 The uses and abuses of the polarity discourse in UK foreign and defence politics – David Blagden — 169

Conclusion: Debating the distribution of power and status in the early twenty-first century – Benjamin Zala — 196

Index — 211

List of figures

3.1 GDP (PPP) of the US and BRICS, 2000 and 2015. Source: Based on International Monetary Fund, 'IMF data', 2017, www.imf.org/en/Data. *page* 70
3.2 Military expenditure of the US and BRICS, 2000 and 2015. Source: Based on Stockholm International Peace Research Institute, 'SIPRI military expenditure database', www.sipri.org/databases/milex, 2016. 71
3.3 Measuring and mapping conceptual stretching. Source: Based on a survey conducted by the author in Brasilia during June 2017. The plot was designed using Mathpix http://grapher.mathpix.com/. 73
3.4 Use of the term 'multipolar' in the Brazilian Congress and the UNGA, 2000–15. Source: Based on an overview of Brazilian politicians' speeches to the Brazilian Congress and Brazilian diplomats' speeches to the United Nations General Assembly, 2000–15. 77
3.5 Use of the term 'multipolar' in academic journal articles, 2000–15. Source: Based on an overview of articles published in *Revista Brasileira de Política Internacional*, *Contexto Internacional*, and in journals with an impact factor of 0.4 or higher as reported in Thomson Reuters Journal Citation Reports 2000–15. 82

List of contributors

David Blagden is Senior Lecturer in the Strategy and Security Institute, Department of Politics, University of Exeter.

Elena Chebankova is Research Fellow in the Centre for Government and Public Management, Carleton University.

H. D. P. Envall is Fellow in the Department of International Relations, Coral Bell School of Asia Pacific Affairs, Australian National University.

Ian Hall is Professor in the School of Government and International Relations, Griffith University.

James Johnson is Assistant Professor in the Department of Law and Government, Dublin City University.

Nicholas Khoo is Associate Professor in the Politics Programme, University of Otago.

Zhang Qingmin is Professor in the School of International Studies, Peking University.

Luis L. Schenoni is Postdoctoral Researcher in the Department of Politics and Public Administration, University of Konstanz.

Benjamin Zala is Research Fellow in the Department of International Relations, Coral Bell School of Asia Pacific Affairs, Australian National University.

Acknowledgements

I am grateful to the wonderful and patient contributors for their excellent work on this volume. I would also like to thank Marylou Hickey for her crucial assistance in the production of the manuscript in addition to her encouragement and characteristic kindness throughout the project. My thanks also to David Brown, Natasha Kuhrt, Donette Murray, Jonathan de Peyer, Richard Sakwa, and Martin Smith for their involvement and advice at various stages of the project. Finally, I am immensely grateful to Rob Byron, Lucy Burns, and the team at Manchester University Press for their assistance and support, and to Anthony Mercer and Angela Grant for their excellent work on the copy-editing and the index respectively.

Ben Zala
Australian National University

List of abbreviations

AI	artificial intelligence
BRI	Belt and Road Initiative
BRICS	Brazil, Russia, India, China, and South Africa
CCP	Chinese Communist Party
COIN	counter-insurgency
CRA	Contingent Reserve Arrangement
CSD	collective self-defence
DARPA	Defense Advanced Research Projects Agency
DCDC	Development, Concepts, and Doctrine Centre
DIUx	Defense Innovation Unit Experimental
DoD	Department of Defense
DPJ	Democratic Party of Japan
EAC	East Asian Community
EAEU	Eurasian Economic Union
EU	European Union
FOIP	Free and Open Indo-Pacific
GDP	gross domestic product
GST	Global Strategic Trends
IMF	International Monetary Fund
INF	Intermediate-Range Nuclear Forces
LDP	Liberal Democratic Party (Japan)
IR	International Relations
MDP	Modernising Defence Programme
MOD	Ministry of Defence
NAM	Non-Aligned Movement
NATO	North Atlantic Treaty Organization
NDB	New Development Bank
NPCPRC	National People's Congress of the People's Republic of China
NSCR	National Security Capability Review
PPP	purchasing power parity
PSDB	Partido da Social Democracia Brasileira

PT	Partido dos Trabalhadores
RAF	Royal Air Force
RN	Royal Navy
SCO	Shanghai Cooperation Organisation
SDR	Strategic Defence Review
SDSR	Strategic Defence and Security Review
UK	United Kingdom of Great Britain and Northern Ireland
UN	United Nations
UNASUR	Union of South American Nations
UNGA	United Nations General Assembly
UNSC	United Nations Security Council
US	United States of America

Introduction: The utility and limits of polarity analysis

Benjamin Zala

In the International Relations (IR) literature, polarity analysis has had many critics but few serious rivals.[1] As one author has noted, it 'offers a stunningly bold way of simplifying the horrendous day-to-day complexities of world politics', by teasing out and pinpointing the fundamental outlines and features of the distribution of power in the inter-state order.[2] One does not need to be a dyed-in-the-wool structural realist to concede that the relations between major powers have a disproportionate impact in shaping the nature of the global order, and that therefore questions about how many major centres of power exist and the nature of their relations are likely to be important factors in world politics. Nor does taking the concept of polarity seriously mean adopting a purely state-centric view of the world. The contemporary global order is shaped by many factors and the social hierarchy between states (often referred to as the inter-state order) is but one, albeit particularly important, factor. Polarity analysis focuses on whether the inter-state order is dominated by one (unipolarity), two (bipolarity), or three or more (multipolarity) centres of power. While states remain important actors in world politics, and while their relations remain structurally anarchical yet socially hierarchical,[3] the number – or indeed absence – of major powers (or 'poles of power') that exist at any given time will continue to matter. While moments in which major power relations are particularly tense tend to result in an upsurge in the use of the concept,[4] assessing the polarity of international society and debating its implications has been, and will continue to be, a mainstay of IR scholarship.

This is reflected in the prevalence of the language of 'polarity', which is apparent in much of the public policy discourse on international affairs: from think tank[5] and private sector[6] reports, to the opinion pages of major newspapers,[7] and the ever-expanding roster of policy-focused blogs.[8] It is also regularly used by practitioners[9] in an effort to capture something of the shape of major power relations, thus making it, in Barry Buzan's words, 'one of those rare concepts used frequently in both the public policy *and* academic debates'.[10] *Contra* Richard Ned Lebow, who believes that '[p]olarity and its alleged consequences are almost entirely a fixation of Americans',[11] the chapters that follow demonstrate that the concept enjoys a global usage and is therefore unlikely to disappear as IR as a discipline continues to globalise.[12]

There are, however, a number of major deficiencies and blind spots in the existing polarity analysis literature. For example, there is little that explores the polarity debates in *both* the scholarly *and* practitioner realms with a view to developing conclusions about its substance, efficacy, and utility in national policy debates. This is, in a nutshell, what this volume seeks to do. In this sense, it may be useful to begin by distinguishing between polarity as an *analytical tool* deployed by scholars engaging in system-level theorising, and as an *ordering concept* used by practitioners.[13] While many of its advocates have tried to establish polarity analysis purely as a form of abstract, parsimonious system-level theorising, the reality is that the concept is not confined to such scholarship.[14] When world leaders and influential commentators talk about the world being unipolar, bipolar, or multipolar, they do so without regard for rigour or parsimony. Their statements are not accompanied by definitions of power, lists of objectively quantified capabilities, or clear thresholds over which a state must pass in order to become a pole of power.

Many of the problems with traditional polarity analysis relate to this issue of measurement. How do we know a pole of power when we see one? The difficulty in answering this question is that there is no objective and universally agreed upon set of criteria for pole status, despite various authors offering their own preferred lists over the years.[15] In turn, this lack of consensus over how to measure polarity leads to a phenomenon that has been insufficiently analysed and thus understood in the traditional literature: the reasons for, and consequences of, the existence of competing perceptions of polarity at the same time. In other words, analysts and practitioners can look at the same international system at the same point in time and describe it in fundamentally different terms: where one sees unipolarity, another identifies bipolarity, while yet another may perceive multipolarity.[16]

In this book, we are interested in investigating the role of multipolar narratives in different national contexts that exist despite the endurance of analyses that offer unipolar[17] (and to a lesser extent even bipolar)[18] assessments of the current order. Interestingly, these contemporary claims and debates about multipolarity have relatively recent precedent. This is a long-expected shift to a multipolar order. For example, in 1990, within months of the Berlin Wall coming down and before the dissolution of the Soviet Union, one study by leading IR scholars proclaimed that 'there can be no doubt that the extreme bipolar structure of the post-war decades is weakening steadily, and in some sectors dramatically, towards a multipolar one'.[19] They were followed by other leading advocates of polarity analysis making predictions about global and regional security based on the firm assumption that the 'natural' successor to the bipolar order would be a multipolar one.[20]

Yet, as what quickly became known as the 'post-Cold War order' (a phrase that captured what had passed but not what was present) progressed, this concept of a return to multipolarity vied with another in academic and popular analysis: unipolarity.[21] While Charles Krauthammer's famous temporal disclaimer of being a 'unipolar moment' was often attached to it, the now unrivalled material power and social status of the United States seemed to suggest that this was anything but a return to 'traditional' balance of power politics.[22]

A combination of the decisive US-led victory in the first Gulf War (1990–91), proclamations of a US-led 'revolution in military affairs', the growing focus on the 'Washington Consensus' on economic development, and the widespread cultural appeal of what came to be called American 'soft power' were all held up as evidence of a unipolar order. Yet despite these developments, it took some time for the scholarly IR community to fully embrace the concept of unipolarity. In large part this was a result of unipolarity being under-theorised in the polarity analysis literature. It was not supposed to occur.[23] The dominance of balance of power theorising in structural approaches to power in the discipline had led to the assumption that an almost automatic anti-hegemonial balancing mechanism would always be at work in the international system.[24]

While becoming the dominant way of characterising the inter-state order from at least the late 1990s onwards, unipolarity was never fully accepted as the most accurate description of the post-Cold War distribution of power. Samuel Huntington, for example, opted for the descriptor 'uni-multipolar' to describe a more complex configuration of relations amongst the leading and emerging powers of the time.[25] As a number of the national case studies included in this volume highlight, outside of the United States, visions of an extant or imminent multipolar order endured throughout this period. For those who clung to the notion of an objective measure of power, such ambiguity about the polarity of the day proved frustrating. By 2002, Stephen G. Brooks and William C. Wohlforth declared that 'if today's American primacy does not constitute unipolarity, then nothing ever will. The only things left for dispute are how long it will last and what the implications are for American foreign policy.'[26]

The issue of measuring polarity of any type leads inevitably to the question of which sources of power have the most salience today. Are we really in an age where economic capacity has become more important than military might? Are demographics the underlying driver of a shift towards a multipolar order? Is the traditional state-based conception of polarity too narrowly conceived for a potential new era of 'civilisational powers'? What about the analytical utility and value of the oft-discussed concept of 'soft power', and the wider social dimensions of power? While various scholars and commentators have offered their own answers to these questions, our approach in this book is to interrogate the words, policies, and actions of the powers – both established and emerging – themselves.

In this volume we are interested in the roles that contemporary narratives about a 'return to a multipolar order' play in the foreign policies of the actors with, potentially, the most to gain (and also, perhaps, lose) from the evolution of such an order. If we are to deal with the fact that the concept of polarity remains salient in public policy discourse, while being sensitive to the difficulties of providing rigorous scholarly analysis of a concept that defies easy definition, then turning to the discourse and actions of our subjects as the main source of empirical data becomes the most appropriate methodological move.

Power, polarity, and the conceptual framework of this book

The conceptual framework for this book does not rely on outlining a preferred combination of material indicators that should be used when defining power or 'pole' status. Instead, this volume represents an eclectic and varied approach to power. Some of the chapters that follow choose to draw a sharp distinction between their preferred view of power and that of their given subjects of analysis. These chapters, conceptually, align more closely with the traditional polarity literature even while emphasising the contested nature of a given national debate about multipolarity today. Others adopt a more constructivist approach to power, where being treated as a 'great power' by the other members of international society is the most relevant marker of pole status. This approach encourages the analyst to interrogate the ways in which decision-makers and those that influence them perceive polarity themselves, rather than engaging in abstract structural theorising or quantitative 'number crunching' in order to analyse the polarity of the international system as an objective 'fact'.

All of the chapters that follow are therefore focused on exploring the 'use and abuse' of multipolar narratives by policymakers and those that influence them in different national contexts. In other words, they adopt a specifically inductive approach to power that is guided first and foremost by the words and actions of those at the 'coalface' of international policy. The approach therefore has much in common with the way that power is treated by a number of scholars associated with the 'status turn' in IR that recognises that status – including great power or 'pole' status – is something conferred on an actor by others.[27] In this sense, as Steven Ward notes, status is an element of an identity narrative and those narratives are created and shaped in interaction with others (for example, through status accommodation behaviour).[28] This kind of approach is captured in what one account refers to as structural power, as distinct from relative (or relational) capabilities. Structural power, in this view, 'describes the balance of advantage built into systems of states' interactions'.[29]

For the purposes of analysing narratives of order, the system becomes multipolar not when three or more states hit a magic number in terms of their economies, militaries, and populations, but when they attain the position of being regarded by others as key order-producing states in their regions, or indeed globally. Their status in this respect will thus depend at least in part on how the other states and actors define both 'polarity' and 'order'. David Baldwin has argued that such approaches are consistent with a broadly Dahlian approach (building on the influential work on power by Robert Dahl) and, among other things: rely on situational analysis; distinguish between resources/capabilities and power itself; and focus attention on the difference between power as an abstract concept on the one hand, and on operational definitions on the other.[30] Such approaches can contain both materialist and ideational definitions of power in an abstract sense while recognising that these definitions are often used inconsistently, or not at all, by actors in the real world.

Our conceptual framework here is thus avowedly analytically eclectic. By engaging with the concept of polarity, in this case with a particular focus on multipolarity, our starting point is the kind of system-level analysis familiar to structural realists. But the chapters in this volume treat multipolarity not simply as an objective description of the distribution of capabilities, but as a flexible and multifaceted *concept* that can be, and is, used and potentially abused in different ways by its proponents and detractors, both within and between different states and societies. Therefore our approach also resonates with elements of the constructivist, English School, and neoclassical realist literatures that focus on perceptions,[31] great power status,[32] and strategic narratives.[33]

In order to get to grips with the way that contemporary concepts of multipolarity are being put to various uses in the foreign policy strategies of the states analysed in the chapters that follow, each author has been invited to organise their analysis around five key questions or question sets:

1 How prominent is the concept of multipolarity in the public discourse of decision-makers and opinion-formers? How do they actually define and describe multipolarity? Do they use different terms/words to describe the same thing? Have their conceptualisations changed over time and if so, how, why, and to what end?

2 Where relevant, how developed are the debates about multipolarity amongst the scholarly and analytical communities, and is there evidence of 'crossover' between these and the practitioner realm?
3 Is multipolarity mainly used as an *objective* description of how power *is* distributed, or as a *normative* aspiration for how power *should be* distributed?
4 In the discourse on multipolarity, is it clear which states are being considered as poles and which are not?
5 Has a discourse on multipolarity led to discernible policy changes at the governmental level? How have these been perceived by other states?

While the individual chapters approach these questions from different angles and the emphasis on one question over another varies in each case study, they all touch on each question in one way or another. This allows for a collective picture to build up of the contemporary debate over the distribution of power and status in international society across both rising and established states.

State-centrism and case selection

One of the many contradictions that arise when we move from theoretical polarity analysis to its employment in policy circles is that only the former specifies that poles of power must be states. As discussed above, adopting the lens of polarity does not mean rejecting the importance of non-state forms of power. But as it relates to the structural distribution of power specifically, the polarity analysis literature has rarely looked beyond the state, as one account sets out succinctly: '[T]he global system is built around powerful states who construct hierarchical systems of political order.'[34] Yet at various times in the post-Cold War period, multilateral groupings of states have found their way onto various lists of the poles that might make up a multipolar order. The most prominent of these has been the European Union (EU), particularly in the late 1990s and early 2000s, and, to a lesser extent, smaller groupings such as the G7/8 or even the rising power grouping referred to as the BRICS. As is discussed further in Chapter 1, at various times states such as China have even floated the idea of a bloc of developing countries acting as a pole of power at the global level.

Around the turn of the twenty-first century, the EU was the most common non-state entity to make it onto lists of the poles expected to make up an imminent multipolar order.[35] A number of analysts believed that the sheer size, and therefore power, of the single European market acting as a trading bloc in the global economy would impel the individual member states to eschew free-riding in favour of (collectively) taking on increasing global responsibilities. For example, David Calleo argued in 2001 that, in time, the implications of European integration would be so profound for the global order that 'a strong European monetary bloc, sporting its own reserve currency as an alternative to the dollar, ought to help stabilize the global system'.[36]

The rhetoric around the EU being part of the evolving multipolar system had the effect of loosening the criteria for pole status, not just between states and non-state actors, but for all aspirants. As Schenoni points out in Chapter 3, one of the effects was to encourage states who might have otherwise considered themselves as potential future rising powers at best, to instead think of themselves as likely poles in the near term. If a multilateral grouping could be thought of as a potential pole in a multipolar world, surely a geographically large and populous state with a growing economy (such as Brazil in the early 2000s) should be thought of as a great power contender?

As time has gone on, serious analysis of the EU's prospects as a pole of power in its own right have decreased significantly, and today it makes the roster of some but not others. By 2013 for example, Karen Smith argued that for the EU to act as an independent pole in a multipolar system, it would need to successfully clear three key hurdles: re-establishing credibility in the wake of the euro crisis; achieving a far greater degree of unity among its member states; and adapting its approach to exercising power and influence in world politics in general at a time when the balance of power is shifting towards non-Western rising powers and the traditional EU tactics of relying on conditionality in its trade and aid policies carries less weight.[37] By the time that the outcome of the 2016 British referendum on EU membership ensured that the second hurdle would not be cleared any time soon, it had already become clear that the institution's ability to address the other two issues was severely limited. For Richard Whitman, while the capabilities of the member states could provide a basis for great power status, the organisation appeared to no longer 'envision itself as an active participant in forging a new balance of power'.[38] Importantly for this volume, however, references to a pan-European pole (whether specifically mentioning the organisation of the EU or simply using the term 'Europe') endure in some limited national contexts. Specific examples can be found in the analysis of the national debates in China, India, and Russia in the pages that follow. More often than not, the actors that list the EU as a potential pole of power are the same ones that are making normative arguments in favour of multipolarity, raising questions about whether they genuinely perceive an independent European pole of power or whether it is simply politically convenient to refer to some kind of European power in such terms.

Other multilateral organisations tend to be thought of less in terms of being potential poles of power in their own right, but rather as important platforms for the performative aspects of great power status. For example, the G7 (known as the G8 between 1997 and 2014 during the period that Russia was a member) has at various times been discussed as evidence of a multipolar distribution of power in the realm of global economics.[39] However, this has been challenged not only by the 2008 global financial crisis, which emanated from within the wealthiest states themselves, but also by the advent of alternative forums to capture the spread of power to non-Western rising powers. As one account notes, it was the newer and larger grouping of the G20 that became the focus of discussions around differentiated responsibilities in the response to the global financial crisis.[40] The rising power grouping of the BRICS (Brazil, Russia, India, China, and South Africa), particularly in the second decade of this century, similarly provided an important platform for these states to signal their willingness to take on the 'special responsibilities' associated with great power status.[41] As is discussed further in Chapter 3, such groupings have become more important for shaping perceptions of which states count as poles in a new multipolar order for certain rising powers, not least Brazil.

Ultimately, in keeping with the framework outlined above, the contributors to this volume adopt an agnostic approach to the question of whether a non-state entity such as a multilateral grouping could become an independent pole of power. However, the choice to focus on national perspectives on multipolarity, by definition, precludes us from including a specific chapter on the EU, G7, or any other multilateral grouping. Instead this volume is specifically focused on the ways in which analysis, debates, and predictions about multipolarity play out in specific national contexts. Multilateral groupings, the EU in particular, appear at various points in the pages that follow depending on the perceptions of those dominating the national discussions at any one moment.

Structure of the book

The chapters that follow are structured around a two-part division between the rising challengers on the one hand, and the established incumbents on the other. Part I brings together perspectives from four key states, all of which have everything to gain from the promotion of a narrative about the onset of multipolarity. China, India, Brazil, and Russia have all, in different ways, developed the notion of a shift to a more diffuse distribution of power and status in which they are joining the ranks of the great powers. Part II reverses this and brings together the perspectives of some of those states with the most to lose from a shift from a unipolar to a multipolar world. Not only does this section investigate how the United States is responding to the notion of the end of unipolarity, but it also examines how this is playing out in two of Washington's most powerful allies, the United Kingdom and Japan. These two allies have their own complicated histories and pathologies associated with great power status. Each therefore provides a unique insight into the costs and benefits of embracing or resisting narratives of a shift towards multipolarity.

Chapter 1 begins this tour of national perspectives by investigating the Chinese discourse on multipolarity and the related concept of 'multipolarisation'. Nicholas Khoo and Zhang Qingmin provide an overview of the history of the use of the concept in both official Chinese discourse as well as academic scholarship, with an emphasis on the 1970s onwards. They focus on the meaning of 'multipolarisation' – a dynamic and potentially long and complicated process through which a multipolar order will emerge – in Chinese discourse and its role in discussions over Chinese foreign policy and grand strategy. Khoo and Zhang distinguish between the state's view of this concept and the views of scholars, highlighting key differences around the respective Marxist and realist interpretations of this structural phenomenon that have emerged over the years. In the scholarly discourse, the authors also highlight the role of critics of the consensus on both the analytical and normative arguments about the prospect of a multipolar order. This section of the chapter focuses principally on the views of two very prominent academics, Ye Zicheng of Peking University and Yan Xuetong of Tsinghua University. Ye has challenged the mainstream Chinese consensus by offering a more nuanced perspective on the process of multipolarisation itself, while Yan has argued that the view that the international structure is moving towards multipolarisation fails to reflect reality, and that bipolarity rather than multipolarity is taking shape. Khoo and Zhang use this and other work to mount a critique of the discourse on multipolarity in China on both theoretical and empirical grounds, and make the case for a more agency-centred approach to the issue that is contingent on the roles adopted by rising powers such as China in shaping the coming global order.

In Chapter 2, Ian Hall argues that India has long sought a multipolar international order. He makes the case that the majority view in its foreign and security policymaking elite is that such an order would be more conducive to India's interests and values than the orders that have prevailed since the country gained independence in 1947 – the Cold War bipolar system and the United States-dominated unipolar system that emerged in its aftermath. Hall makes the case for understanding Indian ideas about multipolarity as being intrinsically bound up with a particular foreign policy strategy which he terms 'multialignment' – an approach aimed at mitigating the risks inherent in a disordered, multipolar world in which the US cannot or will not play a stabilising role and in which other rising or resurgent states are pursuing strategies that aim at regional hegemony. The chapter develops the argument that this understanding of multipolarity is relatively new, having emerged in India's strategic elite only in the past decade, but it draws on key strands of thought that have evolved since Indian nationalists began to think, in the late nineteenth and early twentieth centuries, about possible foreign policies for a postcolonial India. Hall traces these strands with a view to explaining why the majority of India's foreign and security policymaking elite presently conceive of a multipolar world in the way that they do. He looks back in particular to Jawaharlal Nehru's framing of India's role in the world in the immediate post-independence period and the rationale for his policy of 'nonalignment'. The analysis then examines the responses of India's foreign policymaking elite to the brief moment of post-Cold War unipolarity, and the anxieties that underlay them. In the final section of the chapter, Hall explores the emergence of a more confident narrative about multipolarity in India since the early 2000s, and how this has shaped Indian approaches to securing and extending its interests and preferences in contemporary international relations. Specifically, Hall argues that, in Narendra Modi's India, multipolarity has emerged as a useful device for pushing back against Chinese assertiveness, as Beijing seeks to establish some kind of hegemony over its immediate neighbourhood and the wider Indo-Pacific.

In Chapter 3, Luis Schenoni explores the use of the concept of multipolarity in the Brazilian foreign policy debate with an emphasis on the period associated with Brazil's rise to great power status from 2000 onwards. Schenoni analyses documents from Brazilian governmental agencies in order to reconstruct how polarity was thought of and what impact this had on actual policy. He also draws on a series of in-depth interviews with academics and Brazilian public officials to help unravel their understanding of the term and the interests of different actors. This is complemented by a review of the public speeches of politicians and diplomats in forums such as the Brazilian Congress and the United Nations General Assembly, as well as academic articles that discuss the role of Brazil in a scenario of multipolarity, published in the two major Brazilian IR journals and a number of non-Brazilian IR journals. Schenoni argues that the concept of the global order becoming increasingly multipolar – and Brazil playing a key role in the process and outcome – has been emotionally potent and 'sticky' over this time period, despite what he argues is clear empirical evidence to the contrary. He also argues that the concept of multipolarity itself has been subject to an unusually high degree of conceptual stretching in the Brazilian foreign policy debate. After providing a map of the interests involved and a raw measure of conceptual stretching, the chapter outlines a typology of typical ways that the concept has been moulded to suit various causes in Brazil. In addition, Schenoni identifies common themes across actors (what he terms 'discursive coalitions') and uncovers the implicit theoretical framework they use to reinterpret and redefine the concept. Importantly, he finds that rather than a clear separation of the scholarly and the political use of the multipolar discourse emerging, the use and abuse of the concept cuts across the two spheres. In particular, he highlights the central importance of one particular understanding of multipolarity associated with multilateralism, South–South cooperation, and the BRICS grouping which was very effectively used in both informing an expansive foreign policy and in framing the academic debate.

Chapter 4 investigates both Russia's role in cultivating a global debate about the shift to a multipolar order, including the desirability of a more diffuse global order, as well as the use of the concept within Russia. The chapter begins by placing Russian discourse on multipolarity within the larger context of Russian thinking on issues of global order, state power, and modernity. Elena Chebankova uses this background to highlight the discrepancies between the more theoretical/philosophical approaches to global order in Russian discourse on the one hand, and the more immediate, policy-focused arguments about the 'need' for a multipolar order on the other. The argument is pursued that, while proposing an alternative in theoretical terms, Russia has yet to provide a clearly established practical alternative that could make it a meaningful pole of cultural-ideological alternative influence to the United States. Chebankova identifies four central themes that emerge from both official and scholarly Russian arguments about multipolarity. These include debates around the notion of ideological-cultural distinctiveness (and specifically a rejection of Western-led ideological universalism), normative arguments in favour of a more equitable redistribution of power among rising and re-emerging powers, a reassertion of Russian nationalism, and the regionalisation of world politics. Chebankova also examines specific Russian foreign policy initiatives in recent years and their relationship with Russian normative arguments about the need to construct a multipolar order. This includes Russian approaches to multilateral groupings and institutions including BRICS, the Eurasian Economic Union, and the Shanghai Cooperation Organisation. The discussion argues that, at the practical level, official Russian views on multipolarity tend to fall between the ideas of 'multiregionalism' and more traditional notions of great power management, both of which rest on traditional assumptions about the role of the nation-state and state sovereignty in world politics.

Chapter 5 moves the focus from rising and re-emerging powers to the established powers. James Johnson analyses the state of debate about relative

US decline and the 'rise of the rest' from the point of view of the United States. Johnson frames this around three categories of actors involved in creating and shaping the discourse on multipolarity in the United States: 'denialists', 'accepters', and 'resisters'. Denialists argue that unipolarity is in fact durable and that serious US decline is a myth, accepters advocate for retrenchment or strategies of 'offshore balancing' to navigate the inevitable arrival of a multipolar order, and resisters are concerned about the rise of peer competitors but believe that Washington can still stare down the challenge and maintain its hegemonic position. This typology is then used to frame a more specific discussion of how this is currently playing out through the lens of debates over power and high-end technological superiority. Johnson sets up the debate over the rapid diffusion and proliferation of artificial intelligence (AI) capabilities through an exploration of those views that harness these capabilities as a key aspect of efforts to maintain Washington's unipolar dominance. The chapter uncovers a key strand to this which, while often shrouded in the language of multipolarity, is actually based on perceptions of a bipolar order based around a new competitive struggle between Beijing and Washington. The chapter analyses calls from within the US to take action to sustain its primacy in the emerging global AI race in the context of predictions of a shift to a multipolar order. Johnson argues that the rapid acquisition and diffusion of AI amongst great and rising powers will fundamentally influence the future distribution of power, particularly in a manner which is likely to trigger security dilemmas and strategic rivalry between states.

In Chapter 6, H. D. P. Envall investigates the reception of narratives about the rise of a multipolar order in Japan, a state once touted as a potential pole of power in a post-Cold War multipolar order in its own right. Instead, Envall argues that the central framing of debates over multipolarity today in Tokyo is one of fear – fear of the end of unipolarity and the rise of multipolarity signalling an end to the assured peacefulness and prosperity of Northeast Asia, Japan's immediate neighbourhood. Echoing themes from a number of the chapters on rising powers, Envall argues that there is a complex and important interaction between the explanatory and normative sides of the Japanese discourse on multipolarity. How the global distribution of power does and should manifest itself in polarity terms is often difficult to disentangle. Significantly, the chapter highlights the larger debates about order – in particular a specific conception of a liberal rules-based order – that Japanese decision-makers and analysts bring to bear on debates about a future multipolar distribution of power. This implies that the unipolar, US-led order is itself defined by a liberal outlook that needs to be preserved as the global order becomes increasingly multipolar. Envall's chapter highlights the difficulties for Tokyo in holding on to this narrative, not least the Donald Trump administration's decidedly illiberal path in its foreign policy, and the legacy this left for the Biden administration.

The final case study (Chapter 7) by David Blagden presents the discourse around multipolarity in the United Kingdom as perhaps the ultimate symptom of the contested and often contradictory arguments about power and status that define the current global power transition. Reflecting what Blagden describes as 'the country's own tortured concerns with power and status', this chapter pitches discussion around the emergence of a new multipolar order as being a debate about the nature of 'greatness' in international relations itself. This chapter examines London's now decades-long history of attempting to project an image of itself as a pole of power long after the material bases of its formerly unambiguous global status have atrophied. Ultimately, Blagden argues that the United Kingdom's dogged persistence in attempting to cultivate and maintain a role as one of the great powers at the global level has hampered its ability to pursue more narrowly defined economic and security interests. In particular, Blagden outlines a set of what he argues are vital interests that can be secured in a post-unipolar era as long as London can become less fixated on a performative identity divorced from material realities.

The concluding chapter reflects on the implications for both scholarship and policymaking of the contested nature of the multipolar narratives analysed in the previous chapters. It brings together a set of recurring themes and topics from across the case studies and draws out some of the general and longer-term implications that emerge from the individual national contexts. For scholars, it discusses the theoretical and empirical challenge of distinguishing between regional and great (global-level) powers as well as making the case for a more fine-grained focus on the perceptual components of polarity analysis. For policymakers, it highlights the need to be able to deal effectively with ambiguity and subjectivity in net assessments and strategic analysis relating to power transitions. It also discusses the likely policy impacts of the continued salience of narratives of imminent multipolarity on issues such as alliance management.

What follows is a *tour d'horizon* of the different ways that the debate about the shift to a new multipolar order is playing out in different national contexts. Of course, the perspectives on offer here can only provide a partial insight into all the different elements of these national debates. These studies also present each individual author's understanding of how these discussions have emerged in their respective case studies and do not attempt to provide a definitive or exhaustive account of debates in any one country about power, status, and order in world politics. They provide, however, a crucial snapshot into the many, and often varied, ways that what is frequently referred to as 'the' global power transition is understood, embraced, and resisted in different national contexts. These chapters deepen our understanding of important policy debates and shed new light on one of IR's most fundamental concepts – the global distribution of power. The picture that emerges over the chapters that follow is simultaneously more complex and more interesting than the vast majority of the existing literature on this time-honoured topic would lead us to expect.

Notes

1 For critiques, see R. Harrison Wagner, *War and the State: The Theory of International Politics* (Ann Arbor, MI: University of Michigan Press, 2009); Randall L. Schweller, 'Entropy and the trajectory of world politics: Why polarity has become less meaningful', *Cambridge Review of International Affairs*, 23:1 (2010), 145–63.

2 Barry Buzan, *The United States and the Great Powers: World Politics in the Twenty-First Century* (Cambridge: Polity, 2004), pp. 40–1.

3 See David A. Lake, *Hierarchy in International Relations* (Ithaca, NY: Cornell University Press, 2009).

4 Stephen G. Brooks and William C. Wohlforth argue that at the current time 'polarity has arguably never been more popular among academics'. Stephen G. Brooks and William C. Wohlforth, *America Abroad: The United States' Global Role in the 21st Century* (New York: Oxford University Press, 2016), p. 64.

5 Myriam Zandonini, 'Multiple currencies for a multipolar world: All change … or not?', Programme Paper IE 2013/01 (London: Chatham House, April 2013), www.chathamhouse.org/sites/default/files/public/Research/International%20 Economics/0413pp_zandonini.pdf (accessed 3 May 2021).

6 Credit Suisse, 'The end of globalization or a more multipolar world?' (Zurich: Credit Suisse AG, September 2015), www.credit-suisse.com/media/assets/corporate/docs/about-us/research/publications/the-end-of-globalization-or-a-more-multipolar-world-report.pdf (accessed 3 May 2021).

7 Simon Denyer, 'With Brexit, China could be losing its best friend in the EU', *Washington Post*, 2 July 2016.

8 Matthew Dal Santo, 'Russia's success in Syria signals an emerging multipolar world order', *The Interpreter*, 6 April 2016, www.lowyinstitute.org/the-interpreter/russias-success-syria-signals-emerging-multipolar-world-order (accessed 21 August 2019).

9 See, for example, His Excellency Sergey V. Lavrov, Foreign Minister of the Russian Federation, 'Russia in a multipolar world: Implications for Russia–EU–US relations', Address to the Center for Strategic and International Studies, Washington, DC, 12 July 2011, www.csis.org/events/russia-multipolar-world (accessed 21 August 2019).

10 Buzan, *The United States and the Great Powers*, p. 36, emphasis added.

11 'Self-censorship in international relations and security studies: An interview with Richard Ned Lebow', *Journal of Global Security Studies*, 1:4 (2016), 356–60, at 358.

12 For recent examples of all three forms of polarity being used in analysis by three different scholars from (and working in) Latin America, Asia, and Africa respectively, see (unipolarity): Matias Spektor, 'Brazil: Shadows of the past and contested ambitions', in William I. Hitchcock, Melvyn P. Leffler, and Jeffrey W. Legro (eds), *Shaper Nations: Strategies for a Changing World* (Cambridge, MA: Harvard University Press, 2016), pp. 17–35; (bipolarity): Yan Xuetong, 'Why a bipolar world is more likely than a unipolar or multipolar one', *New Perspectives Quarterly*, 32:3 (2015), 52–6; (multipolarity): Eben Coetzee, 'Democracy, the Arab Spring and the future (great powers) of international politics: A structural realist perspective', *Politikon*, 40:2 (2013), 299–318.

13 Benjamin Zala, 'Polarity analysis and collective perceptions of power: The need for a new approach', *Journal of Global Security Studies*, 2:1 (2017), 2–17. In our understanding of 'ordering' in this book, however, we are interested not only in current debates about who is 'at the top', but also the sometimes less-considered issues concerning the quality and complexity of the assets and resources – broadly defined – that underpin a pole's capacities.

14 For this reason, Buzan has stated that the issue of empirical challenges to the approach of quantifying the distribution of capabilities 'was never properly addressed by polarity theory'. Barry Buzan, 'Polarity', in Paul D. Williams (ed.), *Security Studies: An Introduction*, 2nd edn (Abingdon: Routledge, 2013), pp. 155–69, at p. 159. Kenneth Waltz was somewhat contradictory on this point. He admitted that difficulties exist in quantifying and assessing capabilities and that therefore 'we should not be surprised if wrong answers are sometimes arrived at'. Yet at the same time, he maintained that 'historically, despite the difficulties, one finds general agreement about who the great powers of a period are, with occasional doubt about marginal cases'. Kenneth N. Waltz, *Theory of International Politics* (New York: Random House, 1979), p. 131.

15 For prominent examples of such work see, *inter alia*, Waltz, *Theory of International Politics*, p. 131; Robert Jervis, 'International primacy: Is the game worth the candle?', *International Security*, 17:4 (1993), 52–67, at 52; William C. Wohlforth, 'The stability of a unipolar world', *International Security*, 24:1 (1999), 5–41, at 10; Nuno P. Monteiro, *Theory of Unipolar Politics* (Cambridge: Cambridge University Press, 2014), pp. 36–47; Michael Beckley, 'The power of nations: Measuring what matters', *International Security*, 43:2 (2018), 7–44.

16 On this, see Martha Finnemore, *The Purpose of Intervention: Changing Beliefs about the Use of Force* (Ithaca, NY: Cornell University Press, 2003), pp. 92–3; Brooks and Wohlforth, *America Abroad*, pp. 3–4.

17 Brooks and Wohlforth, *America Abroad*.

18 Yan, 'Why a bipolar world is more likely'.

19 Barry Buzan, Morten Kelstrup, Pierre Lemaitre, Elzbieta Tromer, and Ole Wæver, *The European Security Order Recast: Scenarios for the Post-Cold War Era* (New York: Pinter Publishers, 1990), p. 23.

20 See, famously, John J. Mearsheimer, 'Back to the future: Instability in Europe after the Cold War', *International Security*, 15:1 (1990), 5–56; and Kenneth N. Waltz, 'The emerging structure of international politics', *International Security*, 18:2 (1993), 44–79.

21 Joseph Nye was in the vanguard in this respect, perceiving an emerging unipolar power configuration even before the dissolution of the Soviet Union in December 1991. See Joseph Nye, *Bound to Lead: The Changing Nature of American Power* (New York: Basic Books, 1990).

22 Charles Krauthammer, 'The unipolar moment', *Foreign Affairs*, 70:1 (1990/91), 23–33. It is however worth noting that Krauthammer assumed that the so-called 'moment' was likely to last for 'another generation or so' (p. 23).

23 It took until well into the next decade for a serious body of theoretical writing on the topic of unipolarity to be published. For examples from this period, see Thomas S. Mowle and David H. Sacko, *The Unipolar World: An Unbalanced Future* (Basingstoke: Palgrave Macmillan, 2007); Birthe Hansen, *Unipolarity and World Politics: A Theory and its Implications* (London and New York: Routledge, 2011); G. John Ikenberry, Michael Mastanduno, and William C. Wohlforth (eds), *International Relations Theory and the Consequences of Unipolarity* (Cambridge: Cambridge University Press, 2011).

24 The attempts to reckon with the consequences of an order in which balancing appeared less relevant even spawned two high-quality books with the same title! See Coral Bell, *A World Out of Balance: American Ascendency and International Politics in the 21st Century* (Double Bay, New South Wales: Longueville Books, 2003); Stephen G. Brooks and William C. Wohlforth, *World Out of Balance: International Relations and the Challenge of American Primacy* (Princeton, NJ and Oxford: Princeton University Press, 2008).

25 Samuel Huntington, 'The lonely superpower', *Foreign Affairs*, 78:2 (1999), 35–49.

26 Stephen G. Brooks and William C. Wohlforth, 'American primacy in perspective', *Foreign Affairs*, 81:4 (2002), 20–33, at 21.

27 For a good overview, see T. V. Paul, Deborah Welch Larson, and William Wohlforth (eds), *Status in World Politics* (New York: Cambridge University Press, 2014).

28 Steven Ward, 'Status, stratified rights, and accommodation in international relations', *Journal of Global Security Studies*, 5:1 (2020), 160–78.

29 Nicholas Kitchen and Michael Cox, 'Power, structural power, and American decline', *Cambridge Review of International Affairs*, 32:6 (2019), 734–52, at 735.

30 David A. Baldwin, *Power and International Relations: A Conceptual Approach* (Princeton, NJ: Princeton University Press), pp. 176–7.

31 Zala, 'Polarity analysis'.

32 See Paul, Larson, and Wohlforth, *Status in World Politics*.

33 See Alister Miskimmon, Ben O'Loughlin, and Laura Roselle, *Strategic Narratives: Communication Power and the New World Order* (Abingdon: Routledge, 2013).

34 G. John Ikenberry, 'Introduction: Power, order, and change in world politics', in G. John Ikenberry (ed.), *Power, Order, and Change in World Politics* (Cambridge: Cambridge University Press, 2014), pp. 1–16, at pp. 5–6. See also Waltz, *Theory of International Politics*, pp. 130–1; Buzan, *The United States and the Great Powers*, p. 32.

35 See Charles A. Kupchan, 'After Pax Americana: Benign power, regional integration, and the sources of a stable multipolarity', *International Security*, 23:2 (1998), 40–79; Pascal Boniface, 'European power: For a multipolar world', *Strategic Analysis*, 25:3 (2001), 385–92; Buzan, *The United States and the Great Powers*, pp. 116–19; Mark Leonard, *Why Europe Will Run the 21st Century* (London: Fourth Estate, 2005).

36 David P. Calleo, *Rethinking Europe's Future* (Princeton, NJ and Oxford: Princeton University Press, 2001), p. 248.

37 Karen E. Smith, 'Can the European Union be a pole in a multipolar world?', *The International Spectator*, 48:2 (2013), 114–26.

38 Richard Whitman, 'The EU: Standing aside from the changing balance of power?', *Politics*, 30:S1 (2010), 24–32, at 31. For later analysis on what the emergence of a multipolar distribution of power 'means for' (rather than how it is shaped by) the EU, see Megan Dee, *The European Union in a Multipolar World: World Trade, Global Governance and the Case of the WTO* (London: Palgrave Macmillan, 2015).

39 Dries Lesage, 'Is the world imaginable without the G8?', *Internationale Politik und Gesellschaft*, 4 (2007), 107–16.

40 Mlada Bukovansky, Ian Clark, Robyn Eckersley, Richard Price, Christian Reus-Smit, and Nicholas J. Wheeler, *Special Responsibilities: Global Problems and American Power* (Cambridge and New York: Cambridge University Press, 2012), p. 203.

41 Oliver Stuenkel, 'The financial crisis, contested legitimacy, and the genesis of intra-BRICS cooperation', *Global Governance*, 19:4 (2013), 611–30.

Part I

Rising and re-emerging powers

1

'Mirror, mirror on the wall': China and the concept of multipolarity in the post-Cold War era

Nicholas Khoo and Zhang Qingmin

In the familiar Grimm Brothers' fairy tale *Snow White*, the Queen, one of the protagonists, repeatedly asks the mirror how beautiful she is. Before the arrival of Snow White, the mirror delivers a consistently satisfactory answer to the Queen.[1] An observer of the post-Cold War academic discourse in China on international polarity is struck by a similar pattern. Chinese officials, policymakers, and academics occupy a role not unlike the mirror in the fairy tale. How so? They have provided a consistent answer to two specific questions facing them in world politics: Which variant of polarity is the world heading towards? And which variant of polarity is preferred by China? Through the twists and turns of post-Cold War international politics, the mainstream Chinese answer to both questions has been clear.[2] Specifically, the movement towards multipolarity is inexorable, and this development is welcome. This chapter investigates the Chinese discourse on multipolarity and the related concept of multipolarisation. The first section reviews the general Chinese discourse. The second and third sections review the Chinese government's and Chinese scholars' discourse on multipolarisation. Some observations are then drawn from our review in the fourth section. These pertain to the generally overlapping views of the Chinese party-state and Chinese scholars, with a few notable exceptions, and to the need for greater theorisation and empirical case studies to buttress Chinese arguments in favour of multipolarity and multipolarisation.

China's multipolarity and multipolarisation discourse: a short history

It is only a slight exaggeration to say that the debate concerning the stability of various configurations of polarity – be they multipolarity, bipolarity, or more recently unipolarity – is central to the development of International

Relations (IR) theory as an academic enterprise. We can date the origins of this debate at least as far back as the release of the first edition of Hans Morgenthau's *Politics Among Nations* in 1948, where the virtues of multipolarity were advanced in preference to the emerging Cold War bipolarity.[3] Other analysts, notably Edward Gulick, Henry Kissinger, and David Singer and Karl Deutsch, subsequently lent their support to the multipolar position.[4] Kenneth Waltz famously countered this view with his bipolar stability thesis, with William C. Wohlforth further extending the debate in the post-Cold War era with his pitch for the virtues of unipolarity.[5]

The debate rolls on.[6] Whatever one's position in this discourse, logic and empirical evidence suggest strongly that while the impact of polarity can be over- or underemphasised by analysts, we ignore at our peril its role as a structural feature in world politics. This observation is not news to officials and scholars in China. Chinese policymakers and academics pay close attention to structural variables in world politics, not least the concept of multipolarity.[7] Indeed, surveying the Chinese literature in 2004, Brantly Womack noted that 'it [multipolarity] has played an especially important role in China'.[8]

What is the contemporary Chinese view on multipolarity? To answer this question, we need to return to the Cold War era. Some Chinese analysts trace the Chinese discourse on multipolarity back to 1946, when Mao Zedong put forward his intermediate zone theory.[9] According to the theory, the US was separated from the Soviet Union by a vast zone of disparate states.[10] Before it could attack the Soviet Union, the US first had to subjugate this vast zone. According to Mao, 'the objective of the US is to occupy the countries in this vast intermediate zone, bully them, control their economies, establish military bases on their territory, and see that they are increasingly weakened – with Japan and Germany included among them'.[11] By the mid-1960s, Mao had expanded the number of intermediate zones from one to two. The first intermediate zone consisted of Africa, Asia, and Latin America; the second was made up of Europe.[12]

Intermediate zone theory has subsequently been linked to Mao's 1970s era 'Three Worlds' theory,[13] where in a discussion with Zambian President Kenneth Kaunda on 22 February 1974, the Chinese leader characterised the international system as being divided into Three Worlds (*sange shijie huafen*).[14] In Mao's view, the United States and the Soviet Union represented the First World; Canada, Japan, and Europe constituted the Second World; and the Third World covered the undeveloped countries of Africa, Asia, and Latin America.[15] This perspective was formally presented to the international community in a speech delivered by Deng Xiaoping at a special session of the United Nations General Assembly on 10 April 1974.[16] Even as Mikhail Gorbachev's arrival in the Kremlin brought a thaw in the Cold War, the Chinese leadership sensed that structural changes were likely.

Over the course of the 1985–86 period, Huang Xiang, Deng's national security advisor, identified a likely future movement from bipolarity towards multipolarity.[17]

The point worth highlighting here is that there has long been a clear divergence between Chinese aspirations for multipolarity and reality. This aspirational gap continues to exist. Notwithstanding the reality of unipolarity in the post-Cold War era, it remains a widely held Chinese view that the world continues to develop towards multipolarity.[18] What are the main features of the Chinese view of multipolarity? To state the obvious, a movement from unipolarity to multipolarity entails a diffusion of power away from the US. As Zhang Yunling explains, 'the main point of so-called multipolarity is that there exist several power centres with important influence on regional and world affairs'.[19] Multipolarity is broadly viewed as a positive development that China supports. As Pan Zhongqi and Chen Zhimin succinctly observe, 'China favours a multipolar world as a desirable order.'[20]

The goal of multipolarity continues to be referenced by senior figures in both the Chinese Communist Party (CCP) and the government, and there has also been debate about the features of multipolarity.[21] An important twist in the Chinese discussion has occurred, with the concept of multipolarisation (*duojihua*) being emphasised.[22] The first use of the phrase 'multipolarisation' can be identified in the mid-1980s. Huang introduced the concept,[23] and Deng subsequently lent his weight behind it. Commenting on the international situation in 1990, Deng observed a trend towards an increase in the number of poles in the system: 'The situation in which the United States and the Soviet Union dominated all international affairs is changing. Nevertheless, in future when the world becomes three-polar, four-polar or five polar ... in the so-called multi-polar world, China too will be a pole. We should not belittle our own importance: one way or another, China will be counted as a pole.'[24]

Soon after Deng's intervention, a Chinese discourse of multipolarisation developed.[25] Multipolarisation is viewed as a dynamic and potentially long and complicated *process* rather than an end point which has been achieved. Chinese scholars and government officials have not reached a consensus on which countries are considered as the poles in the emerging multipolar structure.[26] While many scholars view the contemporary international structure as 'one superpower and several strong powers', they differ on which entities count as poles.[27] Some hold the view that three poles should be considered, but differ on their identity. Thus, scholars variously count the US, Europe, and East Asia, or the US, Germany, and Japan.[28] Others identify five entities, including the US, Japan, Europe, Russia, and China, while still others opt for six, adding India.[29] At times, the Chinese government has even considered the bloc of developing countries as a pole.[30]

This lack of consensus is not surprising. During the Cold War, American academics debated the various meanings of polarity,[31] with Harrison Wagner even famously posing the 'what was bipolarity?' question immediately after the Cold War.[32] And, it should be noted, American academics either anticipated the arrival of multipolarity, or continued to predict its arrival, long after it was clear that unipolarity reflected the existing structural reality.[33]

A notable feature in Chinese thinking about multipolarisation is that there exists a particularly pronounced economic aspect. Most Chinese scholars concur that a great power cannot become a pole without sufficient military, scientific, and, critically, economic power. Some even hold the view that polarisation is not necessarily limited to the political dimension because a country can only become a pole when it has comprehensive power (economic, military, and technological). Since economic power is the foundation, they contend that political polarisation is a reflection of economic polarisation.[34] In this understanding, if a country is economically weak, it cannot become a pole. The tendency towards an economic understanding of polarisation is likely to reflect the fact that this resonates with China's clear source of strength in the post-1978 reform era, which lies in the economic realm. That is par for the course. But the dangers of such an understanding are clear. Specifically, this borders on an overly economic-centric understanding of multipolarity, bringing with it the distinct possibility of misdiagnosing the fundamental dynamics of world politics. Thus, an overly economic focus obscures more fundamental politically based aspects of world politics such as nationalism, which has increasingly characterised international relations, including inter-state economic relations, as illustrated by Brexit and the US–China tariff dispute.[35]

Multipolarisation: the state's view

The Chinese state's view of multipolarisation is marked by three closely related aspects. First, multipolarisation is an objective reality. Second, multipolarisation is conducive to global peace and stability. Third, promoting multipolarisation is an important aspect of Chinese foreign policy. China's potential partners in the multipolarisation process typically include specific states (Russia, India, and Japan), a multilateral entity (the European Union or EU), and/or a bloc (developing countries). It should be noted that the US is typically viewed as one of the poles in the system, if not necessarily one to cooperate with.

First, multipolarisation is viewed and supported by China as an objective reality. The view that multipolarity was imminent in the early post-Cold War period was shared by many US scholars, and has been reflected in numerous Chinese government and CCP documents and statements.[36] The political report of the 14th National Congress of the Communist Party of China in 1992 (which was the first Party Congress held after the end of the Cold War) pointed out that 'the world today is undergoing a great historical period of change. The bipolar system has come to an end, different forces are restructuring and reconfigured, and the world is moving towards the direction of multipolarisation. It will be a long and complicated process for the new structure to be formed.'[37] Shortly after, in 1994, the National People's Congress of the People's Republic of China (NPCPRC) issued a document stating that 'the trend of multipolarisation within the international structure is becoming more prominent'.[38] The political report of the 15th Party Congress in 1997 noted that 'the process of multipolarisation is taking shape both globally and regionally, and such a trend can be seen in both political and economic fields'.[39] In 1998, the NPCPRC stated that 'the trend of multipolarisation is becoming clearer than ever before'.[40] A report to the National People's Congress in 2002 insisted that 'the trend of world multipolarisation is unchanged'.[41] In 2004 and 2005 respectively, it was declared that China 'strongly promotes world multipolarisation'[42] and 'will continue to promote world multipolarisation'.[43] The political reports of the 17th Party Congress in 2007 and the 19th Party Congress in 2017 both stated that the 'multipolarisation process is irreversible'.[44] Indeed, the political report of the 18th Communist Party Congress was the only major Party Congress report since the end of the Cold War that did not mention the term multipolarisation.[45]

Second, the Chinese government attributes to multipolarisation an almost teleological quality, viewing it as conducive to world peace and stability, prosperity, and even the democratisation of international relations. Thus, during his visit to Russia in 1997, Jiang Zemin stated that multipolarisation 'has become a historical trend that cannot be stopped'.[46] In his speech to the Shanghai Cooperative Organisation summit in 1999, Jiang noted that 'the process to world multipolarisation is a torturous and complicated process, but this trend is unstoppable'.[47] At other times, multipolarisation encapsulates the best ideals in world politics. The joint declaration issued by Jiang and his Russian counterpart Boris Yeltsin in November 1998 stated that 'multipolarity in international relations is conducive for building a new world order featuring balance, stability, democracy, and non-confrontation'.[48] The political report to the 16th Party Congress in 2002, when Hu Jintao replaced Jiang as Secretary General of the CCP Central Committee, stated that China 'is willing to join efforts with international society to actively promote world multipolarisation, promote the coexistence of multiple forces so as to maintain the stability for international society'.[49] Premier Wen Jiabao reiterated that multipolarity is more conducive for world peace and stability and that it is in the interest of the Chinese people and the people of the world at large.[50] In 2011, Hu further promised that China would continue to 'dedicate itself to promoting world multipolarisation and the democratisation of international relations'.[51] Following his ascension to the party leadership in late 2012, Xi Jinping articulated the notion of a 'new type of great power politics' in US–China relations. At the June 2013 Sunnylands summit with US President Barack Obama, Xi explained that the 'new type of great power relations' was based on the principles of 'no confrontation or conflict', 'mutual respect', and 'win-win cooperation'.[52] While still vague and somewhat inchoate, in principle this concept is viewed by Xi as being fully consistent with multipolarisation, with Xi continuing to accord multipolarity an important position in world politics, including it in his keynote speech to the 19th Party Congress on 18 October 2017.[53]

Third, promoting multipolarisation constitutes an integral part of China's post-Cold War foreign policy. Deng emphasised multipolarisation as an important means for achieving a new world order.[54] Leaders since Jiang have not abandoned this policy goal, even as they have added nuanced amendments. As noted above, Jiang made multipolarisation an important part of the democratisation of the international system,[55] while Hu made it an important part of a harmonious society.[56] In his address to the 19th Party Congress in 2017, Secretary General Xi viewed multipolarisation as 'rapidly accelerating', requiring China to respond appropriately as it navigated the international relations of the twenty-first century.[57]

The actors who are viewed as potential partners with China in a multipolarised world are typically Russia, India, Japan, the EU, and the developing countries of the Global South. Implicitly, this represents a critique of the unipolar status quo, and opposition to post-Cold War US unipolarity. In regard to Russia, the 2001 Sino-Russia Treaty of Good Neighbourliness and Friendly Cooperation agreed to by Jiang Zemin and Vladimir Putin stated that the two countries 'will further expand their cooperation in international affairs and promote world peace, stability and the construction of world multipolarisation'.[58] Hu Jintao has continued China's policy of promoting multipolarisation with Russia. The 2003 Sino-Russia Joint Declaration issued by Hu and Putin pointed out that 'world multipolarisation is a general trend of development, but it will be a difficult process which requires the joint efforts of the international community'.[59] The 2005 Sino-Russian Joint Declaration on the Twenty-First-Century International Order noted that multipolarisation is 'an important contemporary trend of human beings' development'.[60]

Interestingly, potential regional rivals of China are sometimes mentioned as partners in multipolarisation. Thus, Hu observed that China and 'India share a comprehensive common interest in promoting multipolarisation, democratisation of the international system, and other important international issues'.[61] The central role of China and India in the BRICS (Brazil, Russia, India, China, and South Africa) organisation that was formally established in 2009 adds a strong element of action to such statements. Nevertheless, the relationship remains complicated by competitive elements, including Indian distrust of the long-standing Sino-Pakistani relationship and Chinese wariness of India's relations with the US, Japan, and Vietnam. Japan is at once China's historical regional rival, and the regional state that has had the deepest economic relationship with China in the post-1978 reform era. Huang Zhengji included Japan as one of the poles in a five-pole world.[62] Interestingly, notwithstanding Hu's comment, there has been a distinct evolution in the Chinese government's and Chinese scholars' view of Japan as a pole of international politics. The 1980s stand out as the high point of Chinese perceptions of Japan, with Tokyo being viewed as a pole or a likely pole at that time. In the 1990s, a distinct shift can be detected where Japan was treated as a 'neighbouring country'. This period coincides with the decline of the Japanese economic model, manifested in its extended economic stagnation.[63] A search of the terms 'Japan' and '*duojihua*' (multipolarisation) in the major books on post-Cold War era Chinese foreign policy and the China National Knowledge Infrastructure (CNKI) database[64] for the same period reveals a distinct trend where Japan was not mentioned as a pole.

Europe is viewed as another prospective Chinese partner in promoting multipolarisation. It has been a long-standing Chinese objective to support European integration. In 2000, Jiang stated that 'European Union development is conducive to world multipolarisation, and to promoting the building of a new international political and economic order.'[65] A 2014 Chinese policy paper on the EU stated that 'China is willing to join the European Union in dedicating to the unity of the two major forces in building world multipolarisation.'[66] In his speech to the EU–China Business Summit in 2015, Premier Li Keqiang observed that 'China has always supported European Union integration. China also respected the road of development that the European Union has chosen. Both sides support world multipolarisation and civilisation diversity. Both insist on settling their differences through dialogue and consultation.'[67]

As a developing country itself, the developing countries constitute the final prospective partner for China in promoting multipolarisation. China has a long-standing tradition of support for developing countries in global affairs and has consistently considered itself a representative of the developing countries. Unsurprisingly, China has emphasised that 'developing countries and the non-aligned movement as a whole are an important force in promoting multipolarisation and stabilising a new world order'.[68] On occasion, Africa and Latin America have even been considered as poles in a multipolar world.[69]

Multipolarisation: scholars' views

Given the prominence accorded by the Chinese government to multipolarisation, it is little surprise that the concept has been a topic of intense interest among Chinese IR scholars. A search of the term '*duojihua*' (multipolarisation) in the CNKI reveals the existence of 401 articles published between 1990 and 2017. That said, the Chinese scholarly community has debated this topic, with distinct characteristics which we elaborate below. As a general statement, on this issue, academics in China have basically echoed the policy of the government. But beyond the symbiotic relationship between the government and scholars, polarity as a concept resonates with Chinese academics because conventional IR theory, not least realist theory, offers a compelling alternative to Marxist theory as a way of understanding the complexities of world politics. Here, Chinese IR theory faces a steep challenge to demonstrate its utility over conventional IR theory.[70]

The vast majority of Chinese scholars hold the view that multipolarisation is a general trend in international politics that is structural in origin, and thus irreversible. In this respect, political multipolarisation and economic globalisation constitute the basis of China's current and foreseeable foreign policy. There is a clear 'balancing' aspect to the Chinese view. A distinct feature in this literature is that a multipolar world is preferable to a unipolar world because multipolarity prevents any one country from imposing its will on other countries.[71] This point, which is elaborated below, is conducive to peace and stability. Relatedly, multipolarity is viewed as facilitating the independence of non-great powers. It does so by safeguarding their sovereignty and independence, allowing them to pursue their own economic and political development.[72]

To varying degrees, the multipolarisation literature has as its focus a shared commitment to alter the status quo in world politics, which is premised on US unipolarity. Some scholars are more explicit than others in viewing multipolarisation as a mechanism to check the US. As Wang Yizhou candidly acknowledged in the *Global Times*, 'one of the fundamental goals of multipolarisation is to prevent the formation of American unipolar hegemonism'.[73] He also noted that 'we must pay attention in our external propaganda that when we talk about multipolarisation, we do not mean to oppose the US'.[74] Luo Huijun also acknowledged that 'multipolarisation has some element of opposition to American hegemonism and unilateralism'.[75]

In terms of its applicability to the realities of world politics, the multipolarisation viewpoint has clearly diverged from empirical reality. A strong case can be made that the first two decades after the end of the Cold War witnessed a distinct tendency towards 'unipolarisation' rather than multipolarisation. The absence of major power balancing against the US documented by unipolarity theorists, and the numerous examples of unilateralism, appears to be difficult to reconcile with the discourse of multipolarisation.[76] One can cite the 1998–99 US intervention in Kosovo as an example. When the US bypassed the United Nations Security Council and went to war against Serbia, countries that China considered as possible poles either did not or could not stop them. The EU supported the US, while Russia protested, but ultimately could not prevent the war. In the face of this reality, China began to emphasise that multipolarisation was 'accelerating', but that it would be a 'tortuous development'.[77] Jiang stated in a November 1999 speech at a Central Committee conference that 'the final formation of the structure of multipolarisation will be a long process full of complicated struggle, but this historical direction is irreversible'.[78] Since then, the Chinese government has been even more cautious in its stance on multipolarisation. Notably, the third volume of Jiang's selected works, which was released in 2006, emphasised that the process of multipolarisation will be 'full of twists and turns'.[79] As the reality of unipolarity became clear, the trend towards US unilateralism accelerated after 9/11, further heightening the divergence between China's multipolarisation discourse and the realities of world politics. One Chinese scholar acknowledged this point when he stated that after 9/11, 'American unilateralism had peaked and that multipolarisation had suffered a significant setback'.[80]

To be sure, there are Chinese scholars who have critiqued the consensus. We focus principally on the views of two academics, Ye Zicheng (Peking University) and Yan Xuetong (Tsinghua University). Ye has challenged the mainstream assumption about multipolarisation and offered a nuanced perspective on the concept, which can be summarised in three points. First, Ye contends that the process of multipolarisation is an objective trend, and is neither good nor bad. Therefore, it should neither be celebrated nor feared. Ye argues that the claim that a multipolar system is better than a unipolar or bipolar system is not definitively supported by theoretical studies or historical evidence. For instance, notwithstanding the advocacy of multipolarity and the related critique of unipolarity among Chinese scholars, Ye points out that the Roman Empire and the pre-1800 China-centred East Asia system appeared to offer counterexamples of stable unipolar systems.[81]

Second, the trajectory of multipolarisation has several possibilities, and uncertainty exists. The international structure is dynamic rather than static. Unipolarity, bipolarity, and multipolarity are comparative rather than definitive concepts, and may even coexist under certain conditions.[82] Interestingly, this understanding is consistent with the view of American scholars such as Samuel Huntington and Joseph Nye, both of whom see much more complexity in our current unipolar era, with multipolarity in the economic sphere coexisting with unipolarity in the military sphere.[83]

Third, both the positive and negative aspects of multipolarisation should be analysed and evaluated in a thorough way. No international structure is perfect. Whatever form multipolarisation may take, it will have both positive and negative aspects. Ye pointed out that the US role in world politics is more complex than that suggested by the multipolarisation consensus, being characterised by both cooperative and conflictual tendencies.[84] On the one hand, there is the well-established and relentless US tendency to practise power politics and interfere in other countries' internal affairs. But in Ye's view, the US has also played a positive role in maintaining world peace and solving world problems.[85] It also merits comment that the US was one of the first to initiate the multipolarity concept, as reflected in the Nixon administration's views on a trend of emerging multipolarity during that phase of the Cold War.[86]

Ye also points out that China should go beyond a 'polarisation' mentality and seek cooperation with major countries.[87] This view is shared by other scholars, who believe that a 'polarity mentality' reflects the logic of 'big powers dominating the world and that neither unipolarity nor multipolarity has seen the demise of power politics'.[88] In this view, polarity and polarisation are Cold War era concepts emphasising tension and confrontation between powers. In Ye's view, we are living in a very complex world, where economic interdependence has led to a significant convergence of interests among major countries. The very nature and source of power has changed and global issues make it imperative for countries to cooperate rather than confront one another.[89] In this view, rather than fixating on polarity, China's diplomacy should focus on being more sophisticated, flexible, and wise.[90]

Academics sympathetic to this viewpoint also caution that the concepts of polarity and multipolarisation should be used carefully since they arguably fail to capture the current world structure accurately.[91] For instance, Yan has argued that the view that international structure is moving towards multipolarisation fails to reflect reality, and that bipolarity rather than multipolarity is taking shape.[92] In his book *Inertia of History*, Yan contends that structural trends lean not towards multipolarisation but towards bipolarisation. This is particularly the case as China continues to rise. Indeed, Yan has argued that bipolarity is already a reality in the Asia-Pacific region, even if it will take longer for such a structure to take shape on a global scale.[93]

Thus, not only does Yan disagree with the multipolarisation perspective, he has further predicted that the focal point of competition in a bipolar Asia-Pacific will be in South East Asia. In this view, China must take the initiative in the region, abandoning its long-held nonaligned foreign policy strategy, and 'try to enter into alliances'.[94] According to Yan, to define alliances as representative of a 'Cold War mentality' is dogmatism, which 'only binds China's own hands'.[95] That said, despite Yan's prominence in the literature, his is a minority view among mainstream Chinese scholars, and has been critiqued.[96]

Observations

First, as this chapter has sought to demonstrate, the Chinese academic literature strongly reflects and buttresses existing government discourse. In this view, multipolarity and the closely related process of multipolarisation are emerging, and this is to be preferred over the alternative structural options of unipolarity and bipolarity. In this important sense, the multipolarity and multipolarisation discourse is aspirational. But is the discourse also propaganda?[97] If so, this would not be the first time that a basic IR concept has been used in such a way.[98] The Collins Dictionary defines propaganda as 'information, often inaccurate information, which a political organization publishes or broadcasts in order to influence people'.[99]

By this standard, the concept does qualify as propaganda. Does anyone doubt that the concepts of multipolarity and multipolarisation have been advanced by the Chinese government, in its capacity as a political actor, to influence world opinion? In a recent joint statement released after a meeting in Beijing between Xi and Putin, it was stated that 'we will continue to advocate a multipolar world order and a more democratic international relations'.[100] This example highlights the reality that the multipolarity and multipolarisation concepts are indeed a critique of the flaws inherent in a US-based unipolarity.

As far as factual accuracy is concerned, while multipolarity may be emerging, there is a compelling case to be made that, however one measures power, the world is still unipolar, even if the US has experienced a relative decline since 2008 and China continues to rise.[101] At a policy level, China currently has to temper its actions to reflect the reality that it exists in a unipolar world where the US has significant power projection capabilities in China's own strategic backyard, East Asia. It stands to reason that Chinese pressure on the status quo in the South China and East China Seas in the post-2012 era would have been even more intense if the US had been merely one of many poles in the system.

Second, there are certainly reasons to suspect that multipolarity could be more stable than a US–China bipolarity or unipolarity in the twenty-first century. But to be convincing, assertions need to be underpinned by rigorous concepts and robust theory. One struggles to find compellingly stated theoretical arguments in the Chinese multipolarisation literature to buttress claims that multipolarity twenty-first-century style will be more stable than the alternatives of bipolarity or unipolarity. On this point, Chinese scholars can profit from re-exploring the long-standing debate on the stability of various configurations of polarity in the IR literature.[102] This is necessary before arguments in favour of multipolarity or other newly introduced Chinese concepts such as a 'new type of great power relations' can be accepted as a basis for policy.[103]

Third, there is a compelling need to relate China's multipolarisation discourse to the empirical realities of world politics. Do Chinese scholars and policymakers fully appreciate what they are asking for when they express approval for multipolarity or multipolarisation? In considering this question, a number of points must be considered.

The existing empirical record on multipolarity is mixed. The 100-year peace between the end of the Napoleonic Wars and the onset of the First World War (1815–1914) is often viewed as a model of great power management and system stability in an era of dramatic change.[104] Nevertheless, while there was no system-wide war during this era, there were numerous regional wars, some involving great powers.[105] While Dale Copeland is correct that the bipolarity thesis has greater resonance only in retrospect, the same point can be made about multipolarity.[106]

In addition to the ambiguous virtues of multipolarity, it should be recognised that these virtues often reside in the eye of the beholder. The often celebrated case of nineteenth- and twentieth-century multipolarity overlaps substantially with the onset of China's century of national humiliation.[107] To the inevitable rebuttal that China is now a rising rather than a declining power, it should be noted that the rising powers of the nineteenth century met vastly different fates. The US and Russia rose to become superpowers while Germany, France, and Japan had a very different experience, and with the benefit of hindsight would probably have made radically different choices. Indeed, contemporary IR theorists such as John Mearsheimer who use the concept of multipolarity make a distinction between balanced and unbalanced multipolarity.[108] Given this discussion, it is not unreasonable to expect more caution from Chinese theorists and policymakers before the vigorous advocacy of multipolarity's virtues is accepted as the basis for policy.

Finally, what is China's back-up plan if multipolarisation and multipolarity turn out to be a quixotic aspiration that never materialises? Notwithstanding

China's extensive discourse on a coming multipolar world, an equally (if not more) likely development in the future of world politics is a movement from unipolarity to bipolarity, with the US and China as the two poles. Why is global bipolarity less preferable to Chinese interests than multipolarity? A post-Cold War era bipolarity will reflect a mix of familiar and distinct sources of friction, but it will have potentially substantial benefits for China.[109] These potential benefits need to be seriously evaluated against those of multipolarity, rather than rejected without serious scrutiny.[110] With the exception of Yan's efforts, why is not at least as much energy and thought being invested by Chinese academics in analysing a global and regional bipolarity? After all, as Robert Ross first claimed in 1999, the regional structure in East Asia is arguably already bipolar, with China and the US as poles. China has relied on its booming economy to systematically modernise its military and strategically consolidate its position in mainland Asia, even as the US maintains a dominant position in maritime Asia.[111]

Even if one's view is that an emerging bipolarity at the regional level is a pathway to a multipolar rather than a bipolar international structure, the process may very well be an extended one, possibly at least as long as the more than four decades long Cold War, and with a very uncertain content and trajectory. As Randall Schweller and Pu Xiaoyu correctly point out:

> a return to multipolarity tells us that several great powers will emerge to join the United States as poles within the international system. That is all. It does not tell us how multipolarity will arrive (whether by means of traditional balancing behavior or as an unintended consequence of inwardly focused states growing at different rates) or what the specific content of international politics will be on the other side of the transition from unipolarity to multipolarity (whether emerging powers will accept or resist the inherited Western order). These issues largely depend on what roles the emerging powers, especially China, decide to play.[112]

That is indeed food for thought. Moving forward, as mentioned above, Xi articulated a bold vision for China in his address to the 19th Party Congress in 2017. This vision is premised on China being a major player in restoring multipolarity.

Conclusion

For much of the post-Cold War era, government and scholarly opinion in the People's Republic of China has expressed a distinct preference for multipolarity, and the closely related concept of multipolarisation, as a structural feature in world politics. This chapter has sought to analyse this perspective. The research presented in the chapter suggests three conclusions. First, there is a strong propagandistic element to this consensus. Second, arguments in favour of multipolarity or multipolarisation have not been buttressed with a sufficiently robust theoretical foundation. Third, questions arise as to whether the advocates of this view have fully explored the implications of their perspective. That said, whether the world remains locked at the global level in an extended era of unipolarity, moves towards a bipolar or multipolar future, or develops along the lines of a variant, it is hard to imagine that China will not play a role.[113] Hence the importance of continuing to reflect, as this chapter has sought to do, on China's perspectives on polarity.

Acknowledgement

The authors would like to thank Peter Grace and John Tai for their comments on this chapter.

Notes

1 Jacob Grimm and Wilhelm Grimm, *The Original Folk and Fairy Tales of the Brothers Grimm: The Complete First Edition*, trans. Jack Zipes (Princeton, NJ: Princeton University Press, 2016).
2 Xu Jin, 'Debates in IR academia and China's policy adjustments', *Chinese Journal of International Politics*, 9:4 (2016), 470–5.
3 For the classic statement on the merits of multipolarity over bipolarity, see Hans J. Morgenthau, *Politics Among Nations: The Struggle for Power and Peace* (New York: Knopf, 1948).
4 Edward Vose Gulick, *Europe's Classical Balance of Power* (New York: W. W. Norton, 1955); Henry Kissinger, *A World Restored: Metternich, Castlereagh, and the Problems of Peace, 1812–1822* (London: Weidenfeld & Nicolson, 1957); David Singer and Karl Deutsch, 'Multipolar power systems and international stability', *World Politics*, 16:3 (1964), 390–406.
5 See Kenneth Waltz, *Theory of International Politics* (New York: McGraw-Hill, 1979); William C. Wohlforth, 'The stability of a unipolar world', *International Security*, 24:2 (1999), 5–41.
6 See, for example, Stephen G. Brooks and William C. Wohlforth, *World Out of Balance: International Relations and the Challenge of American Primacy* (Princeton, NJ: Princeton University Press, 2008); Nuno Monteiro, *Theory of Unipolar Politics* (New York: Cambridge University Press, 2014); Christopher Fettweis, 'Unipolarity, hegemony and the new peace', *Security Studies*, 26:3 (2017), 423–51; Benjamin Zala, 'Polarity analysis and collective perceptions

of power: The need for a new approach', *Journal of Global Security Studies*, 2:1 (2017), 2–17.

7 Xie Yixian (ed.), *Zhongguo dangdai waijiaoshi, 1949–2001* [Contemporary Chinese Diplomatic History, 1949–2001] (Beijing: Zhongguo qingnian chubanshe, 2002); Jiang Lingfei, 'China's international security challenges and response at present and in the coming five years', in Wang Jisi and Zhou Mingmei (eds), *China International Strategy Review* (Beijing: Foreign Languages Press, 2013), pp. 152–73.

8 Brantly Womack, 'Asymmetry theory and China's concept of multipolarity', *Journal of Contemporary China*, 13:39 (2004), 351–66, at 351.

9 Mao Zedong, *Selected Works of Mao Zedong*, Vol. 4 (Beijing: People's Press, 1991), p. 1193; Liu Haijun, 'Woguo duojihua sixiang de yanbian' [Evolution of our country's multipolarisation thinking], *Guoji guanxi xueyuan xuebao* [Journal of Institute of International Relations], 2 (2000), 3–9.

10 Jiang An, 'Mao Zedong's "three worlds" theory: Political considerations and value for the times', *Social Sciences in China*, 34:1 (2013), 35–57.

11 Cited in *ibid.*, 37.

12 Cited in *ibid.*, 38.

13 Li Xiangqian, 'Cong "zhongjian didai" dao "sange shijie"', [From 'intermediate zone' to 'three worlds'], *Shijie Zhishi* [World Affairs], 24 (1993), 10; Michael Sheng, *Battling Western Imperialism: Mao, Stalin and the United States* (Princeton, NJ: Princeton University Press, 1997), pp. 145–60.

14 Central Committee of the Communist Party of China, *Mao Zedong on Diplomacy* (Beijing: Foreign Languages Press, 1998), p. 454.

15 Mao Zedong, 'On the question of the differentiation of the three worlds', 22 February 1974, https://digitalarchive.wilsoncenter.org/document/119307 (accessed 21 August 2019).

16 'Chairman of Chinese delegation', *Peking Review*, 17:16 (16 April 1974), 6–11.

17 As cited in Michael Pillsbury, *China Debates the Future Security Environment* (Washington, DC: National Defense University Press, 2000), pp. 10–11.

18 Zhou Jirong and Wang Ling, '90 niandai guoduxing shijie geju de tedian jiqi dui jianli guoji xinzhixu de yingxiang' [The characteristics of the transitional world structure in the 1990s and its impact on establishing the new international order], *Waijiao xueyuan xuebao* [Journal of Foreign Affairs College], 4 (1991), 19–22; 'Shijie duojihua zai quzhezhong fazhan' [Multipolarisation is developing with twists and turns], *Qiu Shi* [Seeking Truth], 2 (2014), 12–15; Zhou Fangyin, 'Zhongguo xuezhe dui guoji geju de renshi ji zhengming' [Chinese scholars' perception and debate on international structure], *Guoji zhengzhi kexue* [Quarterly Journal of International Politics], 2:2 (2017), 1–32.

19 As cited in Womack, 'Asymmetry theory', 354.

20 Pan Zhongqi and Chen Zhimin, 'Peaceful rise, multipolarity, and China's foreign policy line', in Takashi Inoguchi and G. John Ikenberry (eds), *The Troubled Triangle: Economic and Security Concerns for the United States, Japan and China* (New York: Palgrave Macmillan, 2013), p. 64.

21 Pillsbury, *China Debates the Future*, pp. 56–8.

22 For example, see Xi Jinping, 'Juesheng quanmian jianshe xiaokang shehui, duoqu xinshidai Zhonguo tese shehuizhuyi weida shengli' [Secure a decisive victory in building a moderately prosperous society in all respects and strive for the great success of socialism with Chinese characteristics for a new era], *People's Daily*, 18 October 2017. Premier Li Keqiang also endorsed multipolarity at the China–ASEAN summit in November 2018. 'Full text: Premier of China Li Keqiang's speech at China–ASEAN summit', Xinhua News Agency, 15 November 2018.

23 See Pillsbury, *China Debates the Future*, p. 9.

24 Deng Xiaoping, *Selected Works of Deng Xiaoping*, Vol. 3 (Beijing: People's Press, 1993), p. 353.

25 For further examples, see Zhao Shuisheng, 'Beijing's perception of the international system and foreign policy adjustment after the Tiananmen incident', in Zhao Shuisheng (ed.), *Chinese Foreign Policy: Pragmatism and Strategic Behavior* (Abingdon: Routledge, 2004), p. 142.

26 Yuan Shengyu, 'Cong "wuji" dao "duoji": baijialun geju' [From 'no pole' to 'multipolar': Debates on structure], *Shijie jingji yu zhengzhi luntan* [Forum on World Economics and Politics], 9 (1991), 19–23.

27 Zhou, 'Zhongguo xuezhe dui guoji geju de renshi ji zhengming'.

28 Wang Huaining, 'Guanyu yanjiu shijie zhengzhi he jingji geju de jidian sikao' [Several reflections on the study of world political and economic structure], *Shijie jingji yu zhengzhi* [World Economy and Politics], 7 (1993), 1–4.

29 Ma Xiaojun, 'Dangdai shijie duojihua yu guoji shehui xinzhixu' [Contemporary world multipolarisation and the international new world order], *Zhonggong zhongyang dangxiao xuebao* [Journal of the Party School of the Central Committee of the Chinese Communist Party], 10:1 (2006), 100–4; Xi Runchang, 'Lun lengzhanhou shijie zhengzhi de duojihua yu daguojia de zhanlue jingzheng' [On world political polarisation and strategic competition among major powers], *Jiaoyu yu yanjiu* [Education and Research], 4 (1998), 20–4; Du Xiaoqiang, 'Liangji haishi duoji' [Bipolar or multipolar], *Shijie Zhishi*, 14:4 (1987), 14–15.

30 In a report to the National People's Congress, Li Peng, Chairman of China's National People's Congress, stated that Africa was an important pole in the multipolar structure. Li Peng, 'Li Peng weiyuanzhang fangwen Maoliqiusi, Nanfei, Kenniya, Yiselie, Baleisitan he Aman liuguo de shumian baogao' [Written report on NPC Chairman Li Peng's Mauritius, South Africa, Kenya, Israel, Palestine and Oman], *Renmin ribao* [People's Daily], 27 December 1999. In a speech delivered while on a visit to Pakistan, Jiang Zemin observed that 'the trend of multipolarisation, characterised by the rise of developing countries, is like a powerful current which is unstoppable'. Jiang Zemin, 'Shidai mulin youhao, gongchuang meihao weilai' [Generations of good-neighbourliness and friendship, creating a better future together], *Renmin ribao* [People's Daily], 3 December 1996.

31 Joseph L. Nogee, 'Polarity: An ambiguous concept', *Orbis*, 18:4 (1975), 1193–225.

32 Harrison Wagner, 'What was bipolarity?', *International Organization*, 47:1 (1993), 77–106.
33 Aaron Friedberg, 'Ripe for rivalry? Prospects for peace in a multipolar Asia', *International Security*, 18:3 (1993–94), 5–33; Kenneth Waltz, 'Intimations of multipolarity', in Birthe Hansen and Bertel Heurlin (eds), *The New World Order* (New York: Saint Martin's Press, 2000), pp. 1–17; Barry Posen, 'Emerging multipolarity: Why should we care?', *Current History*, 108:721 (2009), 347–52.
34 Yu Sui, 'Shijie duojihua wenti' [On world polarisation], *Shijie jingji yu zhengzhi* [World Economy and Politics], 3 (2004), 15–16.
35 See the discussion on trade in Nicholas Khoo, 'Interstate rivalry in East Asia', in Derek Reveron, Nikolas Gvosdev, and John Cloud (eds), *The Oxford Handbook of US National Security* (New York: Oxford University Press, 2018), pp. 573–90.
36 See Friedberg, 'Ripe for rivalry?'; John Mearsheimer, 'Back to the future: Instability in Europe after the Cold War', *International Security*, 15:1 (1990), 5–56; Kenneth Waltz, 'The emerging structure of international politics', *International Security*, 18:2 (1993), 44–79.
37 Jiang Zemin, 'Jiakuai gaige kaifang he xiandaihua jianshe, duoqu you Zhonguo tese shehuizhuyi shiye de gengda shengli' [Accelerating the pace of reform, opening up and modernisation to achieve greater victory in the cause of socialism with Chinese characteristics], *Renmin ribao* [People's Daily], 21 October 1992.
38 Li Peng, 'Zhengfu gongzuo baogao 1994' [Political report on the work of government 1997], *Renmin ribao* [People's Daily], 24 March 1994.
39 Jiang Zemin, 'Gaoju Deng Xiaoping lilun weida qizhi, ba jiashe you zhonguo tese shehuizhuyi shiye quanmian tuixiang ershiyi shiji' [Holding high the great banner of Deng Xiaoping theory, promoting the cause of building socialism with Chinese characteristics into the 21st century], *Renmin ribao* [People's Daily], 22 September 1997.
40 Li Peng, 'Zhengfu gongzuo baogao 1998' [Political report on the work of government 1998], *Renmin ribao* [People's Daily], 21 March 1998.
41 Zhu Rongji, 'Zhengfu gongzuo baogao 2002' [Political report on the work of government 2002), *Renmin ribao* [People's Daily], 17 March 2002.
42 Wen Jiabao, 'Zhengfu gongzuo baogao 2004' [Political report on the work of government 2004], *Renmin ribao* [People's Daily], 14 March 2004.
43 Wen Jiabao, 'Zhengfu gongzuo baogao 2005' [Political report on the work of government 2005], *Renmin ribao* [People's Daily], 15 March 2005.
44 Hu Jintao, 'Gaoju zhongguo tese shehuizhuyi weida jizhi,wei duoqu quanmian jianshe xiaokang sheui xinshengli er fendou' [Hold high the great banner of socialism with Chinese characteristics and strive for new victories in building a moderately prosperous society in all respects], *Renmin ribao* [People's Daily], 25 October 2007.
45 Hu Jintao, 'Report to the Eighteenth Party Congress of the Communist Party of China on 8 November 2012', *China Daily*, 18 November 2012.
46 Central Documentary Press, *Jiang Zemin lun you Zhongguo tese shehuizhuyi: zhaunti zhaiyao* [Jiang Zemin on Socialism with Chinese Characteristics: Excerpt on Special Topics] (Beijing: Zhongyang wenxian chubanshe, 2002), p. 513.

47 Jiang Zemin, *Selected Works of Jiang Zemin*, Vol. 2 (Beijing: People's Press, 2006), p. 401.
48 'Shiji zhijiao de zhonge guanxi, Zhong E gaoji huiwu jieguo de lianhe shengming' [Sino-Russian relations at the turn of the century, joint declaration resulting from Sino-Russian summit], *Renmin ribao* [People's Daily], 24 November 1998.
49 Jiang, *Selected Works*, Vol. 2, p. 566.
50 *Ibid.*, p. 108. Premier Wen Jiabao made clear in his report on the government's work to the National People's Congress in 2004 and 2005 that China would promote multipolarisation.
51 'Hu Jintao tong Meideweijiefu huitan' [Hu Jintao holds talks with Medvedev], *Renmin ribao* [People's Daily], 17 June 2011.
52 Ministry of Foreign Affairs of the People's Republic of China, 'Xi Jinping and US President Obama hold joint press conference', 8 June 2013, www.fmprc.gov.cn/mfa_eng/topics_665678/xjpttcrmux_665688/t1049545.shtml (accessed 21 August 2019).
53 'Full text of Xi Jinping's report at 19th CPC National Congress', *China Daily*, 18 October 2017, www.chinadaily.com.cn/china/19thcpcnationalcongress/2017-11/04/content_34115212.htm (accessed 21 August 2019).
54 Deng, *Selected Works*, p. 353.
55 Jiang Zemin, 'Gongtong kaichuang Zhong Lai youhao hezuo de xinshijie' [Work together for a new century of Sino-Latin American friendly cooperation], *Renmin ribao* [People's Daily], 7 April 2001.
56 Foreign Ministry, People's Republic of China, 'Hu Jintao delivers an important speech at the Consultative Council of Saudi Arabia, 23 April 2006', www.fmprc.gov.cn/mfa_eng/wjb_663304/zzjg_663340/xybfs_663590/gjlb_663594/2878_663746/2880_663750/t248648.shtml (accessed 4 January 2019).
57 Xi, 'Juesheng quanmian jianshe xiaokang shehui'.
58 'Zhonghua renmin gongheguo yu Eluosi lianmeng mulin youhao hezuo tiaoyue' [People's Republic of China and Russian Federation Treaty of Good Neighbourliness and Friendly Cooperation], *Renmin ribao* [People's Daily], 17 July 2001.
59 'Zhonghua renmin gongheguo he Eluosi lianbang lianhe shengming [Joint Declaration between the People's Republic of China and the Russian Federation], *Renmin ribao* [People's Daily], 29 May 2003.
60 'Zhonghua renmin gongheguo he Eluosi lianbang guanyu ershiyi shiji guoji zhixu de lianhe shengming [Joint Declaration between the People's Republic of China and the Russian Federation on the Twenty-First-Century International Order], *Renmin ribao* [People's Daily], 2 July 2005.
61 Hu Jintao, 'Xieshou tuozhan hezuo, gongtong chuangzao meihao weilai' [Expanding cooperation jointly, creating a better future together], *Renmin ribao* [People's Daily], 23 November 2006.
62 See Pillsbury, *China Debates the Future*, p. 9.
63 William Grimes, *Unmaking the Japanese Miracle: Macroeconomic Politics, 1985–2000* (Ithaca, NY: Cornell University Press, 2001).
64 The CNKI is a major database of Chinese academic journal articles.

65 'Jiang Zemin huijian Xilake he Puluodi' [Jiang Zemin holds talks with Chirac and Prodi], *Renmin ribao* [People's Daily], 24 October 2000.
66 'Shenhua huli gongying de Zhong Ou quanmian zhanlue hezuo huoban guanxi: Zhongguo dui Oumeng zhenge wenjia' [Deepening mutual beneficial and win-win comprehensive strategic Sino-EU partnership: China's policy paper toward the European Union], *Renmin ribao* [People's Daily], 3 April 2014.
67 State Council, People's Republic of China, 'Le Keqiang zai Zhong Ou gongshang fenghui shang de jianghua' [Le Keqiang's speech at the EU–China Business Summit], 29 June 2015, www.gov.cn/guowuyuan/2015-06/30/content_2886643.htm (accessed 21 August 2019).
68 'Zhong E guanyu shijie duojihua he jianli guoji xinzhixu de lianhe shengming' [Sino-Russian Joint Declaration on World Multipolarisation and Building a New International Order], *Renmin ribao* [People's Daily], 24 April 1997.
69 Li, 'Li Peng weiyuanzhang fangwen'.
70 Qin Yaqing, 'Why is there no Chinese international relations theory?', *International Relations of the Asia-Pacific*, 7 (2007), 313–40.
71 This is also a core theme in balance of power theory.
72 He Fang, 'Shi duojihua haishi "yichaoduoqiang"?' [Multipolarisation or 'one superpower' with several strong powers], *Shijie zhishi* [World Affairs], 17 (1998), 17; Yu Sui, 'Shijie geju yu daguoguanxi ruogan wenti tantao' [Discussion on world structure and major country relations], *Xiandai guoji guanxi* [Contemporary International Relations], 2 (1998), 38–41; Ye Zicheng, 'Zhongguo zai duojihua guochengzhong de diwei, zuoyong he celue' [China's position, role, and tactics in the multipolarisation process], *Guoji pinglun* [International Review], 4 (1999), 12–16; Ma, 'Dangdai shijie duojihua yu guojishehui xinzhixu'.
73 Wang Yizhou, 'Duojihua bingbu dengyu fan Mei' [(Promoting) multipolarisation does not mean opposing the US], *Huanqiu shibao* [Global Times], 6 August 1999.
74 *Ibid.*
75 Luo Huijun, 'Danji, duoji haishi wuji: dangji shijie geju jiqi fazhan qushi zai tantao' [Unipolar, multipolar or no pole at all: Reconsideration of the current world structure and its developmental trends], *Xiangtan daxue xuebao, zhexue he shehui kexue ban* [Journal of Xiangtan University (Philosophy and Social Sciences edition)], 38:1 (2014), 144–9.
76 Brooks and Wohlforth, *World Out of Balance*; Monteiro, *Theory of Unipolar Politics*.
77 Jiang Zemin, *Jiang Zemin lun you Zhongguo tese shehuizhuyi: zhuanti zhaibian* [Jiang Zemin on Socialism with Chinese Characteristics, Excerpt on Special Topics] (Beijing: Zhongyang wenxian chubanshe, 2002), pp. 515–16.
78 *Ibid.*, pp. 515–16.
79 Jiang Zemin, *Selected Works of Jiang Zemin*, Vol. 3 (Beijing: People's Press, 2006), p. 138.
80 Li Qizhen, 'Jiu yaoyao shijian dui dangqian shijie duojihua jincheng de yingxiang 9·11' [The impact of the '9/11' incident on the process of multipolarisation], *Dongnanya xue* [South East Asia Studies], 2 (2002), 77–81.

81 Ye Zicheng, 'Dui Zhongguo duojihua zhanlue delishi yu lilun de fansi' [Reflection on the history and theory of China's multipolarisation strategy], *Guoji zhenzhixue* [Study of International Politics], 1 (2004), 12–14; Zhang Qingmin, 'Zhongguo de guojia texing, guojia juese he duiwai zhenge sikao' [China's national attributes, national role conception, and reflection on its foreign policy], *Taipingyang xuebao* [Pacific Journal], 2 (2004), 54–5.
82 Ye, 'Dui Zhongguo duojihua zhanlue delishi yu lilun de fansi'.
83 Samuel Huntington, 'The lonely superpower', *Foreign Affairs*, 78:2 (1999), 35–9; Joseph Nye, *The Future of Power* (New York: Public Affairs, 2011).
84 Ye, 'Dui Zhongguo duojihua zhanlue delishi yu lilun de fansi', p. 17.
85 Ye Zicheng, 'Dujihua yanjiu zhong de jige wudian' [Several errors in the study of multipolarisation], *Guoji luntan* [International Forum], 1 (1999), 35–40.
86 United States Department of State, *Foreign Relations of the United States, 1969–1976, Vol.1, Foundations of Foreign Policy* (Washington, DC: Office of the Historian, 2018), https://history.state.gov/historicaldocuments/frus1969-76v01/d2 (accessed 25 January 2019).
87 Ye, 'Dui Zhongguo duojihua zhanlue delishi yu lilun de fansi', 14.
88 *Ibid.*
89 *Ibid.*
90 Wang Hongtao, 'Guoji geju zhong de duojihua wenti yanjiu' [Studies on multipolarisation in international structure], *Zhonggong zhongyang dangxiao xuebao* [Journal of the Party School of the Central Committee of the Chinese Communist Party], 13:4 (2009), 106; Liu Jianfei, 'Lun shijie gejuzhong de feijiahua yinsu' [On the depolarisation factors in international structure], *Xiandai guoji guanxi* [Journal of Contemporary International Relations], 4 (2008), 2–5.
91 Xia Anling and Hou Jiehui, 'Chaoyue "jihua" siwei, bawo shijie geju de jiben fangxiang' [Go beyond 'polarisation' mentality, grasp the fundamental trends of world structure], *Guoji zhengzhi yanjiu* [Study of International Politics], 3 (2004), 15–21.
92 Yan Xuetong, 'Bipolar structure has already taken shape in Asian-Pacific region', *International Herald Tribune*, 5 February 2015.
93 Yan Xuetong, *Lishi de Guanxing* [Inertia of History] (Beijing: Zhongxin chubanshe, 2013), pp. 31–55.
94 Interview with Yan Xuetong, 'Zhong Mei jingzheng hui geng jilie ma?' [Can Sino-US confrontation become more intense?], *Huanqiu shibao* [Global Times], 15 July 2016.
95 Hao Weiwei and Liu Lina, 'Hunluan he wuxu zheng chengwei shijie changtai: zhuangfang qinghua daxue guojiguanxi yanjiuyuan yaunzhang yan xuetong' [Confusion and disorder has become a new normal in the world: Interview with Yan Xuetong, Dean of Tshinghua University's Institute of International Studies], *Cankao xiaoxi* [News Reference], 22 June 2018.
96 For instance, Xiao Feng, a research fellow from the International Liaison Department of the CCP Central Committee, offered the rebuttal that China's economy has not developed to the point where it can become another pole, and that China must not succumb to the inevitability of over-pessimism in

US–China relations. Xiao Feng, 'Duojihua jiang zouxing Zhong Mei liangji ma?' [Can 'multipolarity' move to 'China–US bipolarity'?], *Dangdai shijie* [Contemporary World], 10 (2016), 72–5.

97 D. Cameron Watt, 'The proper study of propaganda', *Intelligence and National Security*, 15:4 (2000), 143–63.

98 Ernst Haas, 'The balance of power: Prescription, concept, or propaganda?', *World Politics*, 5:4 (1953), 442–77.

99 See 'propaganda', *Collins' Dictionary*, www.collinsdictionary.com/dictionary/english/propaganda (accessed 19 August 2019).

100 Office of the President of Russia, 'Press statements following Russian–Chinese talks', 8 June 2018, http://en.kremlin.ru/events/president/transcripts/57699 (accessed 19 August 2019).

101 Stephen G. Brooks and William C. Wohlforth, *America Abroad: The United States' Global Role in the 21st Century* (New York: Oxford University Press, 2016).

102 Morgenthau, *Politics Among Nations*; Waltz, *Theory of International Politics*; Wohlforth, 'Stability of a unipolar world'.

103 Jinghan Zeng, 'Constructing a "new type of great power relations": The state of the debate in China (1998–2014)', *British Journal of Politics and International Relations*, 18:2 (2016), 422–42, at 436.

104 Henry Kissinger, *Diplomacy* (New York: Simon & Schuster, 1994).

105 Nicholas Khoo and Michael L. R. Smith, 'A "Concert of Asia"?', *Policy Review*, 108 (2001), 73–83.

106 Dale Copeland, 'Neorealism and the myth of bipolar stability', in Benjamin Frankel (ed.), *Realism: Restatements and Renewal* (London: Frank Cass, 1996), pp. 29–89.

107 John W. Garver, *Foreign Relations of the People's Republic of China* (Englewood Cliffs, NJ: Prentice-Hall, 1993), pp. 2–30.

108 John Mearsheimer, *The Tragedy of Great Power Politics* (New York: W. W. Norton, 2001), p. 44.

109 See Waltz, *Theory of International Politics*.

110 Oystein Tunsjo, 'US–China relations: From unipolar hedging toward bipolar balancing', in Robert S. Ross and Oystein Tunsjo (eds), *Strategic Adjustment and the Rise of China* (Ithaca, NY: Cornell University Press, 2017), pp. 41–68.

111 Robert Ross, 'The geography of peace: East Asia in the twenty-first century', *International Security*, 23:4 (1999), 81–118.

112 Randall L. Schweller and Xiaoyu Pu, 'After unipolarity: China's visions of international order in an era of US decline', *International Security*, 36:1 (2011), 41–72, at 42.

113 See Nye's articulation of alternatives in Nye, *Future of Power*.

2

India: Seeking multipolarity, favouring multilateralism, pursuing multialignment

Ian Hall

> Well before a multipolar world actually came into being, we believed in its desirability and even its inevitability.[1]

India has long sought a multipolar international order. The majority view in its foreign and security policymaking elite is that such an order would be more conducive to India's interests and values than the orders that have prevailed since the country gained independence in 1947 – the Cold War bipolar system and the United States-dominated unipolar system that emerged after the collapse of the Soviet Union.[2] But India's present conception of a multipolar order is distinct from the Russian and Chinese understandings discussed elsewhere in this book. Today, it is not reflexively anti-American, and values – for the most part – Washington's contributions to sustaining key elements of our contemporary international order by providing a range of public goods.[3] It also favours multilateral methods of managing global challenges, rejecting the argument implicit in some Chinese and Russian thinking that rising and resurgent powers should be permitted to carve out regional orders dominated by hegemonic states or 'spheres of influence'.[4] This is not to say, however, that this Indian conception is naive to the realities of power politics or major power ambition. It recognises that India must play a role in balancing against some threats to order. With that in mind, it advocates a strategy of 'multialignment' that aims to mitigate the risks inherent in a disordered, multipolar world in which the US cannot or will not play a stabilising role, and in which other rising or resurgent states are pursuing regional hegemonies.

This understanding of multipolarity is relatively new, having emerged in India's strategic elite only in the past decade or so, but it draws on key strands of thought that have evolved over more than a century, since Indian nationalists began to think about possible foreign policies for a postcolonial India. This chapter traces these strands with a view to explaining why the majority of India's foreign and security policymaking elite presently conceive of a multipolar world in the way that they do. In particular, it looks to Jawaharlal Nehru's framing of India's role in the world in the immediate post-independence period and the rationale for his policy of 'nonalignment'. It then examines the responses of India's foreign policymaking elite to the brief moment of post-Cold War unipolarity, and the anxieties that underlay them. In the last section, it explores the emergence of a more confident narrative about multipolarity in India since the turn of the twenty-first century, and the manner in which this has shaped Indian approaches to securing and extending its interests and preferences in contemporary international relations.

Independent India in the world

On 15 August 1947, India was one of the first European imperial possessions to gain its independence. As such, its leaders had few clear precedents on which to draw in establishing a foreign policy for a postcolonial state.[5] Indian nationalists were understandably keen to distance themselves from British ways of conducting international relations – these were patently immoral, they argued, pointing to British acquisitiveness and belligerence. In any case, they were clearly unsuited to an economically poor and militarily weak state.[6] Indian history prior to the establishment of the Raj also offered little help. Before the British, much of modern India had been controlled by the Mughals – Muslim emperors of Central Asian origin who ruled from 1536 until the remnant of their regime was abolished by the British after the so-called Mutiny – or First War of Independence – in 1857.[7] Since modern India was a Hindu-majority state carved out of the wider British Raj by partition, and given controversies about Mughal rule and its impact on non-Muslims, and, more immediately, given the communal violence that had accompanied the creation of India and Muslim-majority Pakistan, the Mughal example was not palatable to India's postcolonial elite.[8]

In this context, India's leaders were forced to look much further back in history – and beyond South Asia – for the resources with which to construct a foreign policy. Here Nehru, prime minister from 1947 until his death in 1964, played a key role, drawing on a disparate collection of ideas of both Indian and Western origin to construct an 'idea of India' and a conception of how it ought to behave in international relations.[9] He drew on Buddhist thought and invoked the statecraft of the ancient Mauryan emperor Ashoka, who converted to Buddhism during his reign and sought thereafter to rule by its principles, as an exemplar.[10] He drew too on the idiosyncratic and syncretic political philosophy of his fellow campaigner for

Indian independence, Mohandas Karamchand Gandhi – the Mahatma or 'Great Soul'.[11] And Nehru made extensive use of ideas gleaned from his time as a schoolboy at Harrow, student at Cambridge, and lawyer in London, as well as those derived from the Western literature – philosophical, historical, political, economic, and scientific – that he read and digested during the inter-war period, the war years, and afterwards.[12] In particular, he made extensive use of British socialist and international thought, especially that of the Fabians and Harold Laski, as did a number of other influential Indian politicians, including Nehru's confidante and erstwhile emissary, V. K. Krishna Menon.[13]

From these sources, Nehru constructed a radical and internationalist world view, with a hard pragmatic edge.[14] It was notably hostile to amoral versions of political realism, which, as A. P. Rana noted in 1969, Nehru thought underpinned 'the methods of the defunct empires, which he labelled policies of the balance of power, or simply power politics'.[15] He argued that European history and the track record of European colonialism amply demonstrated that power politics merely generated ever-worsening cycles of violence, and that, in any case, modern warfare rendered such methods self-defeating and obsolete. Indeed, in contemplative works like *The Discovery of India* (1946), written while interned in British jails, he mocked thinkers like Walter Lippmann or Nicholas Spykman who believed that power politics represented 'realism or practical politics'.[16]

Nehru welcomed the creation of the United Nations (UN), placing great faith in the UN Charter's capacity to provide security for the weak and its restraining effect on power politics. He quickly recognised that the UN provided a useful forum for weak states like India for both airing their concerns about the behaviour of the strong, and campaigning for substantive change in international norms and rules. Drawing on the accumulated wisdom of the subcontinent, as well as contemporary Western internationalism, Nehru believed that India could and should lead Asia in particular, and the world more broadly, towards a different kind of international relations, characterised by mutual respect, non-aggression, cooperation, solidarity, and opposition to colonialism and racism.[17] That way, India could further the cause of what Nehru called 'One World', ideally in the form of some kind of world federation.[18]

Nehru argued that Indian foreign policy must proceed from the recognition that India is materially weak, but could play a significant and positive role in world affairs, drawing on its substantial reserves of wisdom accumulated over thousands of years of Indian history and its recent struggle against European imperialism.[19] Although India could not impose its will by economic or military means, he believed, it could and should act as a kind of 'normative power' or 'moral power', campaigning to change the norms and rules of international relations to align with more progressive ideals.[20] To be able to perform this role, however, India must avoid both entanglement in the conflicts of the major powers, which would be likely to have devastating consequences, and dependence on other states, which might bring about its effective recolonisation. By keeping a free hand and pursuing economic self-reliance, India could minimise the need to expend scarce resources on building and maintaining military power, and maximise its autonomy in foreign policy.[21]

Bipolarity and nonalignment

This expansive Nehruvian world view proved remarkably resilient, persisting until the end of the Cold War, if not beyond, despite the failures of Nehru's diplomacy and those of his successors and significant changes in India's circumstances.[22] It gave rise, during the late 1940s and early 1950s, to the controversial strategy that became known as 'nonalignment'.[23]

This strategy was cast by Nehru as the only logical response for a new and relatively weak state to the regrettable continuance of power politics and the post-war emergence of bipolarity. In a classic text first published in 1970, the Bengali diplomat-turned-scholar Jayantanuja Bandyopadhyaya presented the problem and India's solution thus:

> By 1947 the major segment of international politics had become bipolarized and the Cold War had set in ... and soon afterwards an attempt was being made by each bloc to draw ... the newly independent states of Asia and Africa into the vortex of the Cold War by cajolery, threats and temptations ... This situation was largely out of India's control, but it was within the boundary conditions of this given international milieu, desperate and terrifying, yet inescapable, that Indian foreign policy had to be formulated after 1947. To India and other newly independent states, the choice during this period was limited to two broad alternatives. On the one hand, there was the choice of participating in the Cold War, inevitably including the military alliances and counter-alliances, possibly compromising to a considerable extent the newly won sovereignty ... and probably also sliding inexorably ... into the vortex of a totally destructive third world war. There was the choice, on the other hand, of keeping out of bipolar confrontation, preserving the newly won sovereignty and playing an independent role in international affairs, concentrating on domestic economic development and state-building, and endeavouring to reduce tension and control conflict situations through the United Nations and outside of it.[24]

India chose the second path, pursuing nonalignment, avoiding alliance or alignment with the great powers, seeking instead to have cordial relations with them, and using diplomatic suasion, especially within the UN system, as an instrument to articulate its interests and ideals.[25]

This approach to Cold War bipolarity was not cost-free, especially in India's relations with the West. In the 1950s and 1960s, European states found India's aspiration to act as a normative power irksome, as it campaigned against colonialism worldwide and racism in South Africa in particular. At the same time, many in the United States came to view India's unwillingness to align with it against the Soviet Union as amoral 'neutralism', or worse still, as evidence that Nehru and his government were themselves communists or fellow travellers.[26] That Nehru also pressed for recognition of the People's Republic of China during the late 1940s and 1950s merely deepened American suspicion, as did the nagging sense that India was playing the superpowers off against each other for its own advantage in terms of aid, technical assistance, and arms, at best, and free-riding on US efforts to underpin international peace and security, at worst.[27]

Nehru and his followers responded by arguing that India wished all well and was simply striving to act in a principled way, consistent with its obligations under the UN Charter. They insisted that India was driven as much by strong ethical and ideological beliefs formed during the independence struggle as by calculations of strategic interest. But Nehru acknowledged that nonalignment was also intended to put India in a good position to negotiate for aid and assistance, maximising its chances of getting what was required for economic and social development by placing the superpowers in competition for New Delhi's favour. And he believed that this competition could be exploited to boost India's security. As A. P. Rana has noted in his brilliant analysis of nonalignment, Nehru's view was that a 'free India … was secure by virtue of the rivalry of the great powers in potential (if not actual) conflict over her, and through such a conflict, a free but otherwise susceptible India could achieve and maintain her security … if she knew how to play her cards well'.[28]

In other words, Nehru's strategy was, as Rana rightly argued, a 'particular type of a balance of power policy', albeit one designed for the unusual circumstances of Cold War bipolarity and implemented by a weak actor. Stripped of the ethical and ideological baggage with which Nehru had (quite sincerely, for the most part) loaded it, the strategy was analogous to Britain's approach to European power politics in the nineteenth century, when it stood aloof from the squabbles of the continental states, intervening only when its interests or (occasionally) values were perceived to be at stake.[29] Nehru, a keen student of history, knew this strategy very well. By remaining outside alliances, India was, in theory at least, preserving its freedom to pick and choose what stance to take depending on the issues at stake in any given circumstances, criticising and sanctioning what it considered bad behaviour, even to the point of committing what military force it had to support one superpower bloc or another if, say, an act of aggression had taken place.

In practice, during the 1950s and for the rest of the Cold War, India found both this delicate geopolitical balancing act and the role of 'normative power' more challenging than Nehru had anticipated. India's leadership of the decolonising and postcolonial world was contested by China, despite Nehru's assiduous championing of China's claim on international recognition and China's seat on the UN Security Council (UNSC). Beijing's radicalism soon proved more appealing to other 'Third World' nationalists than Nehru's socialist-inflected liberalism, making for uncomfortable exchanges at the Bandung Conference in April 1955 and meetings of what later became the Non-Aligned Movement (NAM).[30] Unlike Nehru, these more radical nationalists were keen to see the nonaligned engage in power politics as a third pole, especially after the Sino-Soviet split began to emerge from 1960 onwards, and forge a new multipolar order.[31] At the same time, Nehru also struggled with the ideological preferences of his own representatives. The contrasting responses given by India's UN ambassador and Nehru confidante, V. K. Krishna Menon, to the two great crises of 1956 – Suez, which was roundly condemned, and Hungary, which was more mildly criticised – embarrassed the prime minister and left him open to accusations of pro-communist bias. Standing aloof and choosing sides according to conscience was increasingly difficult in such circumstances, as the Cold War deepened.

The 1962 war with China was, however, the crucial turning point. Menaced by the People's Liberation Army, which quickly overran India's forces on the northern border, Nehru was dismayed to discover that the United States and others, to which he turned for help, were unwilling to commit troops to defend India, a non-ally, despite what he saw as their obligations under the UN Charter.[32] A hard lesson was learned: India had to bolster its own capacity to deter potential adversaries and defend itself, if necessary. China's acquisition of a nuclear weapon in 1964 and Pakistan's adventurousness, leading to a brief war with India in 1965 and the forging of 'all weather friendship' with Beijing, simply reinforced that message.[33] After Nehru's death in 1964 – if not before – India was forced to admit that nonalignment had not brought it the advantages that it had promised. It had delivered neither security nor (arguably) greater access to aid and assistance, leaving India exposed to Chinese coercion and Pakistani belligerence.

This acknowledgement took time. In the mid-1960s, the lessening of Cold War tensions after the Cuban Missile Crisis, the re-emergence of Europe and Japan as economic powers, and nuclear tests by China and France, as well as the institutionalisation of NAM, gave rise in some quarters to the (in retrospect, mistaken) notion that bipolarity was about to be replaced by what Indian analysts termed 'polycentrism'.[34] In mainstream policymaking circles, this was seen as a potential boon to India, which could continue to pursue nonalignment with regard to the superpowers while taking advantage of new opportunities for aid, assistance, and arms from emerging sources.[35] In retrospect, however, this heralding of polycentricism and the hope of new partnerships that went with it was premature. Between 1962 and the end of the Cold War, India was forced to give up key elements of the Nehruvian strategy of nonalignment and to internalise certain logics imposed on New Delhi by great power politics, embracing instead a version of realism.[36] The hope – expressed at a high-level gathering of diplomats and scholars in 1966 – that this apparently emerging polycentrism would give India the chance to simultaneously 'end our increasing dependence on the United States and the Soviet Union … take suitable initiatives to solve our disputes with Pakistan and China, and establish closer ties with our other neighbours in Asia' was vain.[37]

In fact, the circumstances in which Indian policymakers laboured deteriorated in the latter part of the Cold War, as the economy stagnated (despite a growing population), the political system began to fragment as the hold of the Congress Party weakened, and international relations became even more challenging. The lesson partially learned in the crushing defeat inflicted by China were driven home by Pakistan's attack on India in 1965. Pakistan had adopted a very different foreign policy and national security strategy after 1947, becoming the 'most allied ally' of the US, a member of the Central Treaty Organization and the Southeast Asia Treaty Organization from 1955 until their respective demises (in 1979 and 1977). These ties, combined with extensive American military aid, gave Pakistan the leeway and means to pursue its territorial ambitions, especially its desire to subsume the two-thirds of Jammu and Kashmir governed by India after partition. Although Pakistan lost, New Delhi was forced once again to confront the reality that weak states faced by belligerent neighbours must either divert scarce resources to acquiring the means of defence and deterrence, or align or ally themselves with a stronger state, preferably one of the great powers.

In the end, New Delhi did both. It doubled the size of its military to over a million personnel, pushed its defence expenditure to about 3.5 per cent of gross domestic product, and began its own nuclear weapons programme.[38] Economic pressures and defence needs also drove New Delhi to consider a more robust partnership with one of the superpowers that would provide it with much needed markets, technical assistance, and technology. India made approaches to both superpowers, requesting aid, assistance, and arms. It received some help from the US, but the relationship faltered as Indira Gandhi, Nehru's daughter and prime minister from 1966 to 1977 and then again from 1980 to 1984, became a vocal critic of American conduct in

Vietnam. In response, the US cut off military aid to India, but carried on supplying it to Pakistan. Left with no alternative, New Delhi turned instead to the Soviet Union.[39]

In August 1971, India concluded a Treaty of Peace, Friendship and Cooperation with the Soviet Union. It was an admission, of sorts, that Cold War bipolarity necessitated making the choice that Nehru had thought avoidable and unnecessary between one bloc and another. The treaty did not constitute an alliance – indeed, Article IV specifically stated that the USSR respected 'India's policy of non-alignment'.[40] India and the USSR agreed not only to 'abstain from any aggression' but also to 'abstain from providing any assistance to any third party that engages in armed conflict' with the other or entering into obligations that might be prejudicial.[41] More importantly, from New Delhi's point of view, the treaty gave India the economic assistance and defence technology it needed, as well as the implied promise of Soviet diplomatic assistance at the UN.

These expedients did not solve the problems generated for relatively weak states under conditions of bipolarity, but they did at least mitigate their worst effects. Their potential efficacy was soon demonstrated in the crisis that erupted in December 1971 in what was then East Pakistan. Faced with a major humanitarian crisis – some 10 million refugees entered India as Pakistani forces suppressed a secessionist movement – and seeing an opportunity to hobble its rival, Indira Gandhi launched a military intervention that led to the rapid defeat of the Pakistani army and the creation of the independent state of Bangladesh.[42] This act was met with outrage in Washington, which had backed Pakistan with political support and military aid, and covertly sought its help in making an approach to Mao Zedong's China to normalise relations and shift the Cold War balance of power.[43] But with tacit – if not enthusiastic – Soviet cover, India was able to establish a kind of imperfect regional hegemony over South Asia, a key part of what became known as the 'Indira Doctrine' that shaped Indian thinking until the late 1980s.[44]

There were, of course, limits to New Delhi's new confidence, best illustrated by its so-called 'peaceful nuclear explosion' – essentially a nuclear weapons test – in 1974. Because India was not a treaty ally of the Soviet Union, it was not covered by extended nuclear deterrence, unlike members of the Warsaw Pact or North Atlantic Treaty Organization (NATO). The advent of the Nuclear Non-Proliferation Treaty, first signed in 1968 and in force from 1970, thus posed a dilemma for India, with a proximate nuclear threat coming from China, a possible although improbable one from the US, and an emerging one from Pakistan. New Delhi was faced with a choice between seeking a full alliance – as opposed to the tacit alignment it had with the Soviet Union – that might give it extended deterrence, but at the cost of diminished autonomy, or pursuing its own deterrent at the cost of reputational damage and further stress on a hard-pressed budget. In the event, New Delhi found a third way: demonstrating that it had the technology to build a bomb, but not pursuing a full deterrent too quickly, which allowed India to maintain a measure of autonomy while managing the financial costs involved in developing the weapons and delivery systems. It was an uneasy solution that showed up – among other things – the limits of its partnership with the Soviet Union and curbed its capacity to present itself as a 'normative power' in international relations.

In these ways, India struggled to cope with the pressures of state-building at home and the shifting dynamics of the Cold War abroad, downgrading its earlier effort to lead the postcolonial world into eschewing power politics, accommodating itself in part to bipolarity with its quasi-alignment with Moscow, and accepting that it needed to bolster its own military power. These compromises each had costs, however: undermining its influence in the developing world, complicating its relations with the West and – in different ways – with East Asian states, and imposing costs on an increasingly fragile economy. As a result, as S. D. Muni observed, India became increasingly 'marginal to the emerging world order', as it spent the remainder of the Cold War in a reactive mode, trying to limit the 'damage potential' of shifts in power and alignment to New Delhi's interests and preferences.[45]

Uncomfortable India in the unipolar moment

The end of the Cold War did not ease India's woes.[46] Indeed, in many ways, it exacerbated them. During 1991, India arguably reached its lowest ebb.[47] Its governments had grown weaker during the 1980s, as the fragmentation of the Indian party system progressed, and so had the economy, as the contradictions of the so-called 'licence raj' – heavy-handed bureaucratic regulation of commerce and industry – took their toll.[48] Abroad, India found itself in deepening diplomatic trouble, as Moscow and Beijing resolved some of their differences, the Soviets looked to reset their relations with the West, and East Asia's economic miracle gathered pace. New Delhi struggled to accommodate itself to these rapid changes and to the 'New World Order' they brought into being. During 1990 and 1991, India was left isolated and estranged from both the West and the Soviets over the equivocal position it struck concerning Iraq's invasion of Kuwait and the UNSC-sanctioned war to expel Saddam Hussein's forces.[49] At the same time, the spike in oil prices caused by the crisis eroded Indian foreign currency reserves to a dangerous level, forcing an embarrassing bailout from the International Monetary Fund that involved transporting some of its gold reserves to

Europe as collateral. Then in late December 1991 came the collapse of the Soviet Union, which greatly diminished the influence and capacity of India's principal economic and military partner.[50]

In the background, two other major emerging challenges loomed. The first was radical Islamism, which began to impinge on New Delhi's interests in several different ways – affecting its access to oil from the Middle East and directly threatening the many Indian workers in that region; destabilising Afghanistan, Pakistan, and perhaps even Central Asia more broadly in the wake of the Soviet withdrawal; potentially reviving insurgency in Kashmir; and even reshaping Hindu–Muslim relations in the rest of India. The other was China's economic transformation. These developments, combined with what some saw as New Delhi's laxity about defence preparedness, suggested to some analysts, like Bharat Karnad, that India's future was 'imperilled'.[51]

At the dawn of what Charles Krauthammer famously called the 'unipolar moment',[52] India found itself in a serious predicament. This was made worse by deep concerns in New Delhi about the role that the US and its allies might now play in international relations. A significant portion – although by no means all – of India's foreign and security policymaking elite was gripped by a profound sense of insecurity induced by unipolarity and what it might entail. The 1991 Gulf War raised fears about a new interventionist activism led by the West. In India, this generated specific worries about heightened international scrutiny of its governance of its part of Kashmir and other restive regions, and its rough handling of internal security problems, like its counter-insurgency campaign against Sikh secessionists in the 1980s.[53] At the same time, the dissolution of the multinational Soviet and Yugoslav states, and the apparent relaxation – at the behest of the West – of key international norms concerning national self-determination also challenged India, given its patchwork of ethnic, linguistic, and religious identities.[54]

Moreover, America's military capabilities, displayed to devastating effect in Kuwait, were met with acute anxiety in India about the capacity of its own Soviet-supplied forces to stand up to their Western equivalents, should the need arise.[55] While the end of the Cold War slowed the flow of weapons to Third World proxies and allies, the so-called 'revolution in military affairs' threatened a new and different arms race, in which postcolonial states were well behind the West in terms of access to advanced military technologies, forcing them to look to cruder alternatives.[56] The blunt response of General Krishnaswamy Sundarji, then one of India's most senior officers, when asked what he thought was the main lesson of the Gulf War, was telling: '[I]f a state intends to fight the US', Sundarji declared, 'it should avoid doing so unless and until it possesses nuclear weapons.'[57]

Insecurity was, however, only one driver of Indian concern about the US in the post-1991 'New World Order'. Ideology was the other. The emergence of a sole superpower was met with dismay in those parts of India's elite wedded to broadly Nehruvian, socialist, or Third World-ist views, as well as among the avowed 'realists' who worried about the unprecedented amount of power now concentrated in Washington's hands. The veteran analyst S. D. Muni, for example, who taught at the traditionally left-leaning Jawaharlal Nehru University from the mid-1970s until the 2000s, argued that if India was to retain its strategic and economic autonomy in the post-Cold War world, it needed 'to rediscover [its] Nehruvian elan', keep its distance from the US, keep its options open, and cooperate with Washington only on the basis of shared interests.[58] That way, he suggested, India could position itself to take advantage of the multipolar order that he thought would eventually follow the unipolar moment, acknowledging 'the reality of newly emerging power centers, such as Europe, China, Japan, and a number of "regional influential" actors in the Third World'.[59]

This vision of a multipolar order as the principal alternative to a US-dominated unipolar system persisted through the 1990s and after, despite the rise of more pragmatic ways of conceiving Indian foreign policy and India's relationship with the US during that period.[60] In the Nehruvian and socialist versions, it built on earlier visions of what Bandyopadhyaya had called – harking back to the 1960s – 'polycentrism', in which the nonaligned were willing and able to resist the push to ally with great powers, and advance the causes of anti-imperialism, anti-racism, mutual respect and non-interference, disarmament, the disbanding of military alliances, and the global redistribution of wealth against Western ideologies and interests, in particular.[61] Updated for the post-Cold War world, this vision involved a renewal of the spirit and practice of nonalignment and resistance to the various elements of American – and more broadly, Western – hegemony: political, economic, and military.

These ideas were influential throughout the 1990s and afterwards, despite significant improvements in relations with the United States in the early years of the twenty-first century. They informed India's opposition to various Western attempts to rewrite elements of the international order put in place after 1945, which aimed at aligning them with a more overly liberal internationalist agenda.[62] The 'humanitarian interventions' of the 1990s, in Yugoslavia and elsewhere, were met with scorn by Indian commentators, who questioned the motives of Western states, implying they were, at root, imperialistic.[63] At the UN, India condemned NATO's bombing of Kosovo in 1999 as 'a return to anarchy, where might is right'.[64] India also showed a marked reluctance to endorse the extension of international criminal law, attempting to derail the negotiation process that led to the Rome Statute establishing the International Criminal Court, and refusing to sign when it was agreed.[65] It behaved in a similar manner during the talks that led to the endorsement by the 2005 World Summit of the principle of the

'Responsibility to Protect', although in that case it reluctantly agreed to the final communique that endorsed the concept.[66]

At the same time, India worked to stymie international agreement in other areas, notably in the Doha Round of global trade talks which began in 2001, and in climate change negotiations, especially at Copenhagen in 2009. In particular, New Delhi's vehement opposition to lowering tariffs on agricultural goods and exposing its many poor and comparatively inefficient farmers to global competition is one of the major reasons why the World Trade Organization's Doha Round has failed to reach agreement, despite nine ministerial-level meetings over fifteen years.[67] India's collaboration with China at Copenhagen was the principal cause of the last-minute collapse of a US-sponsored deal on climate change at that meeting, although it should be noted that New Delhi has since modified its position to one that is more cooperative and amenable to Western agendas.[68]

This 'soft balancing' against US or European interests on a range of political and economic issues was complemented in Indian policy by efforts to maintain New Delhi's 'strategic autonomy' in a unipolar world that undercut Western-led efforts to improve international security.[69] Above all, this involved the development of a fully fledged nuclear deterrent. In May 1998, India tested five nuclear devices and subsequently made clear that it intended to build sufficient weapons for a nuclear triad.[70] While this expedient was principally undertaken to deter a rising China from military aggression against India, it threw efforts to defend and extend the nuclear non-proliferation regime, in which the US had taken the lead during the 1990s, into disarray.[71]

The immediate effects of the nuclear tests were not positive for India. Diplomatic protests were lodged and sanctions imposed. Pakistan moved to test six devices of its own and accelerated its missile programmes, allowing Islamabad the flexibility to develop a deterrent that might counterbalance India's superior conventional forces and to exploit the 'stability–instability' paradox by stepping up its support for terrorist groups willing to attack India in Kashmir and elsewhere.[72] Relations with Beijing suffered lasting damage, especially after the leak of a letter to President Bill Clinton from Indian Prime Minister Atal Bihari Vajpayee, which pointed to the threat from China as the main reason for the tests.[73] Over time, however, India's fortunes improved, as the US decided to re-engage New Delhi in a dialogue which eventually led to a bilateral nuclear deal that effectively recognised its right to possess nuclear weapons and permitted it to trade in civilian nuclear technology.[74] Moreover, this dialogue soon broadened, opening up new areas of political, economic, and defence cooperation between the US and India that were unprecedented in scale and scope.

India emerged from the unipolar moment in a much stronger position than it had been in at its start, in the early 1990s, despite reservations held by the Indian elite about American power and Western agendas. In the early 2000s, if not before, however, a new challenge was looming: coping with the implications of the rise of China as a challenger to American power and influence in the Asia-Pacific, which might or might not herald a multipolar or polycentric order advantageous to India.

Multipolarity and multialignment

At the end of the Cold War, as we have seen, leading Indian thinkers like S. D. Muni saw more opportunities than challenges in the multipolar order he predicted would follow the unipolar moment.[75] At the close of the 1990s, however, despite a decade of economic growth and burgeoning confidence about India's chance of emerging as a major power, the mood had shifted. To be sure, many analysts were convinced, as Gurmeet Kanwal put it, that 'the international order is gradually, but inexorably, changing to a polycentric system'. But this prediction was tempered by a stark warning about the effects that China's growing military and economic power might have on India's security in the context of this new order.[76] During the late 1990s and early 2000s, this concern was compounded by the growing realisation that Moscow's or Beijing's preferred version of multipolarity did not necessarily align with New Delhi's. The responses of China and India to the Russian proposal, made by Yevgeny Primakov in 1998, to form a 'strategic triangle' to 'counter ... increasing US hegemony', were telling. As Kanwal observed: 'India responded in a lukewarm manner', and 'China dismissed it out of hand'.[77]

New Delhi's ambivalence was a function of disagreement within the strategic elite about how best to handle the manifold challenges posed by China and thereby realise a multipolar or polycentric order that secured and promoted India's interests and values. In the 2000s and 2010s these questions pressed on India's policymakers as Beijing's power grew. During this period, four different schools of thought contended for influence and, at different points, underpinned India's China policy: one basically Nehruvian; one that was broadly liberal (or, for some, 'neoliberal' or 'liberal globalist'); one that was essentially realist; and one derived from Hindu nationalist ideology.[78] While they all agreed that a multipolar order was desirable from an Indian perspective, they differed over how to achieve it and what it might involve, in terms of both the balance of power and the rules of the game, as China's shadow loomed. The Nehruvians favoured dialogue with Beijing and were wary about Washington and its intentions.[79] The liberals argued that globalisation was transforming international relations, that India needed to open up if it was to develop, that greater economic interdependence with

China would help reduce the likelihood of conflict, that New Delhi should work with Beijing to rewrite the rules of global governance, but that India also needed to build a closer strategic partnership with the US.[80] The realists argued that the liberals were being overly optimistic – though they too generally favoured more economic liberalisation and strong defence and security ties with the US – and called for India to bolster its military capabilities to defend its interests and deter possible adventurism by Beijing.[81] The Hindu nationalists, for their part, were sceptical about globalisation and wary of greater economic interdependence with China. They agreed with the realists that military modernisation and stronger ties with the US were needed, but held too that India needed to bolster its 'soft power' in East and South Asia to counter Chinese influence.[82]

From the late 1990s to the late 2010s, each of these schools of thought in turn shaped India's approach to China and its wider strategy. Under the Hindu nationalist-led government of Vajpayee (1998–2004) realism mostly prevailed, as New Delhi acquired nuclear weapons in an effort to deter China from encroaching on India's interests, and to give India some breathing space for further social and economic development and room to negotiate more confidently with the major powers abroad, including both China and the US.[83] During Manmohan Singh's first term in office (2004–2009) the liberals were in charge.[84] They argued that economic considerations did and should drive relations between the major powers, and that India ought to embrace globalisation and economic interdependence to a greater degree, including with China.[85] At the same time, as a hedge, New Delhi worked to construct a strategic partnership with the US. In Singh's second term, however, Beijing's growing assertiveness, concern over the state of the US economy, and worries about India's own circumstances led to a partial return to a more realist approach, with moves to bolster military power. Under his successor, Narendra Modi, who came to power in mid-2014, this new realism was blended with Hindu nationalist thinking which rendered Sino-Indian competition – and indeed international relations as a whole – as a struggle involving both soft and hard power.[86]

Beneath these shifts in policy, however, there remained a basic consensus that a multipolar order was a 'good thing', provided that India was one of the poles, and the system was not unbalanced at either the global or regional level by an overpowerful state. As a result, there was a basic continuity of approach in Indian strategy, despite shifts in policy or emphasis concerning one major power or another. 'Multialignment' replaced 'nonalignment' during the 2000s, as New Delhi tacked backwards and forwards, deepening partnerships in some sectors with both Beijing and Washington at the same time, forging them with others, like Tokyo, and playing a bigger role in multilateral contexts.[87] This behaviour reflected the growing belief that the greatest challenge to Indian interests was not a US-dominated unipolar order, as it had been in the 1990s, but rather a Sino-US-dominated bipolar global order in which China emerged as the dominant power in Asia. As Mohan Malik observed in 2012, this view increasingly put New Delhi 'at odds' with Beijing (and Moscow, for that matter), where 'multipolarity is often expressed in terms of "saving others from US hegemony"'. In India, by contrast, 'multipolarity' was by the early 2010s understood 'in terms of "saving itself and others" from American and Chinese hegemony'.[88]

New Delhi's frequently reiterated commitments to a multipolar 'world order' – such as the one it made during Modi's summit with Russian President Vladimir Putin in early October 2018 – should be seen in that light.[89] New Delhi's new conception of multipolarity is quite distinct from Russia's or China's: in contrast to earlier versions, it no longer implies a diminution of Washington's global role or its vision of a 'rules-based order'. Instead, it now supports a continued US role as a security provider and as a leader in global governance – a position that contrasts with the mixed and often hostile ones taken by New Delhi during the 1990s. To be sure, it recognises that American power is declining relatively as China rises and rearms.[90] As Modi argued in an important speech at the Shangri-La Dialogue in early June 2018, India now shares the US 'vision of an open, stable, secure and prosperous Indo-Pacific Region'. It seeks an order that is grounded in 'sovereignty and territorial integrity, as well as equality of all nations, irrespective of size and strength' in which 'rules and norms should be based on the consent of all, not on the power of the few'.[91] And making such an order a reality, many in India's elite now believe, requires multipolar balances at both the regional and global levels.

Conclusion

As China's new assertiveness has become ever more apparent and disagreements between Beijing and New Delhi have multiplied, the appeal to India of a multipolar order that retains the US as a significant player in the Indo-Pacific has patently deepened. Xi Jinping's signature policy – the Belt and Road Initiative (BRI) – has played a central role in this process, as New Delhi has become increasingly uncomfortable about Chinese economic statecraft in general and about BRI 'connectivity' projects in particular.[92] New Delhi has pushed back on Chinese claims that the BRI is a 'multilateral' enterprise, with the then foreign secretary, S. Jaishankar, taking pains to describe it as a 'national Chinese initiative' in comments following a high-profile speech in July 2015.[93] At the Raisina Dialogue six months later, India's then external affairs minister, Sushma Swaraj, reinforced this point, calling for a 'cooperative rather than unilateral approach' that creates 'an environment of trust and confidence', and warning against using 'connectivity as an exercise in hard-wiring that influences choices'. She went on to emphasise that, in India's view, multilateralism was the best means to create and sustain a multipolar order:

> Connectivity should diffuse national rivalries, not add to regional tensions … Indeed, if we seek a multi-polar world, the right way to begin is to create a multi-polar Asia. Nothing could foster that more than an open minded [*sic*] consultation on the future of connectivity.[94]

These pleas fell, of course, on deaf ears in Beijing, as did New Delhi's complaints about the specifics of the China–Pakistan Economic Corridor, central to the BRI, which runs through territory in Kashmir that India claims as its own.

In Modi's India, multipolarity has thus emerged as a useful device for pushing back against Chinese assertiveness, as Beijing seeks to establish some kind of hegemony over its immediate neighbourhood and the wider Indo-Pacific. But as I have argued, a desire for a multipolar or polycentric world can be located in earlier debates about India and its global role. Conscious of relative weakness but eager to set an example of a more enlightened approach to foreign policy, and to create circumstances in which India could eventually take its rightful place in the world as the inheritor of an extraordinary civilisational legacy, Nehru's government pursued nonalignment as a means of challenging Cold War bipolarity and undermining its polarising logic. Keen to defend its independence and its perceived interests after the Cold War, in the unipolar moment New Delhi looked to build its capabilities and to resist, where it could, attempts to impose more liberal rules and norms on developing states, whether in the form of freer trade or the extension of international criminal justice. India's appeal for a multipolar order today, in the face of what some see as a drive for Chinese regional hegemony, has similar drivers: a desire for autonomy and the time and space to develop the country to its full potential, matching a recognition that an order dominated by one or two powers would not provide the best circumstances in which to realise those ambitions.

Notes

1 Subrahmanyam Jaishankar, 'Speech by foreign secretary at Second Raisina Dialogue in New Delhi', Ministry of External Affairs, India, 18 January 2017, https://mea.gov.in/Speeches-Statements.htm?dtl/27949/Speech_by_Foreign_Secretary_at_Second_Raisina_Dialogue_in_New_Delhi_January_18_2017 (accessed 10 August 2017). As foreign secretary, Jaishankar was the Ministry of External Affairs' highest-ranking official.

2 For an eloquent recent expression of this view by someone who has been both India's top diplomat and its foreign minister, see Subrahmanyam Jaishankar, *The India Way: Strategies for an Uncertain World Order* (New Delhi: HarperCollins, 2020).

3 This point is well made by C. Raja Mohan in *Crossing the Rubicon: The Shaping of India's New Foreign Policy* (New York: Palgrave Macmillan, 2003), especially pp. 57–115.

4 See especially Waheguru Pal Singh Sidhu, Pratap Bhanu Mehta, and Bruce Jones (eds), *Shaping the Emerging World: India and the Multilateral Order* (Washington, DC: Brookings Institution Press, 2013).

5 This is not to say that Indians had not thought about international relations prior to 1947. As Rahul Sagar and others have shown, they had. See Rahul Sagar, 'Before midnight: views on international relations, 1857–1947', in David M. Malone, C. Raja Mohan, and Srinath Raghavan (eds), *The Oxford Handbook of Indian Foreign Policy* (Oxford: Oxford University Press, 2015), pp. 65–79.

6 See especially Sneh Mahajan, 'The foreign policy of the Raj and its legacy', in Malone et al. (eds), *Oxford Handbook of Indian Foreign Policy*, pp. 51–64. Of course, there were some continuities between the foreign and defence policies of British and postcolonial India. For an overview, see Pallavi Raghavan, 'Historiography of South Asia's international relations', in Mischa Hansel, Raphaëlle Khan, and Mélissa Levaillant (eds), *Theorizing Indian Foreign Policy* (Abingdon: Routledge, 2017), pp. 15–28.

7 Jayashree Vivekanandan provides a useful account of Mughal thinking in 'Strategy, legitimacy and the Imperium: framing the Mughal strategic discourse', in Kanti Bajpai, Saira Basit, and V. Krishnappa (eds), *India's Grand Strategy: History, Theory, Cases* (New Delhi: Routledge, 2014), pp. 63–85.

8 Mughal strategic thought did, of course, shape Pakistani thinking. See especially C. Christine Fair, *Fighting to the End: The Pakistan Army's Way of War* (New York: Oxford University Press, 2014).

9 For an overview, see Paul F. Power, 'Indian foreign policy: the age of Nehru', *Review of Politics*, 26:2 (1964), 257–86. See also Sunil Khilnani, *The Idea of India* (New Delhi: Penguin, 1997).

10 Adda B. Bozeman, 'India's foreign policy today: reflections upon its sources', *World Politics*, 10:2 (1958), 256–73, at 265–6. Ashoka's wheel – his *dharmachakra* or wheel of *dharma* (loosely, righteousness) – was integrated into the flag of the Republic of India and his distinctive Lion Capital made India's national emblem.

11 Andrew Bingham Kennedy, *The International Ambitions of Mao and Nehru: National Efficacy Beliefs and the Making of Foreign Policy* (New York: Cambridge University Press, 2012), pp. 139–72. The literature on Gandhi's political thought is vast, but see Bhikhu Parekh, *Gandhi's Political Philosophy: A Critical Examination* (Basingstoke: Macmillan, 1989).

12 On Nehru's thought, see M. N. Das, *The Political Philosophy of Jawaharlal Nehru* (London: George Allen & Unwin, 1961). See also S. Gopal, 'The formative

ideology of Jawaharlal Nehru', *Economic and Political Weekly*, 11:21 (1976), 787–9, 791–2.

13 Bozeman, 'India's foreign policy today', 269–70. On Laski and Menon, see Ian Hall, '"Mephistopheles in a Saville Row suit": V. K. Krishna Menon and the West', in Ian Hall (ed.), *Radicals and Reactionaries in Twentieth-Century International Thought* (New York: Palgrave Macmillan, 2015), pp. 191–216.

14 This world view is still best approached via Nehru's speeches. See especially Jawaharlal Nehru, *India's Foreign Policy: Selected Speeches, September 1946–April 1961* (New Delhi: Publications Division, Ministry of Information and Broadcasting, Government of India, 1961).

15 A. P. Rana, 'The intellectual dimensions of India's nonalignment', *Journal of Asian Studies*, 28:2 (1969), 299–312, at 302.

16 Jawaharlal Nehru, *The Discovery of India* (New Delhi: Penguin, 2004 [1946]), pp. 600–1.

17 Ian Hall, 'Normative power India?', in Jamie Gaskarth (ed.), *China, India and the Future of International Society* (Lanham, MD: Rowman & Littlefield, 2015), pp. 89–104, at pp. 94–7.

18 Manu Bhagavan, *India and the Quest for One World: The Peacemakers* (Basingstoke: Palgrave Macmillan, 2013). Nehru borrowed the slogan 'One World' from Franklin D. Roosevelt's wartime special envoy, Wendell Willkie.

19 India might be an 'infant State', Nehru argued in 1949, but it is a 'very ancient country' with 'a history in which she has played a vital part not only within her own vast boundaries, but in the world and in Asia in particular'. See Jawaharlal Nehru, 'India and Asia' (1949), in Nehru, *India's Foreign Policy*, pp. 21–3, at p. 21, and see also the excellent summary of Nehru's understanding of Indian greatness in Tobias F. Engelmeier, *Nation-Building and Foreign Policy in India: An Identity–Strategy Conflict* (New Delhi: Foundation Books, 2009), pp. 210–21.

20 Hall, 'Normative power India?' On India as a 'moral power', see Priya Chacko, *Indian Foreign Policy: The Politics of Postcolonial Identity from 1947 to 2004* (Abingdon: Routledge, 2012), pp. 19–106.

21 For a helpful account of how Nehru conceived state-building in India, see Kennedy, *International Ambitions of Mao and Nehru*, pp. 139–237.

22 Ian Hall, 'The persistence of Nehruvianism in India's strategic culture', in Ashley J. Tellis, Alison Szalwinski, and Michael Wills (eds), *Strategic Asia 2016–17: Understanding Strategic Cultures in the Asia-Pacific* (Washington, DC: National Bureau of Asian Research, 2016), pp. 141–68. Pratap Bhanu Mehta argues that the persistence of the Nehruvian framework is due to a lack of alternatives. See Pratap Bhanu Mehta, 'Still under Nehru's shadow? The absence of foreign policy frameworks in India', *India Review*, 8:3 (2009), 209–33.

23 See especially Itty Abraham, 'From Bandung to NAM: Non-alignment and Indian foreign policy, 1947–65', *Commonwealth and Comparative Politics*, 46:2 (2008), 195–219.

24 J. Bandyopadhyaya, *The Making of India's Foreign Policy: Determinants, Institutions, Processes and Personalities*, 2nd edn (New Delhi: Allied Publishers, 1979), pp. 100–1.

25 For an early account of nonalignment, see Jawaharlal Nehru, 'We lead ourselves' (1948), in Nehru, *India's Foreign Policy*, pp. 29–37.
26 The charge that Nehru's policy was neutralist was also made domestically. For a characteristic response, see Jawaharlal Nehru, 'The larger scheme of things' (1952), in Nehru, *India's Foreign Policy*, pp. 55–64, especially pp. 58–9.
27 As Michael Edwardes noted in the mid-1960s, during much of the previous decade nonalignment was a 'dirty word', especially to American Secretary of State, John Foster Dulles. See Michael Edwardes, 'Illusion and reality in India's foreign policy', *International Affairs*, 41:1 (1965), 48–58, at 48. For a useful discussion of nonalignment and neutralism, see Peter Lyon, *Neutralism* (Leicester: Leicester University Press, 1963).
28 Rana, 'Intellectual dimensions', pp. 305–6.
29 *Ibid.*, p. 302. For the comparison with British foreign policy, see also p. 308. For a similar take on Nehru's nonalignment policy, characterised as 'liberal realism', see Srinath Raghavan, *War and Peace in Modern India* (New York: Palgrave Macmillan, 2010).
30 See Abraham, 'From Bandung to NAM'.
31 This interpretation of the operation of NAM was and remains, of course, contested. Radical Nehruvians like Bandyopadhyaya, for example, argued that NAM was 'a counterforce to the balance of power', a 'futuristic movement' that signalled the beginning of a new era in international relations, and a signal that bipolarity had been replaced in the late 1950s by 'polycentrism'. See Jayantanuja Bandyopadhyaya, *North over South: A Non-Western Perspective of International Relations* (New Delhi and Madras: South Asian Publishers, 1982), p. 197. On Nehru's opposition to a 'third force', see Jawaharlal Nehru, 'No "third force"' (1957), in Nehru, *India's Foreign Policy*, pp. 77–9.
32 See especially Rudra Chaudhuri, *Forged in Crisis: India and the United States since 1947* (London: Hurst & Company, 2014). The US did, of course, provide arms and ammunition.
33 On this relationship, see Andrew Small, *The China–Pakistan Axis: Asia's New Geopolitics* (London: Hurst & Company, 2015).
34 See the summary of a discussion between Indian diplomats and scholars at the School of International Studies in Delhi in July 1966, in Bimla Prasad, 'A fresh look at India's foreign policy', *International Studies*, 8:3 (1967), 277–99.
35 *Ibid.*, p. 277.
36 There is a very active debate about how 'realist' Indian foreign policy was after Nehru. See especially Surjit Mansingh, 'Indira Gandhi's foreign policy: hard realism?', in Malone et al. (eds), *Oxford Handbook of Indian Foreign Policy*, pp. 104–16.
37 Prasad, 'Fresh look', p. 286. For a more pessimistic view, see Bandyopadhyaya, *Making of India's Foreign Policy*, pp. 101–3.
38 On modernisation, see Hall, 'Persistence of Nehruvianism', p. 156; on the nuclear programme, see George Perkovich, *India's Nuclear Bomb: The Impact on Global Proliferation*, updated edn (Berkeley and Los Angeles, CA: University of California Press, 1999), pp. 60–85.

39 Bruce Riedel, *Avoiding Armageddon: America, India, and Pakistan to the Brink and Back* (New Delhi: HarperCollins, 2013), p. 69.
40 'Treaty of Peace, Friendship and Cooperation between the Government of India and the Government of the Union of Soviet Socialist Republics', 9 August 1971, Article IV, http://mea.gov.in/bilateral-documents.htm?dtl/5139/Treaty+of+ (accessed 10 August 2017).
41 *Ibid.*, Articles VIII, IX.
42 See, *inter alia*, Srinath Raghavan, *1971: A Global History of the Creation of Bangladesh* (Cambridge, MA: Harvard University Press, 2013).
43 Gary J. Bass, *The Blood Telegram: Nixon, Kissinger, and a Forgotten Genocide* (New York: Random House, 2014).
44 For an overview of Indian regional strategy in this period, see Mohammed Ayoob, 'India in South Asia: the quest for regional predominance', *World Policy Journal*, 7:1 (1989/1990), 107–33.
45 S. D. Muni, 'India and the post-Cold War world: opportunities and challenges', *Asian Survey*, 31:9 (1991), 862–74, at 862–3.
46 See especially the first line of the veteran politician, former soldier, and erstwhile Defence, External Affairs and Finance Minister Jaswant Singh's landmark article 'Against nuclear apartheid': 'While the end of the Cold War transformed the political landscape of Europe, it did little to ameliorate India's security concerns.' See Jaswant Singh, 'Against nuclear apartheid', *Foreign Affairs*, 77:5 (1998), 41–52, at 41.
47 In Ramesh Thakur's words, India 'cut a sorry figure' – it was 'friendless and forlorn'. See Ramesh Thakur, 'India after nonalignment', *Foreign Affairs*, 71:2 (1992), 165–82, at 165.
48 On Indian politics during this period, see especially Pradeep K. Chhibber, *Democracy without Associations: Transformation of the Party System and Social Cleavages in India* (Ann Arbor, MI: University of Michigan Press, 2001).
49 J. Mohan Malik, 'India's response to the Gulf crisis: implications for Indian foreign policy', *Asian Survey*, 31:9 (1991), 847–61.
50 For a useful overview of the challenges faced and their impact, see James Chiriyankandath, 'Realigning India: Indian foreign policy after the Cold War', *The Round Table: The Commonwealth Journal of International Affairs*, 93:374 (2004), 199–211.
51 Bharat Karnad, 'Introduction', in Bharat Karnad (ed.), *Future Imperilled: India's Security in the 1990s and Beyond* (New Delhi: Viking, 1994), pp. 1–15, at pp. 4–6.
52 Charles Krauthammer, 'The unipolar moment', *Foreign Affairs*, 70:1 (1990/91), 23–33.
53 On Kashmir and India's approach to counter-insurgency more broadly during this period, see Sumit Ganguly and Kanti Bajpai, 'India and the crisis in Kashmir', *Asian Survey*, 34:5 (1994), 401–16.
54 Mohammed Ayoob, *The Third World Security Predicament: State Making, Regional Conflict, and the International System* (Boulder, CO: Lynne Rienner, 1995), pp. 165–88.

55 See, *inter alia*, V. K. Nair, *War in the Gulf: Lessons for the Third World* (New Delhi: Lancer, 1991).

56 On the relief that the end of the Cold War might bring, see Muni, 'India and the post-Cold War world', p. 864; for an assessment of the 'revolution in military affairs' and its implications for India's region, see especially Paul Dibb, 'The revolution in military affairs and Asian security', *Survival*, 39:4 (1997), 93–116.

57 Quoted in Thanos P. Dokos, *Countering the Proliferation of Weapons of Mass Destruction: NATO and EU Options in the Mediterranean and the Middle East* (Abingdon: Routledge, 2015), p. 94.

58 Muni, 'India and the post-Cold War world', p. 867.

59 *Ibid.*, p. 868.

60 See Mohan, *Crossing the Rubicon*.

61 Bandyopadhyaya, *North over South*, pp. 197–236.

62 On India and the liberal order, see Ted Piccone, *Five Rising Democracies and the Fate of the International Liberal Order* (Washington, DC: Brookings Institution Press, 2016), pp. 71–96.

63 See, for example, M. S. Rajan, '"The new interventionism"?', *International Studies*, 37:1 (2000), 31–40.

64 Ian Hall, 'Tilting at windmills? The Indian debate over the responsibility to protect after UNSC Resolution 1973', *Global Responsibility to Protect*, 5:1 (2013), 84–108, at 91.

65 Usha Ramanathan, 'India and the ICC', *Journal of International Criminal Justice*, 3:3 (2005), 627–34. India's position aligned with the US, which did sign the Rome Statute in 2000, but has since refused to ratify it.

66 Hall, 'Tilting at windmills?', p. 93.

67 Andrew Hurrell and Amrita Narlikar, 'A new politics of confrontation? Brazil and India in multilateral trade negotiations', *Global Society*, 20:4 (2006), 415–33.

68 In general, and for helpful comparisons with the positions of other developing states, see Andrew Hurrell and Sandeep Sengupta, 'Emerging powers, North–South relations and global climate politics', *International Affairs*, 88:3 (2012), 463–84.

69 On 'soft balancing', see T. V. Paul, 'Soft balancing in the age of US primacy', *International Security*, 30:1 (2005), 46–71; on the concept of 'strategic autonomy' and its relationship with 'nonalignment', see Teresita C. Schaffer and Howard B. Schaffer, *India at the Global High Table: The Quest for Regional Primacy and Strategic Autonomy* (Washington, DC: Brookings Institution Press, 2016).

70 For a useful early discussion of India's nuclear doctrine and implied force structure, see P. R. Chari, 'India's nuclear doctrine: confused ambitions', *Nonproliferation Review*, 7:3 (2000), 123–35.

71 William Walker, 'International nuclear relations after the Indian and Pakistani test explosions', *International Affairs*, 74:3 (1998), 505–28.

72 On these dynamics, see S. Paul Kapur, 'India and Pakistan's unstable peace: why nuclear South Asia is not like Cold War Europe', *International Security*, 30:2 (2005), 127–52.

73 'Nuclear anxiety; Indian's letter to Clinton on the nuclear testing', *New York Times*, 13 May 1998. Andrew B. Kennedy offers a detailed analysis of the Indian calculations. See Andrew B. Kennedy, 'India's nuclear odyssey: implicit

umbrellas, diplomatic disappointments, and the bomb', *International Security*, 36:2 (2011), 120–53.
74 See especially Dinshaw Mistry, *The US–India Nuclear Agreement: Diplomacy and Domestic Politics* (Cambridge: Cambridge University Press, 2014).
75 Muni, 'India and the post-Cold War world'.
76 Gurmeet Kanwal, 'China's long march to world power status: strategic challenge for India', *Strategic Analysis*, 22:11 (1999), 1713–28, at 1713.
77 *Ibid.*, p. 1714. For an in-depth but sceptical assessment of the concept, see Harsh V. Pant, 'The Moscow–Beijing–Delhi "strategic triangle": an idea whose time may never come', *Security Dialogue*, 35:3 (2004), 311–28.
78 For a useful account of these schools, see Deepa M. Ollapally and Rajesh Rajagopalan, 'India: foreign policy of an ambiguous power', in Henry R. Nau and Deepa M. Ollapally (eds), *Worldviews of Aspiring Powers: Domestic Foreign Policy Debates in China, India, Iran, Japan, and Russia* (New York: Oxford University Press, 2012), pp. 73–113.
79 For a Nehruvian view, see Alka Acharya, *China and India: The Politics of Incremental Engagement* (New Delhi: Har Anand, 2008).
80 For a liberal view, see Sanjaya Baru, *India and the World: Essays on Geoeconomics and Foreign Policy* (New Delhi: Academic Foundation, 2016), especially chapter 9, as well as Jairam Ramesh, *Making Sense of Chindia: Reflections on China and India* (New Delhi: India Research Press, 2005) and Prem Shankar Jha, *Crouching Dragon, Hidden Tiger: Can China and India Dominate the West?* (New York: Soft Skull Press, 2010).
81 See, for example, Harsh V. Pant, 'India comes to terms with a rising China', in Ashley J. Tellis, Travis Tanner, and Jessica Keough (eds), *Strategic Asia 2011–12: Asia Responds to its Rising Powers: China and India* (Seattle and Washington, DC: National Bureau of Asian Research, 2012), pp. 101–30.
82 See, for example, Tarun Vijay, *India Battles to Win* (New Delhi: Rupa, 2009), pp. 217–21.
83 See especially Mohan, *Crossing the Rubicon*.
84 Ian Hall, 'China in India's strategic thought', in Kanti Bajpai, Manjari Chatterjee Miller, and Selina Ho (eds), *Routledge Handbook of China–India Relations* (London and New York: Routledge, 2019).
85 Sanjara Baru, *The Accidental Prime Minister: The Making and Unmaking of Manmohan Singh* (New Delhi: Penguin, 2014), pp. 165–7.
86 Ian Hall, *Modi and the Reinvention of Indian Foreign Policy* (Bristol: Bristol University Press, 2019).
87 Shashi Tharoor uses the term 'multialignment' in his *Pax Indica: India and the World of the 21st Century* (New Delhi: Penguin, 2012), pp. 406–28.
88 Mohan Malik, 'India balances China', *Asian Politics & Policy*, 4:3 (2012), 345–76, at 361.
89 Ministry of External Affairs, 'India–Russia joint statement during visit of President of Russia to India', 5 October 2018, https://mea.gov.in/bilateral-documents.htm?dtl/30469/IndiaRussia_Joint_Statement_during_visit_of_President_of_Russia_to_India_October_05_2018 (accessed 18 February 2020).
90 This is very clear, for example, in Jaishankar, *The India Way*.

91 Ministry of External Affairs, 'Prime minister's keynote address at Shangri La Dialogue', 1 June 2018, https://.mea.gov.in/Speeches-Statements.htm?dtl/29943/Prime+Ministers+Keynote+Address+at+Shangri+La+Dialogue+June+01+2018 (accessed 18 February 2020).

92 For a critical assessment of China's economic statecraft, see Robert D. Blackwill and Jennifer M. Harris, *War by Other Means: Geoeconomics and Statecraft* (Cambridge, MA: Belknap, 2016), pp. 93–151.

93 S. Jaishankar, comments following 'India, the United States, and China', IISS Fullerton Lecture, 29 July 2015, www.youtube.com/watch?v=et2ihw8jHaY&feature=youtu.be&t=46m27s, at 46 mins (accessed 18 February 2020).

94 Quoted in Tanvi Madan, 'What India thinks about China's One Belt, One Road initiative (but doesn't explicitly say)', *Brookings Institution*, 14 March 2016, www.brookings.edu/blog/order-from-chaos/2016/03/14/what-india-thinks-about-chinas-one-belt-one-road-initiative-but-doesnt-explicitly-say/ (accessed 18 February 2020).

3

Brazil: Pursuing a multipolar mirage?

Luis L. Schenoni

Ai, esta terra ainda vai cumprir seu ideal:
Ainda vai tornar-se um império colonial!
[Oh, this land will still accomplish its ideal:
It will still become a colonial empire!]
Chico Buarque, *Fado Tropical*

Introduction

In this chapter, I explore the use of the concept of multipolarity in the Brazilian foreign policy debate from 2000 to 2015. To do so, I draw on four sources. First, I analyse documents from Brazilian government agencies to reconstruct how polarity was thought of and what impact this had on actual policy. Second, I rely on a series of in-depth interviews conducted in June 2017 with academics and Brazilian public officials to help unravel their understanding of the term and the interests of different actors. Third, I systematically review the public speeches of politicians and diplomats in forums such as the Brazilian Congress and the United Nations General Assembly (UNGA). Fourth, I examine academic articles that discuss the role of Brazil in a multipolarity scenario, published in the two major Brazilian International Relations (IR) journals and in non-Brazilian IR journals with a measured high impact.

Two main conclusions can be drawn from this review of the Brazilian discourse on multipolarity. The first is that it has been emotionally potent and 'sticky', despite evidence to refute it. Arguably, it was the thirst for global recognition and grandeur reflected in the ironic quote of Chico Buarque's *Fado Tropical* that initially led Brazilian scholars, diplomats, and politicians to believe in the multipolar mirage. This mirage metaphor highlights the idea that the aspiration was genuine in the early 2000s, but has since become unrealistic because of domestic problems in Brazil and, most importantly, the evolution of the international system towards a *bipolar* distribution of capabilities.[1] Nowadays, the popular saying that 'Brazil is the country of the future, and always will be' better captures both structural trends and the mood of public opinion. Yet scholars and practitioners of Brazilian foreign policy have had a difficult time accepting the new reality. Unlikely as it may seem, the multipolar discourse continues to resonate in everyday foreign policy discussions in Brasilia even after the arrival of President Jair Bolsonaro. This strange phenomenon suggests a deep emotional attachment to the unfulfilled expectations of the recent past, and the successful resistance of powerful interest groups and many individuals who have invested their careers in the prospects of an expansive diplomacy.[2] Even when Brazilian foreign policy started a retraction with President Michel Temer, which arguably continues,[3] the *saudade* of an expansionist foreign policy is still evident in, for example, the messianic discourse of Foreign Minister Ernesto Araújo.

The second conclusion is that multipolarity has been subjected to an impressive degree of conceptual stretching in the Brazilian foreign policy debate.[4] Practitioners and academics – most of them analysts and diplomatic historians unfamiliar with IR theory – should take a step back and rethink fundamentally what they mean when using the term. My interviews with members of the foreign policy community in Brasilia reveal a great divergence in their understanding of multipolarity. In particular, their conceptions about multipolarity seem to be at odds with that of realism, the school in which the idea of polarity originated, and the only one to provide a consensual, empirical definition of the concept.

In this chapter I trace the evolution of this debate, identifying the different uses and misuses of the concept by influential scholars and practitioners of Brazilian foreign policy. After providing a map of the interests involved and a raw measure of conceptual stretching, I offer a typology of typical misapprehensions. I also discern common themes across actors – discursive coalitions – and the implicit theoretical framework they use to reinterpret and redefine the concept. Although one might expect a clear separation between the scholarly and political uses of the multipolar discourse – the first being more rigorous – my findings suggest that it cuts transversally across the two spheres. In particular, one understanding of multipolarity associated with multilateralism, South–South cooperation, and the BRICS (Brazil, Russia, India, China, and South Africa) group, was very effective in both informing an expansive foreign policy and in framing the academic debate.

The chapter is structured as follows. The first section shows how the evolution of the international system and domestic politics undermined the initial hopes that Brazil would become a pole in a multipolar world. The second section deals with the problem of conceptual stretching and presents a sketch of the interests and coalitions that benefited from the misperception of material capability distribution in the international structure. The third and fourth sections deal with the misuse of the term in the political and academic spheres. Finally, I briefly discuss the 'hangover' that took place after the multipolar carnival ended in 2015, the drivers of stubbornness, and some lessons learned.

The multipolar mirage

Some academic fashions and political moods, like carnivals, begin rather quietly, grow into a frenzy, and end in hangovers. Excitement about the idea of a multipolar world in which Brazil would play a central role was apparently one of these bubbles. Unfortunately, we are now left with the consequences of the excesses of that era, which are amplified by the current economic and political crises in Brazil. Looking back, evidence that the world was rapidly becoming bipolar, *not* multipolar,[5] was apparent before the Brazilian crisis, and a better assessment of structural variables could have prevented both the exaggerations of the past and the present despondency.

Not everything about the multipolar illusion is regrettable. Intellectually, it was a period of some fertility in which academics and practitioners of Brazilian foreign policy rethought their position in the world – as the world rethought the international role of Brazil. At the beginning, their main conclusions were correct: the early 2000s opened a window of opportunity for a more assertive foreign policy and presented multipolarity as a possible future scenario for the long term. But at some point multipolarity became a normative objective,[6] and the enterprise to reinterpret and redefine the concept, if it ever existed, was truncated by the overwhelming force of political interests. These interest groups then log-rolled for a foreign policy of overexpansion, creating what we could effectively call a myth of multipolarity.[7]

Although any periodisation is arbitrary, one could sensibly locate the rise and fall of the multipolar debate roughly between the years 2000 and 2015.[8] Before 2000, references to the term were scant in the political realm. On taking up the presidency in 1995, President Fernando Henrique Cardoso publicly declared that the US was the sole superpower and that any fight Brasilia put up against Washington would automatically be lost. As Fernando Collor de Mello and Itamar Franco before him, the newly elected president understood the post-Cold War era as unipolar, perhaps even hegemonic, and even more clearly so in the western hemisphere.

It was only at the beginning of his second mandate that Cardoso started to reinterpret the international environment in ways that would give Brazil, now stabilised economically, space for a more vigorous diplomacy. Brazilian diplomacy played an active role in sustaining the Paraguayan democracy in 1999 and 2001. In 2000, Cardoso launched the Initiative for the Integration of the Regional Infrastructure of South America, planting the seed of what would become the Union of South American Nations (UNASUR). Presidential trips skyrocketed; Brazil began to use the platform of a regional leader with global projection to represent South American interests in multilateral forums like the World Trade Organization Doha Round and started to entertain the idea of a permanent seat on the United Nations Security Council.[9] Moreover, after a short burst of solidarity following the terrorist attacks in the US on 11 September 2001 (9/11), Cardoso became one of the harshest detractors of the US-led 'war on terror', ending a period of acquiescence vis-à-vis the US.

By that time, the American scholar Samuel Huntington had published an influential article in *Foreign Affairs*, claiming that the world was not clearly unipolar, as some had previously argued, but uni-multipolar.[10] This meant that the US, despite its material superiority, would need to coordinate with other major states to get things done. This watered-down concept of multipolarity proved a useful frame in which the newest Brazilian foreign policy turn towards regional leadership and soft balancing against the hegemon could be placed. Matias Spektor stated that 'throughout the early 2000s, the *new* emphasis on multipolarity did set the tone of the conversation in the Brazilian foreign policy community'.[11]

Early discussions about multipolarity in Brazil were not delusional. Goldman Sachs had included the country in its famous report about the 'BRICs',[12] and euphoria had originated outside Brazil. Moreover, both academics and diplomats emphasised that a Brazilian rise to the status of a pole was not clear. In those early moments even the most stringent ideologue of multipolarity remarked that if the rise of Brazil to great power status were to happen, it had to be preceded by the resolution of important domestic and international constraints, and would be a long-term process at best.[13]

However, general enthusiasm for this new idea had begun to grow after the Partido dos Trabalhadores (PT) won the presidency in Brazil. Two factors combined to produce this. On the one hand, the US became bogged down in the Iraqi civil war, which led many Americans to believe that the unipolar moment – allegedly reinforced after 9/11 – had finally begun its eclipse.[14] On the other hand, by the mid-2000s Brazil was riding the wave of Chinese-led economic growth in Latin America. The country's gross domestic product (GDP) expanded to 5.8 per cent in 2004 – the highest growth rate since 1986 – and the commodity boom kept up the pace during the next five years or so. Then President Luiz Inácio Lula da Silva initiated an era of audacity.[15] By about 2005, the idea of a rising Brazil became broadly accepted, leading many to think of the country as a regional activist, leader, power, unipole, and even hegemon.[16] A few bold scholars even argued that Brazil was rising as a great power in the dawn of a multipolar era,[17] an idea that captured the imagination of almost everyone in Brasilia. The excitement was epitomised in a cover of *The Economist*, entitled 'Brazil takes off', which pictured the statue of Christ the Redeemer taking off from Mount Corcovado.[18]

But the same magazine published a very different cover in 2013 entitled 'Has Brazil blown it?', showing Christ falling down.[19] The crisis that ensued has only grown, making erstwhile excesses more evident. In the period under review, forty-eight embassies were opened (one-third of Brazil's current total) and the Brazilian Cooperation Agency became involved in 108 projects abroad. The Brazilian National Bank for Economic and Social Development invested US$14 billion (five times the current fiscal deficit) in eleven Latin American and African countries, supporting Brazilian businesses sponsored by an active economic and presidential diplomacy. It is not surprising that this notable expansion was linked to the corruption and fiscal crisis that has been bleeding Brazil dry.[20]

The reasons for selecting 2015 as the end point of my series are also both global and particular to Brazil. Although growth rates had been meagre since 2011, and some had already seen the meek foreign policy of President Dilma Rousseff as a testament of decline,[21] the real shock came when the Brazilian economy entered into recession in 2014 and shrank by 3.8 per cent in 2015. As the country started to experience the worst economic crisis since 1981, a serious corruption scandal arose. Now world-famous, Operation Car Wash expanded considerably in 2015, leading to the imprisonment of many members of the Brazilian elite and the impeachment process against President Rousseff. The country has since experienced a general discrediting of the political class, which ended in the election of the extremist partial outsider Bolsonaro in 2018.

Globally, 2015 was also a turning point. As many other 'emerging powers' such as South Africa, India, and Russia were experiencing similar economic and political difficulties, the trend towards multipolarity was also questioned abroad. Nowadays, outside a narrow circle of 'emerging powers' scholars, the academic consensus is that the world is becoming bipolar, not multipolar.[22] There is strong empirical evidence to support this claim. Figure 3.1 shows the distribution of GDP (purchasing power parity) in the US and BRICS countries in 2000 and 2015. Although a path towards multipolarity can be seen in 2000, it is clear that by 2015 the world economy had become bipolar and that Brazil had made little progress relative to China.

Further, a revival of realism in recent years has brought military power back into the equation. Traditionally, the distribution of material capabilities

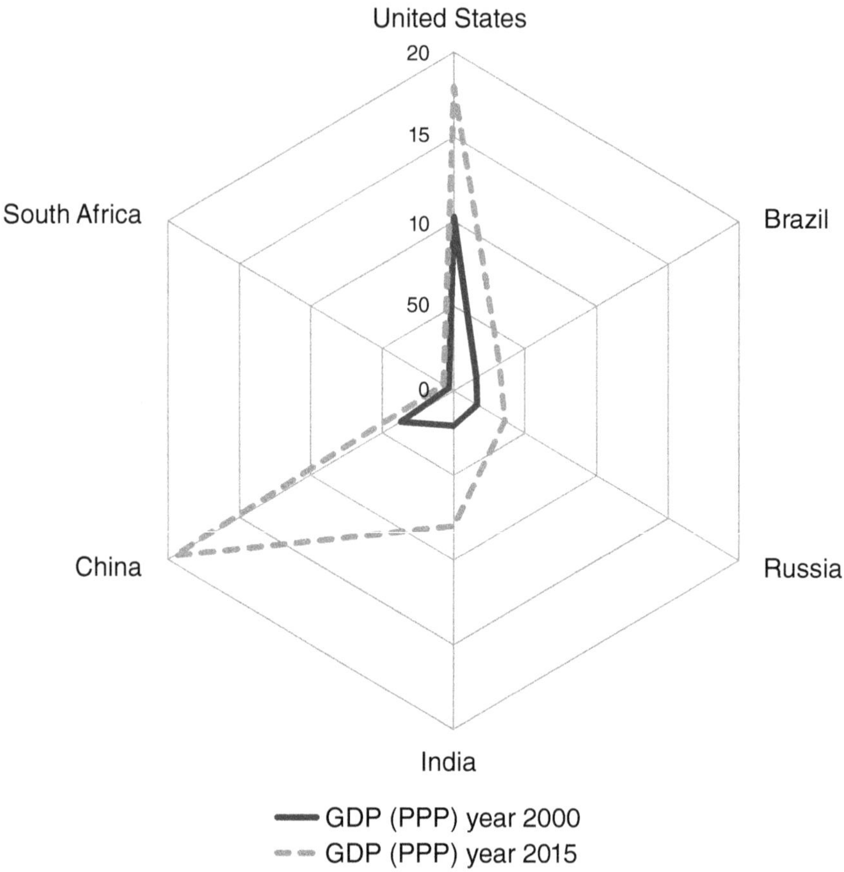

Figure 3.1 GDP (PPP) of the US and BRICS, 2000 and 2015. Note: PPP (purchasing power parity). Numbers represent US$ trillion (2015).

in the international system had been understood as a synonym for military strength,[23] but this understanding changed when economic considerations overshadowed military force, particularly during the two decades following the end of the Cold War.[24] However, the increasing assertiveness of the Russian strategic stance in Eastern Europe and the Middle East, as well as Chinese naval deployments and other activities in the South China Sea and beyond, have brought military considerations back to the centre of the scene. In general, this contributed to a weakening of the multipolar – and even the bipolar – discourse. The consideration of military capabilities greatly damaged the status of a military dwarf like Brazil. Moreover, military capabilities are unlikely to become less important in the future.

In short, the US has remained unchallenged in the military realm. India, Russia, and most prominently China have taken steps to call Washington's primacy into question, but Brazil has lagged far behind. Figure 3.2 illustrates this trend with a widely used proxy of military power (military expenditure). The figure shows how the impressive military might of the US compared to a tiny Brazil in both 2000 and 2015. It also shows the Chinese rise in this realm, which has monopolised the attention of the Americans.[25]

As Figures 3.1 and 3.2 show, all potential BRICS great powers, besides China, were eliminated in the race to great power status. Even Russia, which holds a privileged position regarding cybersecurity and nuclear issues, is now seen as a secondary concern in Washington.[26] For any dispassionate analyst it should be apparent that bipolarity, *not* multipolarity, lies on the horizon, both in the economic and military realms. Yet prominent diplomats and academics of Brazilian foreign policy usually insist on the reality of the multipolar mirage.

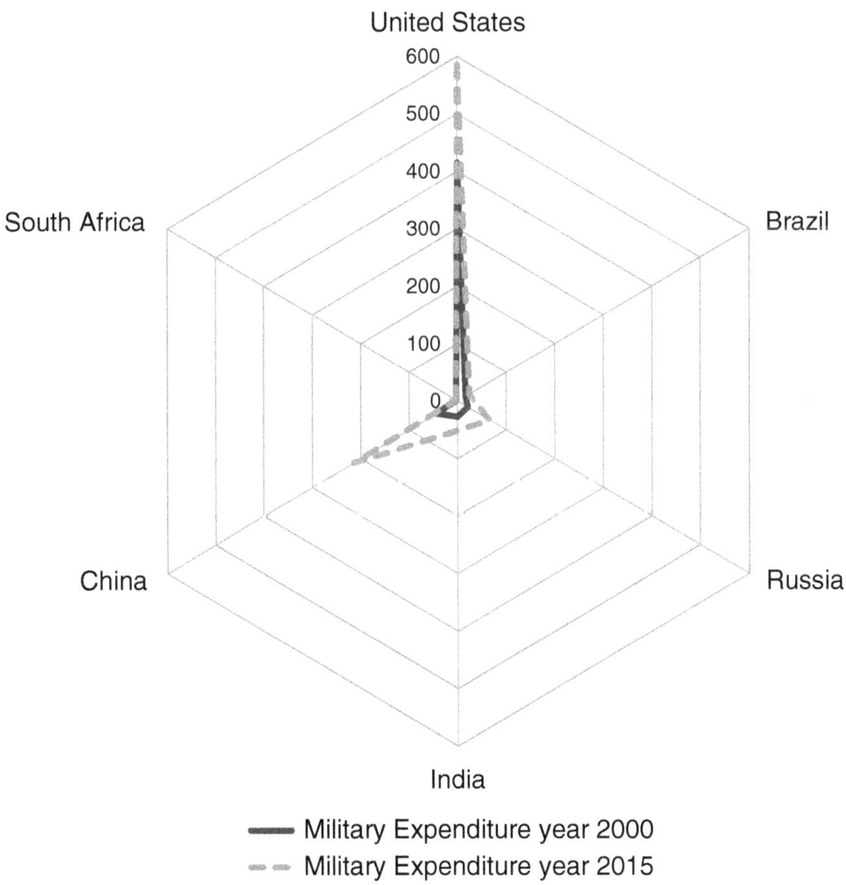

Figure 3.2 Military expenditure of the US and BRICS, 2000 and 2015. Note: numbers represent US$ billion (2015).

Conceptual stretching and interest groups

Why didn't the multipolar debate just fade away as this reality became evident? Why do some intelligent people persist with this discourse despite overwhelming empirical evidence to the contrary? The answers seem to lie in the enduring influence of certain interest groups and their capacity to reproduce the practice of conceptual stretching – relaxing the original empirical definition of the term to fit additional cases.[27]

Conceptually, the general neglect of a substantial literature on multipolarity that preceded the 2000–15 multipolar mood was necessary for the aforementioned hyperbole to take place. As with any other concept, the term 'multipolarity' only makes sense within a theoretical framework that determines its definition and causal relations with other phenomena. Realism and, more precisely, some variants of neorealism provide such a framework.[28]

The concept of multipolarity describes the existence of three or more great powers in the international system. Realist theory specifies that this structural configuration is determined by the distribution of *material capabilities* (i.e. the empirical definition or observational implication of multipolarity), and predicts a *higher conflict-proneness* in any given international system (i.e. the causal definition or its normative implication) due to a series of inefficiencies that are introduced in balancing behaviour when there are more than just two great powers in the system. As I argue, the Brazilian foreign policy debate neglected all of this. In Brazilian terms, multipolarity seems to convey a multilateral system in which middle or regional powers can sit at the negotiating table with great powers to discuss certain issues. But such a definition has nothing to do with the original concept. In a best-case scenario, it would have to be theorised consistently and given a different name.

Twenty-eight members of the Brazilian foreign policy community[29] were asked about their understanding of 'multipolarity' along three dimensions: theoretical, normative, and empirical. To unravel their theoretical understanding, I asked whether a definition of polarity had to consider material capabilities or ideational indicators.[30] This first question helps us understand how the interviewees see what Giovanni Sartori called the 'intention' of the concept – the set of meanings and attributes that define the category and determine membership.[31] To get a grasp of the normative dimension, I asked whether they thought multipolarity was essentially positive (for example, generating equality) or negative (for example, generating miscalculation and conflict, as realism argues).[32] This provided an approximation of the interviewees' causal definition of multipolarity – i.e. which consequences one can expect from it or, in other words, to which phenomena it is related as a cause.[33] Finally, I asked how they saw the distribution of military and economic might nowadays, to get an idea of how updated and accurate their perception of capabilities distribution was.[34] This last question illuminated the 'extension' of the concept – that is, the set of entities in the world to which it refers.[35] As with the first two questions, possible answers were designed to fit a five-point scale ranging from the realist definition of polarity to its complete opposite.

Figure 3.3 shows the distribution of all responses (dark points) between the realist ideal type of what multipolarity means – point (1, 1, 1) in the upper left-hand corner – and the opposite of a realist definition – point (5, 5, 5) in the lower right-hand corner. The Euclidean distance between the two points is 6.92 – the maximum possible misunderstanding of the definition.

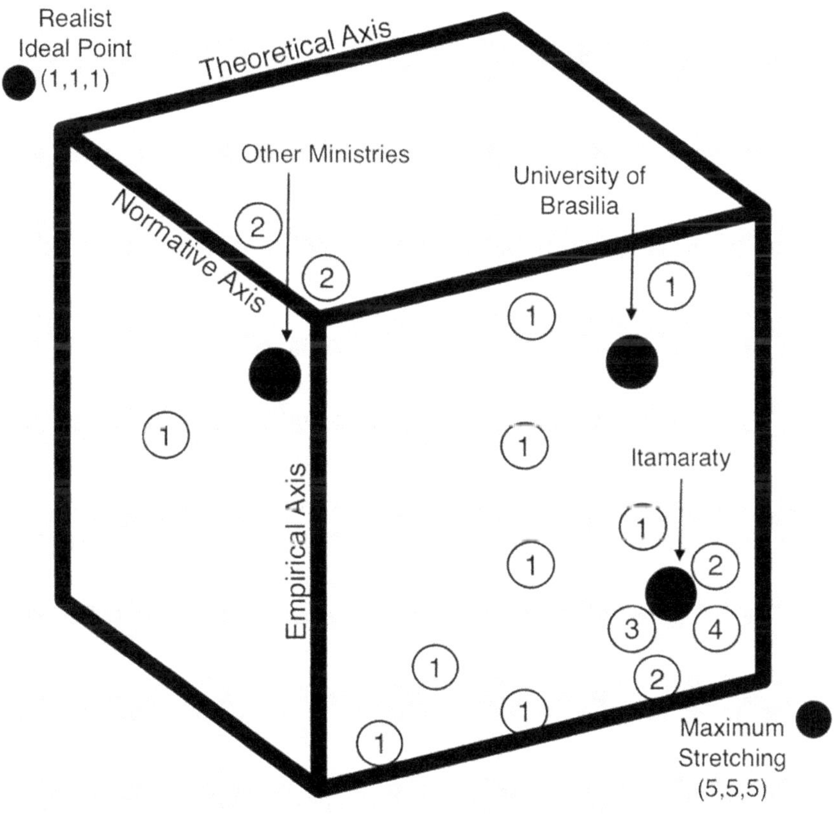

Figure 3.3 Measuring and mapping conceptual stretching. Note: points in the three-dimensional space represent the position of interviewees. If more than one occupies the same space, the number of overlapping respondents is indicated. White circles show the mean respondent from relevant institutions.

Diplomats were, on average, at 5.83 points from the realist ideal, and just 1.09 from the complete opposite to the academic understanding of the term. They were followed by university professors (4.12), faring relatively well in the empirical axis, and other public officials at the Ministry of Defence and the Presidency (2.44), who had a moderately more realist – but still very much biased – understanding of the concept.

Can multipolarity be understood in different terms? Why is it not possible to have an alternative, non-realist understanding of it? Multipolarity *could* mean something else in other IR theories besides realism – as similar phonemes have different meanings in different languages. However, the multipolar discourse in Brazilian foreign policy debates combined a misunderstanding of the original definition *and* a lack of alternative theorisation. In other words, attempted reinterpretations of the term have not been paired with new conceptualisations – much less new theoretical frameworks – leading to conceptual stretching.[36] The best alternative to refer to a different thing would have been to use a different term and take the time to define it properly. Using 'multipolarity' without redefining it was a grave mistake. It turned a social science concept into a buzzword.[37]

If the error is so flagrant, how has this practice been reproduced with such impressive success? One possible answer is that political discourse misappropriated the word. As with most political concepts, the empirical content of multipolarity has now been diluted to signify a vague emotional appeal to Brazilian grandeur that benefits specific actors. A non-exhaustive list of beneficiaries of this purposive deception includes Itamaraty (Ministry of Foreign Affairs), ministries that expanded their transgovernmental activity, educational institutions closely related to the foreign service (for example, the University of Brasilia and private institutions like the Getulio Vargas Foundation that offer training for prospective diplomats), and think tanks that have based their reputation on the multipolar discourse (for example, the BRICS Policy Center, the Agarapé Institute, and the Alexandre de Gusmão Foundation, among others). Indirectly, it would be fair to say that all Brazilian IR academia benefited from the multipolar mirage. To be even fairer, the *mea culpa* should include academics like myself, based outside Brazil but writing about the multipolar mirage, together with the many Brazil institutes and programmes opened in tertiary institutions such as Harvard University, the University of Oxford, and King's College London. However, on the ladder of responsibility, four particular actors stand out: Itamaraty, Brazilian multinational corporations, the PT, and China.

The diplomatic corps benefits from an expansive foreign policy in terms of more positions abroad, more personnel at home, and higher budgets and social status. Moreover, as the role of diplomats grows, the more important they are in policy debates, and the more locked-in their benefits become.

An expansive and indispensable diplomacy grants Itamaraty a central role in Brazilian politics that it has always claimed, and had marginally lost since democratisation.

Brazilian corporations also benefited from this world view. The so-called *campeões nacionais* (national champions) – the biggest Brazilian multinational enterprises in sectors like food manufacturing, construction, mining, oil, and transportation – benefited greatly from the support of the diplomatic corps, from their participation in state visits, and from low-interest loans to expand their investments and exports in mostly African and Latin American markets. As unveiled by recent investigations, these businesspeople largely financed major parties and systematically bribed politicians. Since most of these investments and presidential visits took place in countries governed by leftist or anti-apartheid leaders and during the years that the PT was in power, the defence *à outrance* of the multipolar illusion has become one of the bastions of the *petistas* since the impeachment of Rousseff.

Finally, the multipolar mirage has proven an invaluable source of legitimacy for China – arguably, the most powerful financer behind it – as it disguises its steady rise to the rank of great power. The functioning of the BRICS group illustrates these dynamics nicely. Besides the regular meetings between the five heads of state, there is little actual coordination between these very different countries. However, the cooperation that takes place is often financed by China. In the Contingent Reserve Arrangement (CRA), China is the largest contributor.[38] BRICS' Shanghai-based New Development Bank (NDB), like the Asian Infrastructure Investment Bank, relies on Beijing's (and perhaps Delhi's) financial solidity given their steady growth, relatively low debts, and high levels of foreign exchange reserves. Without China, the existence of the NDB would simply not be possible. Indeed, Brazil has to make enormous efforts even to participate as a shareholder. Beijing is also the largest financer and organiser of all kinds of inconsequential meetings where the brand of BRICS is publicised but almost no compromises are reached. It has proposed the expansion of the BRICS membership (for example, China promoted the inclusion of South Africa, which Brazil initially opposed), the participation of non-members, and an increased interaction with civil society. Thanks to this sponsorship, most well-known Brazilian IR scholars have travelled to China, which has contributed to the reproduction of the multipolar discourse.

The use and misuse of the term 'multipolarity' in the policy debate

In this and the following section, I undertake a systematic longitudinal analysis of the period 2000–15 to illustrate the rise and fall of this debate in the political and academic spheres respectively. My intention is to offer a typology of typical misconceptions, and to continue debating the interests involved in these two spheres, now looking at the evolution of the multipolar discourse across time.

When one looks at the declarations of Brazilian diplomats and politicians over time, three further inaccuracies in the interpretation of the concept of multipolarity appear repeatedly that might explain their detachment from reality.[39] During this period, policymakers seemed to think that state groupings, such as the European Union (EU), could become poles in the international system; that Brazilian agency could bring about a change in polarity; and that multipolarity was a strategy – like multilateralism – rather than a structural condition. This divergence from a realist understanding of multipolarity might have contributed to the inflation of its plausibility and the Brazilian role in it.

Figure 3.4 illustrates the evolution of the multipolar discourse in the Brazilian Congress and in the UNGA. We can see that the multipolar policy debate started roughly around 2002 and had not faded by 2015, despite overwhelming evidence against the multipolar hypothesis and its virtual abandonment in other countries.

Regions as poles

First, the most frequent misconception in the policy discourse about multipolarity was the belief that regional blocs and even regions themselves could become poles of the international system. While most policymakers appear to recognise that the US would continue to be a pole in an emerging multipolar order, they consistently think of the EU and South America as *regional* poles. For example, legislator Norberto Requião (of the Partido do Movimento Democrático Brasileiro) stated that 'the formation of the European Union contains the seeds of a new multipolar order',[40] and his colleague Inácio Arruda (of the Partido Comunista do Brazil) argued that the accession of Venezuela to Mercosur was important to consolidate the regional bloc and accelerate 'the projection of the subcontinent as a pole in a multipolar world'.[41]

This idea was equally common in the diplomatic corps and even amongst prominent intellectuals in those circles. Ambassador Samuel Pinheiro Guimarães, one of the most important foreign policy officials in the PT administrations, stated that it was necessary to 'work consistently to favour the emergence of a new global multipolar system in which South America would be one of the poles'.[42] In just one phrase, Guimarães confused system and structure, overstated agency, and misidentified the actors of polarity theory. No wonder Lula da Silva would say in his address to the UNGA

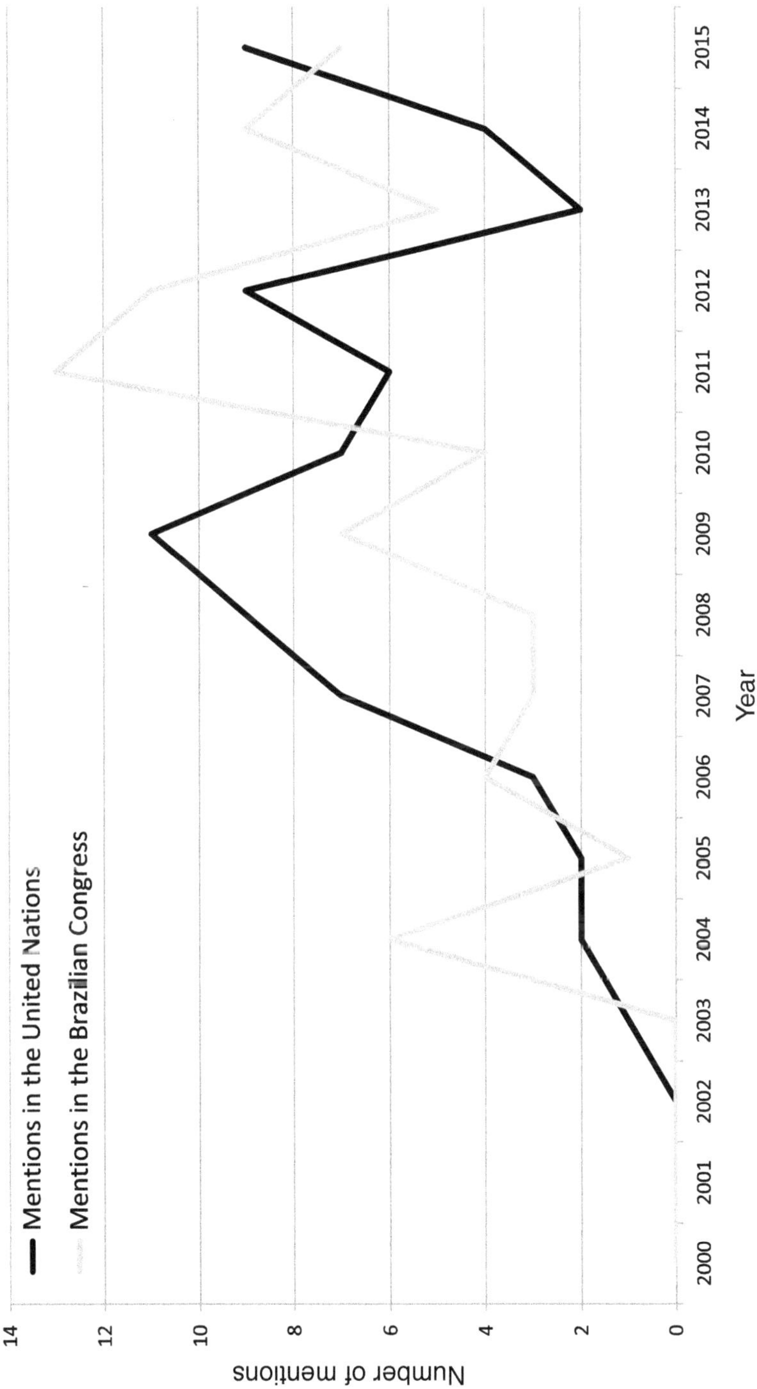

Figure 3.4 Use of the term ‘multipolar’ in the Brazilian Congress and the UNGA, 2000–15.

that '[the world] is also a multipolar world, as demonstrated by experiences in regional integration such as South America's experience in creating the UNASUR'.[43]

Multipolarity refers to the distribution of power among *states*. If common markets like the EU could be considered poles, the world would have been bipolar since its formation by virtue of the 1992 Maastricht Treaty. It is understandable, however, how this idea led to an overestimation of Brazilian capabilities. While Brazil ranks eighth in the world in terms of GDP, South America as a whole is fourth behind China, the US, and India. Thinking of the world in terms of regions diminishes the relative power of the US, and inflates the power of other regions like Europe. Since Brazil represents 50 per cent of all the territory, economy, and population below Panama, a world of regions also inflates the importance of the South American giant, which is otherwise a global pygmy. Unfortunately, however, there is no theory on which to base such claims. Being big in its own subsystem, even if integrated, does not compensate for structural pettiness at the systemic level.

Multipolarity as a foreign policy goal

Second, wishful thinking seems to have been a common error in the Brazilian foreign policy debate. Multipolarity (a structural situation in which states find themselves) is often treated as a situation that can be brought to reality even by a country like Brazil, which accounts for roughly 2.5 per cent of the world's material capabilities. This is based on a misunderstanding of the assumptions of polarity theory, summarised in Thucydides's classic statement 'the strong do what they *can* and the weak suffer what they must'.[44] Notice that there are things that even the strong great power *cannot* do. Changing polarity voluntarily is one of those things.

In Guimarães's unfortunate phrase, as in almost every speech analysed here, the implicit or explicit idea is that Brazil can make the world more multipolar by promoting certain policies. In extreme cases, multipolarity itself is seen as a policy that Brazil should pursue. Senator Vanessa Grazziotin (of the Partido Comunista do Brazil), for example, thought that 'the BRICS group was created with the objective of turning the world multipolar'.[45] For former Foreign Minister Patriota, 'Brazil has defended the establishment of … multipolarity'.[46]

Thinking of polarity as something that states can produce makes polarity change seem more reachable. The problem is that polarity is the product of unforeseen critical junctures and strategic interaction, and states – even great powers – typically adjust to its constraints. Polarity changes have taken place after systemic wars and territorial disintegration of great powers, but almost never as a direct result of alliance formation or the development of single countries. For example, Brazil could develop its national capabilities (internal balancing), but this will not necessarily lead to multipolarity unless the US fails to increase its own capabilities in turn. Brazil could also ally with other rising powers (external balancing), but that does not affect polarity in any way. On the contrary, from the standpoint of polarity theory, unipolarity drives Brazil to conform to an alliance,[47] and an eventual change in capability distribution – for example, the distinctive rise of China amongst the BRICS[48] – might cause the collapse of such alliances. Put simply, polarity is a structural variable and a change in structure is the product of complex strategic interaction over the long term. Most of the time, great powers only adapt to it. Middle-sized or small states can certainly do very little to change it. Saying that multipolarity is an objective of Brazilian foreign policy is profoundly at odds with the meaning of the term.

Multipolarity as a strategy

The third misconception held by Brazilian diplomats and politicians was to confuse multipolarity – the underlying structure of the international game – with a strategy to be played. In most of my interviews, diplomats mistook multipolarity for multilateralism, and this misconception appeared frequently in the 2000–15 period. Arthur Virgílio (of the Partido da Social Democracia Brasileira (PSDB)), for instance, thought of multipolarity as a 'third way' between Caracas's and Washington's plans.[49] President Lula da Silva interpreted multipolarity as a sort of South–South multilateralism when he stated at the UNGA: 'simply by using direct dialogue with no mediation by major powers, developing countries have stepped into new roles in designing a multipolar world'.[50] Patriota stated that he promoted 'multipolarity, so that different actors could converse and dialogue'.[51] These statements confuse capability distribution with mere diplomatic strategy.

The political coalition

One feature of the multipolarity discourse in the political realm has been the diffusion of the term since the early twenty-first century, and a relative decline in its usage since 2012, which almost mimics the rise and fall of domestic enthusiasm with the PT's international strategy. Another interesting feature of this discourse is polarisation. All of the politicians' quotations in this section come from members of the government or the PT coalition in Congress. Almost 83 per cent of the mentions of the term 'multipolarity' in Congress from 2000 to 2015 can be attributed to a member of the incumbent coalition. Sometimes, members of the opposition used the term critically. For example, a senator of the opposition party PSDB stated: 'I have seen people juggling with words, saying that it would be good for Brazil … to pursue the way of multipolarity. I am not convinced, though.

When it comes to bidding processes there has to be correctness. I do not want to discuss if it is multipolar or unipolar, I want to discuss if the law was followed or not!'[52] The indiscriminate and careless use of the term 'multipolar' enraged audiences well beyond purists of polarity theory, as it was used to justify collusion between public and private interests.

In the political realm the multipolar discourse varied in its sophistication depending on the setting in which it was being used and the time span since it entered the political lexicon. Regarding the setting, while usage of the term in the Brazilian Congress was shallow, it was slightly more consistent in diplomatic circles, and much more consistent in specific forums where interlocutors held a traditional understanding of what the term implied. For instance, Patriota did not misinterpret the term before the United Nations Security Council; he even framed it in the realist tradition,[53] which understands multipolarity as a negative, conflict-prone configuration of power:

> Two hundred years have passed since the Congress of Vienna, when an exercise in multipolar coordination, albeit circumscribed to the European continent, was conceived, fostering a century of relative peace. We also remember 100 years since the onslaught of the First World War, a war considered today by many historians as having been avoidable and the result of a failure of leadership and diplomacy.[54]

Time also appears to have been an important factor in consolidating an understanding of multipolarity in the Brazilian foreign policy debate. An analysis of the diplomatic speeches shows that diplomats took some time to make sense of the new discourse and to frame the word 'multipolar' in a way that was coherent with its traditional meaning and the objectives of Brazil's foreign policy. This can be seen when contrasting Lula da Silva's and Rousseff's speeches at the United Nations.[55] By the end of 2015, statements had become quite realist, suggesting an increasing sophistication in the higher spheres of the Planalto and Itamaraty. This trend was also noticeable in Congress, suggesting, if not coordination, at least some acculturation of the rank and file of the PT and sectors of the political elite.

While domestic alliances were often implicit, external allies were more explicitly mentioned in the multipolar discourse. President Lula da Silva, for instance, said that multipolarity examples included 'the IBSA [India, Brazil, South Africa], the G20 at the WTO [World Trade Organization], the summits between South America and Africa and between South America and Arab Countries and the BRIC countries'.[56] The identification of multipolarity with BRICS (as the group was called after the introduction of South Africa in 2010) was one of the most blatant conceptual 'sleights of hand' of the era, confusing a statement about the state of the world with the necessity of a particular foreign alliance. While polarity is always a given, alliances are usually a choice.

As argued in the following section, this idea permeated the academic debate as well. Many in Brazil came to believe that multipolarity could be constructed with BRICS, without questioning the underlying conditions of this alliance, the effects it would have on specific domestic groups, the alternatives to it, or whether it meant anything beyond expensive summitry and an inefficient allocation of precious financial resources – for example, Brazil's shares in the NDB and the CRA. The multipolar fiction continues to shield and propel these policy choices today.

The use and misuse of the term 'multipolarity' in the academic debate

One can indulge politicians for not knowing what multipolarity means in IR theory, but scholars should know better. Academic scholarship is subjected to a minimum level of conceptual clarity by peer-review and other disciplinary mechanisms. However, in my review of articles published in the two major Brazilian IR journals – *Revista Brasileira de Política Internacional* (which frequently publishes work by diplomats) and *Contexto Internacional* – some scholars suggested that non-states could be seen as poles,[57] that states could change the international structure,[58] and that multipolarity was a strategy similar to multilateralism.[59] The problem is not universal; Diniz, for example, provided a remarkable state of the art of the polarity debate, and shows adroitness in the use of the terms.[60]

Scholars that are outside the scope of this study include those who have used the term multipolarity correctly, but have erred in their predictions (even when it was clear that China would be the only great power rival to the US),[61] and those who have tried to justify their reinterpretation of the traditional definition, reviewing the realist literature and criticising it more or less compellingly. For instance, after a remarkable literature review, Fernandes decides to use the term *multiblocos* – instead of multipolar – which he defines in his own way, showing how it better adapts to his argument.[62] I focus instead on IR scholars that have fallen short of providing a new definition of multipolarity and who have used the term incorrectly.

Figure 3.5 shows the evolution of the academic debate on multipolarity. The sources reviewed were articles published in the two major Brazilian IR journals, as mentioned earlier, and in any non-Brazilian journal with an impact factor of 0.4 or above[63] that mentioned the word multipolarity while discussing Brazilian foreign policy. The pattern correlates with that of Figure 3.4, showing some synchronicity between the academic and policy debates. *Revista Brasileira de Política Internacional* appears to have pioneered the

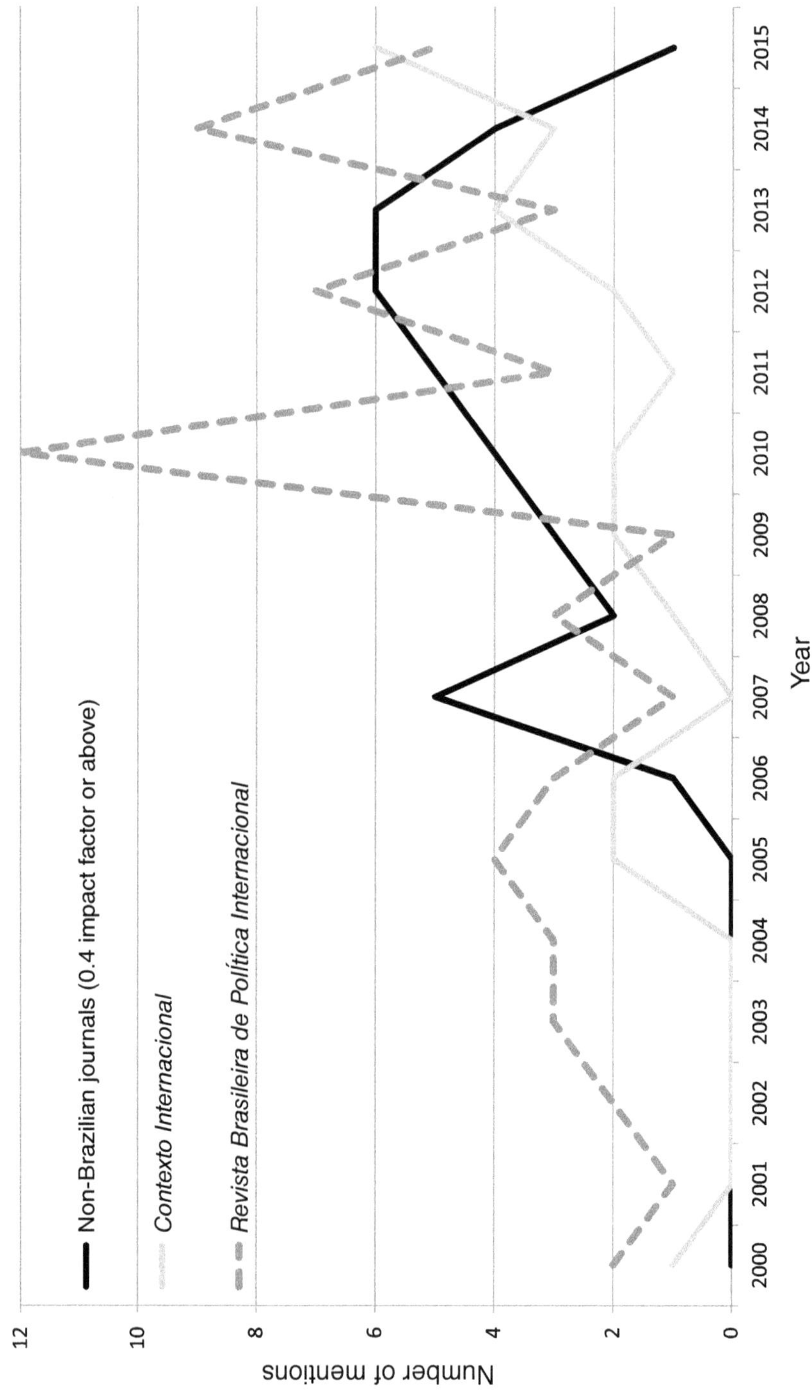

Figure 3.5 Use of the term 'multipolar' in academic journal articles, 2000–15.

debate. But while the multipolar discourse seems to have faded away in non-Brazilian journals, the use of the term multipolarity in the Brazilian journals has remained quite high.

In line with my analysis of conceptual stretching, academics should have been clear about three important questions before using the term 'multipolar': How do we know multipolarity when we see it? What are the expected consequences of multipolarity? What causes polarity change? These questions situate the concept of multipolarity within a theory, and therefore give the concept empirical and causal meaning.[64]

Measuring multipolarity

The first step in defining any concept is to give the reader a clue about how to know it when one sees it. The lack of operationalisation, measurement, and contextualisation of Brazilian relative capabilities has been one of the most recurrent errors in the academic literature on this subject. With only a few exceptions,[65] authors consistently failed to measure their claims about polarity. As we saw in Figures 3.1 and 3.2, it is very difficult to argue that Brazil is a pole of the international system or could become one in the near future, unless we radically stretch the concept. In multipolarity, each pole is a great power, and has to account for a significant proportion of national capabilities to be considered as such. As a convention, some have considered one-third of the greatest power's capabilities to be a relevant threshold,[66] separating great powers from non-great powers. Looking at the numbers, it is impressive that anyone could mistake Brazil, although a giant in its region, for a potential great power in the globe.[67]

Nowadays, this idea is just wrong. While China has almost 20 per cent of the world's capabilities and the United States has roughly 14 per cent, Brazil's composite index of national capabilities puts it alongside South Korea, with a mere 2.5 per cent of the world's material power.[68] Nominal GDP is another usual measure of economic size that IR scholars have used to calculate polarity. In this regard, the US is at the top of the list (US$18 trillion), followed by China (US$12 trillion), with Brazil ninth (barely US$1.7 trillion).[69] Brazil's military expenditure of US$24 billion is dwarfed by China's US$215 billion and the United States' US$596 billion.[70] To think of Brazil as a pole is indeed curious.

The consequences of multipolarity

Academics studying Brazilian foreign policy usually hold a positive view of multipolarity. This is intriguing, since multipolarity is the distribution of power that is considered the most perilous and conflict-prone in IR theory.

Waltz explains in great detail why multipolarity is not desirable, highlighting the benefits of bipolarity – small numbers, as he puts it – instead.[71]

Waltz argues that with fewer great powers in a system, the relative size of individual great powers grows bigger, increasing their chance of survival; second-tier states are less likely to achieve great power status; the costs of bargaining decrease because there are fewer dyads; the incentives to free-ride on third party bargains decrease; each great power acquires a larger stake in the system, becoming more pro status quo; the costs of enforcing agreements and collecting gains decrease; with fewer dyads the difficulty of reaching agreements also decreases; surveillance is easier; and great powers can more easily predict and detect deals made to their disadvantage.[72] All of this makes great powers more secure, which in turn reduces the probability of great power war. Ergo, multipolarity is undesirable.

Furthermore, a system of *two* great powers is less war-prone than any other system because it precludes the possibility of external balancing. States cannot realign, military interdependence (the dependence on other states to wage war) is low, and it is clear who is a danger to whom.[73] Since the two great powers will be intensely focusing on each other's moves, bipolarity further decreases the risk of great power war by miscalculation, while promoting overreaction in the context of minor, peripheral crises but generating incentives for the bipoles to manage those.[74]

In sum, since the causes of great power war in structural realism are inextricably linked to anarchy and the number of great powers that results from the distribution of material capabilities in the system, the sources of optimism in the Brazilian academic debate on multipolarity remain a mystery.[75] If the point is that it would be best for Brazil to be a great power, what place does polarity play in that?

An overlap between polarity theory – a positive theory – and some normative imperative derived from dependency theory or some other critical approach appears to be at the root of this problem. Spektor agrees that '[i]mbued in this discourse was a powerful normative belief that multipolarity was morally superior to any other distribution of global power'.[76] The underlying idea seems to be that multipolarity would be more fair and equal. But if so, scholars have failed to provide evidence of multipolar systems that, by virtue of polarity, were more equitable or just. The causal link between multipolarity and fairness is missing. 'Brazil's leaders have never articulated their own coherent vision of a global order beyond voicing their abstract aspirations for an international system based on "benign multipolarity" that "promotes peace and development for all".'[77]

This is an important point, because multipolarity could bring more inequality to international politics. For instance, I have argued elsewhere that a transition to multipolarity at the systemic level – for example, a rise of

Brazil – could increase the power disparity between Brazil and its neighbours.[78] In fact, history seems to be on the side of the multipolarity pessimists. Colonialism and imperialism were characteristic of multipolar structures and, according to some scholars, could have been caused by the stringency of competition between more than two poles.[79]

The causes of multipolarity

Scholars of Brazilian foreign policy have confused the coordination of foreign policy strategies amongst minor states with the dynamics that brought polarity change in the past. In particular, scholars have erred in the belief that a certain coordination of foreign policies could peacefully bring about multipolarity. This view is closely related to the view of multipolarity as something that Brazil could generate itself. Academics, however, understand that a single country cannot produce such change. Instead, they have proposed a more sophisticated account by which unipolarity – pictured as essentially unstable – could result in a type of coordinated balancing against the unipole that might restore multipolarity.[80]

Persuaded by this old argument – that, in the end, unipolarity resulted in a stable configuration of power[81] – some academics on the periphery have interpreted forms of soft balancing and loose coalition-building under unipolarity as if they were balancing coalitions against a potential hegemon – a recurrent strategy in unbalanced multipolarity, at least in modern European history.[82] This, in turn, provided a certain agency to produce structural change. However, these hopes were proven wrong when states that were militarily and economically stronger than Brazil – such as the UK, Germany, France, Saudi Arabia, South Korea, and Japan – did not balance against the US. The costs of balancing under unipolarity, scholars concluded, were higher than expected.[83] Although the BRICS group was often presented as the poster child of this type of soft balancing, none of the BRICS initiatives could be interpreted as constituting a counterbalancing strategy; and even if they were, the alliance could never assure the equal rise of all members. Internal balancing, not external balancing, can change polarity. Despite the many multi- and minilateral strategies, Brazil failed to increase its material power and so lost its place as a potential pole.

The fading of the soft balancing debate[84] in the US shows how interest is now focused on internal balancing, rather than external balancing, and on China rather than on the BRICS. Even so, discussions about how this affects polarity are heated, because some think that the US will not give up military primacy without a fight.[85] Thus, when one looks at the problem that China is having in giving birth to bipolarity, it becomes clear how multipolarity was nothing but a mirage for Brazil.

Conclusion

The use of the term 'multipolarity' in the Brazilian academic and political discourse has been fraught with problems, the most important of which seems to be its incongruity with the evolution of world politics since 2000. While in the 2000s one could hope that the world would become multipolar, the 2010s have been characterised by the relentless growth of China but other BRICS have lagged behind. It seems clear now that multipolarity was nothing more than a mirage. In the bipolar world to come, secondary states like Brazil will play a more subservient role, hence the fiscal and emotional 'hangovers' that the Brazilian foreign policy elite is enduring. Although sobriety should become the norm after the excesses of the multipolar carnival, the messianic discourse of Foreign Minister Araújo has somehow come to play a cathartic role in a new context of general retraction from the world.

My empirical contribution in this chapter concentrates mostly on a review of the use of the term multipolarity as applied by the Brazilian political and intellectual elites. After describing the evolution of this discursive practice from 2000 to 2015, I have provided a measure of the degree of conceptual stretching, a summary of the actors involved and their interests, and identified six common misconceptions that might have contributed to inflating the role of Brazil in the world. Politicians often ignored the idea that the term multipolarity denotes that states are the main units in the international system, that polarity constrains the agency of the actors and cannot be moulded by them, and that multipolarity is a structural configuration of power, an exogenous constraint, and not a strategy like multilateralism. Academics did not operationalise and measure power capabilities. Therefore, they were unable to describe polarity and the place of Brazil in it, did not consider that the theoretically expected consequence of multipolarity is instability instead of equity, and failed to consider that multipolarity is caused by the material rise of two or more powers, not by simple soft balancing behaviour.

From the point of view of realism, the one and so far only polarity theory, when all of these misrepresentations take place, a foreign policy is bound to end in overstretch or overexpansion. The lack of realism would not necessarily be a problem if authors had proposed a different definition of multipolarity together with an alternative theory. However, no scholar of Brazilian foreign policy has engaged in such an endeavour. The consequence of this confusion has become apparent: Brazil is not, nor it can be, a pole in a future multipolar system. The idea that the world is moving in a multipolar direction is itself very questionable. Material capabilities actually point in the direction of a bipolar system in which China and the US will be the exclusive poles.

If one could deduce a policy recommendation from all this, it would be that scholars should think about the consequences of future bipolarity. In bipolar systems, the poles are interested in maintaining their position, and in preventing anyone else from reaching that position. Furthermore, each of the two poles is expected to have a favourite subordinate state in each different world region, which might lead to the rise of a regional competitor to Brazil. By pursuing the multipolar mirage, Brazilian scholars, diplomats, and politicians might have lost sight of the storm hiding behind Bolsonaro and heading towards them – a bipolar world that can undermine Brazilian global aspirations as well as its primacy in South America.

Acknowledgements

This chapter benefited from comments from professors Amado Cervo, Eugenio Diniz, Antonio Carlos Lessa, Andrés Malamud, Carlos Pio, Eiti Sato, and Eduardo Viola. I would also like to acknowledge the support of the Kellogg Institute for International Studies (University of Notre Dame). Generous funding provided by the Kellogg Institute's graduate research grant allowed for a final round of interviews to be conducted in Brasilia and São Paulo in June 2017.

Notes

1 A brief survey of the main IR journals such as *International Security* – which has long dealt with the polarity issue explicitly – shows that a new consensus has emerged that China is the only prospective great power besides the US. See William Z. Y. Wang, Stephen G. Brooks, and William C. Wohlforth, 'Correspondence: debating China's rise and the future of US power', *International Security*, 41:2 (2016), 188–91.

2 To get an idea of the expanding set of state and non-state actors involved in Brazilian foreign policymaking, see Sean Burges, *Brazil in the World: The International Relations of a South American Giant* (Manchester: Manchester University Press, 2017); Dawisson Belem Lopes, *Politica Externa e Democracia no Brasil* (São Paulo: Editora Unesp, 2013).

3 Luis Schenoni, 'Brasil contrae su política exterior', *La Nación*, 12 July 2017.

4 Since conceptual stretching is arguably the greatest problem fostering a very damaging multipolar myth, I propose a method to measure the degree of conceptual stretching that different actors incur when using the concept.

5 John J. Mearsheimer, 'The gathering storm: China's challenge to US power in Asia', *Chinese Journal of International Politics*, 3:4 (2010), 381–96; Christopher Layne, *After the Fall: International Politics, US Grand Strategy, and the End of*

the Pax Americana (New Haven, CT: Yale University Press, forthcoming); Graham T. Allison, *Destined for War: Can America and China Escape Thucydides's Trap?* (New York: Houghton Mifflin Harcourt, 2017); cf. Stephen G. Brooks and William C. Wohlforth, 'The once and future superpower: why China won't overtake the United States', *Foreign Affairs*, 95:3 (2016), 91–104.

6 Some critics (for example, post-positivists) might say that all concepts are normative, and that might be true. However, the concept of multipolarity – unless redefined – is now at odds with reality, even as a normative possibility.

7 See Jack Snyder, *Myths of Empire: Domestic Politics and International Ambition* (Ithaca, NY: Cornell University Press, 1993).

8 Cf. Andrés Malamud, 'Foreign policy retreat: domestic and systemic causes of Brazil's international rollback', *Rising Powers Quarterly*, 2:2 (2017), 149–68.

9 Andrés Malamud and Júlio César Cossio Rodriguez, 'Straddling the region and the world: Brazil's dual foreign policy comes of age', in Marc Herzog and Philip Robins (eds), *The Role, Position and Agency of Cusp States in International Relations* (Abingdon: Routledge, 2014), pp. 111–28.

10 Samuel Huntington, 'The lonely superpower: US military and cultural hegemony resented by other powers', *Foreign Affairs*, 78:2 (1999), 35–49; Charles Krauthammer, 'The unipolar moment', *Foreign Affairs*, 70:1 (1990/91), 23–33.

11 Matias Spektor, 'Brazil: shadows of the past and contested ambitions', in W. I. Hitchcock, M. F. Leffler, and J. W. Legro (eds), *Shaper Nations: Strategies for a Changing World* (Cambridge, MA: Harvard University Press, 2016), pp. 17–35, at p. 26, emphasis added.

12 Jim O'Neill, *Building Better Global Economic BRICs*, Global Economics Paper No. 66 (New York: Goldman Sachs, 2001).

13 Samuel Pinheiro Guimarães, *Desafios brasileiros na era dos gigantes* (Rio de Janeiro: Contraponto, 2006).

14 Charles Krauthammer, 'The unipolar moment revisited', *The National Interest*, 70:Winter (2002/03), 5–17; Robert A. Pape, 'Soft balancing against the United States', *International Security*, 30:1 (2005), 7–45.

15 This era was characterised by the consolidation of the BRICS, a strong Brazilian presence in the Doha world trade conference, a push for United Nations Security Council reform to grant Brazil a permanent seat, and the attempt by Brasilia to be the main broker in a deal between the West and Iran, among other objectives. These goals became paroxysmal between 2008 and 2010, with a substantive expansion of the diplomatic corps' budget, salaries, and embassies abroad.

16 Matias Spektor, 'Ideias e ativismo regional: a transformação das leituras brasileiras da região', *Revista Brasileira de Política Internacional*, 53:1 (2010), 25–44; Andrés Malamud, 'A leader without followers? The growing divergence between the regional and global performance of Brazilian foreign policy', *Latin American Politics and Society*, 53:3 (2011), 1–24; Maria Regina Soares de Lima and Mônica Hirst, 'Brazil as an intermediate state and regional power: action, choice and responsibilities', *International Affairs*, 82:1 (2006), 21–40; Luis L. Schenoni, 'Rise and hegemony: some observations on emerging powers from a South American perspective', *Revista Brasileira de Política Internacional*, 55:1

(2012), 31–48; Sean W. Burges, 'Consensual hegemony: theorizing Brazilian foreign policy after the Cold War', *International Relations*, 22:1 (2008), 65–84.

17 See Kwang Ho Chun, *The BRICs Superpower Challenge: Foreign and Security Policy Analysis* (London: Routledge, 2013).

18 'Brazil takes off', *The Economist*, 14 November 2009.

19 'Has Brazil blown it?' *The Economist*, 27 September 2013.

20 Fábio Zanini, *Euforia e Fracasso do Brasil Grande: Política Externa e Multinacionais Brasileiras na Era Lula* (São Paulo: Contexto, 2017).

21 Amado Luiz Cervo and Antônio Carlos Lessa, 'O declínio: inserção internacional do Brasil (2011–2014)', *Revista Brasileira de Política Internacional*, 57:2 (2014), 133–51.

22 Or is going through a hegemonic power transition. See Mearsheimer, 'The gathering storm'; Allison, *Destined for War*.

23 J. David Singer, Stuart Bremer, and John Stuckey, 'Capability distribution, uncertainty, and major power war, 1820–1965', in Bruce M. Russett (ed.), *Peace, War, and Numbers* (Beverly Hills, CA: Sage, 1972), pp. 19–48.

24 Stephen G. Brooks, 'Dueling realisms', *International Organization*, 51:3 (1997), 445–77.

25 Brooks and Wohlforth, 'The once and future superpower'; Wang et al., 'Correspondence'; Layne, *After the Fall*.

26 Caitlin Talmadge, 'Would China go nuclear? Assessing the risk of Chinese nuclear escalation in a conventional war with the United States', *International Security*, 41:4 (2017), 50–92.

27 Cf. Giovanni Sartori, 'Concept misformation in comparative politics', *American Political Science Review*, 64:4 (1970), 1033–53; David Collier and James E. Mahon, Jr, 'Conceptual "stretching" revisited: adapting categories in comparative analysis', *American Political Science Review*, 87:4 (1993), 845–55.

28 Kenneth N. Waltz, *Theory of International Politics* (New York: McGraw Hill, 1979); John J. Mearsheimer, *The Tragedy of Great Power Politics* (New York: W. W. Norton & Co., 2001).

29 Five professors, eight public officials, and fifteen highly ranked diplomats.

30 Question 1 (theoretical dimension): 'Multipolarity could be understood in strictly material terms – i.e., as the existence of more than two great powers given their military and economic might – or in more ideational terms – i.e., considering status, prestige, and other non-material elements. According to you, multipolarity is best defined: 1) in purely material terms, 2) in material terms but not only, 3) as a combination of both, 4) in ideational terms but not only, 5) in purely ideational terms.'

31 Sartori, 'Concept misformation'.

32 Question 2 (normative dimension): 'Multipolarity could be seen positively or negatively. On the one hand multipolarity could make coordination between great powers more complex and difficult. On the other hand, it could lead to more equality. According to you, multipolarity generates: 1) more conflict and no equality, 2) more conflict and only some equality, 3) a combination of both, 4) more equality and only some conflict, 5) more equality and no conflict.'

33 Gary Goertz, *Social Science Concepts: A User's Guide* (Princeton, NJ: Princeton University Press, 2006), p. 53.

34 Question 3 (empirical dimension): 'According to the distribution of economic and military might – i.e., raw material capabilities – which of the following best describes the polarity of the international structure: 1) unipolarity – with the US as the only great power, 2) bipolarity – with China and the US as great powers, 3) multipolarity – with other actors but without Brazil, 4) multipolarity – with Brazil as one of the great powers, 5) multipolarity – with South Africa as one of the great powers.'

35 Sartori, 'Concept misformation', p. 1041.

36 Interestingly, none of the scholars that were reviewed proposed an alternative theory of polarity to justify his or her new use of the term. This could have been done. Sean Burges, for example, redefined the term 'hegemony' as understood in mainstream IR theory, provided his own definition and theory, and then applied that to Brazil. See Burges, 'Consensual hegemony'; Sean W. Burges, 'Revisiting consensual hegemony: Brazilian regional leadership in question', *International Politics*, 52:2 (2015), 193–207. Even if one disagrees with the use of the term 'hegemony' in Burges's theory, privileging a more traditional use (cf. Luis Leandro Schenoni, 'The Argentina–Brazil regional power transition', *Foreign Policy Analysis*, 14:4 (2018), 469–89), authors have the right to define their own terms. Unfortunately, even if the intention to redefine multipolarity is implicit in many of the articles I reviewed, no scholar of Brazilian foreign policy provided such an alternative.

37 I return to this point in the final section.

38 Carlos M. Cozendey, 'Vision or mirage? The Development Bank and Reserve Agreement on the BRICS' horizon', in Renato Baumann, Flávio Damico, Adriana Erthal Abdenur, Maiara Folly, Carlos Márcio Cozendey and Renato G. Flôres, Jr (eds), *BRICS: Studies and Documents* (Brasilia: Alexandre de Gusmão Foundation, 2017), pp. 113–35.

39 This section relies on material from three main primary sources in which the term 'multipolarity' was explicitly mentioned – the speeches of Brazilian legislators before Congress, the addresses of Brazilian diplomats to the UNGA, and presidential speeches on foreign policy. One hundred and sixty-three speeches were evaluated for the tone and evolution of the multipolar discourse in Congress, Itamaraty, and the Planalto (the President's Office), from 2000 to 2015.

40 Norberto Requião, 'Speech', *Diario do Senado Federal*, 201, Congresso Nacional, 10 December 2015, p. 182. All translations from Portuguese are my own.

41 Inácio Arruda, 'Speech', *Anais do Senado Federal*, 33(58), Congresso Nacional, 29 October 2009, p. 56.

42 Guimarães, *Desafios brasileiros na era dos gigantes*, p. 275.

43 Luiz Inácio Lula da Silva, Statement by the President of the Federative Republic of Brazil, at the General Debate of the 64th Session of the United Nations General Assembly, New York, 23 September 2009, p. 3.

44 Luis Schenoni and Carlos Escudé, 'Peripheral realism revisited', *Revista Brasileira de Política Internacional*, 59:1 (2016), 1–18, at 8, emphasis added.

45 Vanessa Grazziotin, 'Speech', *Diario do Senado Federal*, 87, Congresso Nacional, 9 July 2015, p. 237.
46 United Nations Security Council, '7015th Meeting', S/PV.7015 (Resumption 1), New York, 6 August 2013, p. 4.
47 Pape, 'Soft balancing against the United States'.
48 Fernando Mouron, Francisco Urdinez, and Luis Schenoni, 'Sin espacio para todos: China y la competencia por el Sur', *Revista CIDOB d'afers internacionals*, 114 (2016), 17–39.
49 Arthur Virgílio, 'Speech', *Diario do Senado Federal*, 42, Congresso Nacional, 9 September 2009, p. 124.
50 Luiz Inácio Lula da Silva, Statement by the President of the Federative Republic of Brazil, at the General Debate of the 63rd Session of the United Nations General Assembly, New York, 23 September 2008, p. 2.
51 António Patriota, 'Speech', *Diario do Senado Federal*, 71, Congresso Nacional, 16 May 2013, p. 71. In the same speech, Patriota mentioned the term 'multipolarity' thirteen times, repeating all of the misconceptions mentioned earlier, such as calling the EU a pole.
52 Virgílio, 'Speech', p. 124.
53 Patriota's attempt to frame post-Napoleonic Europe as a scenario of multipolarity – rather than one of British hegemony – could also be interpreted as representing a subtle posture from someone with a sophisticated understanding of polarity theory and other strands of realism. Some people in Itamaraty, therefore, knew what they were talking about.
54 United Nations Security Council, '7247th Meeting', S/PV.7247, New York, 21 August 2014, p. 25.
55 For example, acknowledging that the space for agency is very limited and that multipolarity is a conflictive scenario, Rousseff opined: 'We must work to ensure that in the multipolarity that comes to prevail, cooperation predominates over conflict.' Dilma Rousseff, Statement by the President of the Federative Republic of Brazil, at the Opening of the General Debate of the 67th Session of the United Nations General Assembly, New York, 25 September 2012, p. 6.
56 Lula da Silva, Statement by the President of the Federative Republic of Brazil, at the General Debate of the 63rd Session of the United Nations General Assembly, p. 2.
57 Abelardo Arantes, 'O paquistão e as estratégias ocidentais para a Asia Meridional', *Revista Brasileira de Política Internacional*, 46:1 (2003), 182–207, at 200; Miriam Gomes Saraiva, 'A União Européia como ator internacional e os países do Mercosul', *Revista Brasileira Política Internacional*, 47:1 (2004), 84–111; Raquel Patricio, 'As relações em eixo – novo paradigma da teoria das relações internacionais?', *Revista Brasileira de Política Internacional*, 49:2 (2006), 5–24, at 21.
58 Steen Fryba Christensen, 'The influence of nationalism in Mercosur and in South America – can the regional integration project survive?', *Revista Brasileira de Política Internacional*, 50:1 (2007), 139–58, at 154; Luiz A. P. Souto Maior, 'Desafios de uma política externa assertiva', *Revista Brasileira de Política Internacional*, 46:1 (2003), 12–34, at 22; Andrés Rivarola Puntigliano, '"Going

global": an organizational study of Brazilian foreign policy', *Revista Brasileira de Política Internacional*, 51:1 (2008), 28–52, at 32; Graciela Zubelzú de Bacigalupo, 'As relações russo-brasileiras no pós-Guerra Fria', *Revista Brasileira de Política Internacional*, 43:2 (2000), 59–86, at 86.

59 Diego Pautasso and Lucas Kerr de Oliveira, 'A segurança energética da China e as reações dos EUA', *Contexto Internacional*, 30:2 (2008), 361–98, at 368; Alexander Zhebit, 'A Rússia na ordem mundial: com o Ocidente, com o Oriente ou um pólo autônomo em um mundo multipolar?', *Revista Brasileira de Política Internacional*, 46:1 (2003), 153–81.

60 Eugenio Diniz, 'Relacionamentos multilaterais na unipolaridade: uma discussão teórica realista', *Contexto Internacional*, 28:2 (2006), 505–65.

61 See Randall L. Schweller and Xiaoyu Pu, 'After unipolarity: China's visions of international order in an era of US decline', *International Security*, 36:1 (2011), 41–72.

62 Antônio José Fernandes, 'O Brasil e o sistema mundial de poderes', *Revista Brasileira de Política Internacional*, 44:1 (2001), 94–111. This is the type of conceptual move that Amitav Acharya adopted in the global debate about multipolarity when he developed the term 'regiopolarity'. See Amitav Acharya, 'Regional worlds in a post-hegemonic era', Keynote speech to the 3rd GARNET Annual Conference, Bordeaux, 17–20 September 2008. Despite these reformulations, many scholars outside Brazil have continued to use the term 'multipolar' (see Jorge F. Garzón, 'Multipolarity and the future of economic regionalism', *International Theory*, 9:1 (2017), 101–35, at 105), incurring conceptual stretching. For instance, while multipolarity refers to the existence of three or more great powers, these authors include bipolarity in the realm of possible multipolarities (Garzón, 'Multipolarity', p. 111).

63 According to the journal citation reports by Thomson Reuters.

64 Goertz, *Social Science Concepts*.

65 Júlio César Cossio Rodriguez, 'Chacal ou Cordeiro? O Brasil frente aos desafios e oportunidades do Sistema Internacional', *Revista Brasileira de Política Internacional*, 55:2 (2012), 70–89; Lucas Pereira Rezende, 'Brazil: a unipolar actor in South America?', *Revista Carta Internacional*, 11:1 (2016), 274–95.

66 Cf. Randall L. Schweller, *Unanswered Threats: Political Constraints on the Balance of Power* (Princeton, NJ: Princeton University Press, 2008); Bruce Bueno de Mesquita, 'Measuring systemic polarity', *Journal of Conflict Resolution*, 19:2 (1975), 187–216.

67 Luis L. Schenoni, 'Unveiling the South American balance', *Estudos Internacionais*, 2:2 (2014), 215–32.

68 Singer et al., 'Capability distribution'; Correlates of War Project, 'Data sets: national material capabilities (v5.0)', 2017, www.correlatesofwar.org/data-sets/national-material-capabilities/national-material-capabilities-v4-0 (accessed 18 July 2017).

69 International Monetary Fund, 'IMF data', 2017, www.imf.org/en/Data (accessed 17 July 2017).

70 Stockholm International Peace Research Institute, 'SIPRI military expenditure database', 2016, www.sipri.org/databases/milex (accessed 17 July 2017).

71 Waltz, *Theory of International Politics*.
72 *Ibid.*, pp. 135–6.
73 *Ibid.*, pp. 163, 169, 170.
74 *Ibid.*, pp. 172, 194; cf. Harold D. Lasswell, 'The prospects of cooperation in a bipolar world', *University of Chicago Law Review*, 15:4 (1948), 877–901.
75 Offensive realism shares this intuition about the importance of raw numbers. Mearsheimer agrees that bipolarity is the most stable configuration of power, but he differs from Waltz in two important respects. First, he introduces *fear* as the mechanism that ultimately increases the probability of war. Second, this fear can be affected by factors other than the number of great powers – such as their possession of nuclear weapons, their geographic location, and, most importantly, power asymmetries between them. See Mearsheimer, *The Tragedy of Great Power Politics*, pp. 45, 346, 42, 44. Mearsheimer offers a slightly more parsimonious account that leaves geography and technology aside: '[w] hat matters most is *the number of great powers* and *how much power each controls*' (Mearsheimer, *The Tragedy of Great Power Politics*, p. 337, emphasis added).
76 Spektor, 'Brazil', p. 26.
77 *Ibid.*, p. 34.
78 Schenoni, 'Rise and hegemony'.
79 Jeffry A. Frieden, 'International investment and colonial control: a new interpretation', *International Organization*, 48:4 (1994), 559–93.
80 See John J. Mearsheimer, 'Back to the future: instability in Europe after the Cold War', *International Security*, 15:1 (1990), 5–56; Kenneth N. Waltz, 'The emerging structure of international politics', *International Security*, 18:2 (1993), 44–79; Christopher Layne, 'The unipolar illusion: why new great powers will rise', *International Security*, 17:4 (1993), 5–51.
81 William C. Wohlforth, 'The stability of a unipolar world', *International Security*, 24:1 (1999), 5–41.
82 Jack S. Levy and William R. Thompson, 'Hegemonic threats and great-power balancing in Europe, 1495–1999', *Security Studies*, 14:1 (2005), 1–33.
83 Huntington, 'The lonely superpower'; Wohlforth, 'The stability of a unipolar world'.
84 Cf. Pape, 'Soft balancing against the United States'.
85 Mearsheimer, 'The gathering storm'.

4

Multipolarity in Russia: A philosophical and practical understanding

Elena Chebankova

The idea of a multipolar world order has become increasingly popular among politicians and analysts around the world. Practically, the term multipolarity signifies the number of effective centres of global hegemonic influence. This number represents a significant structural factor in international relations that has far-reaching consequences for international affairs. Academic literature often debates the impact that the shift in the number of centres of influence has on international stability, flexibility of domestic political systems, state sovereignty, the hierarchy of states in the international arena, and discursive interpretations of world affairs. While no clear theory of multipolarity has been developed, Russia considers the multipolar world order an ideal form for future international relations grounded in the normative principles of equality, fairness, plurality of cultures, and the 'great variety of interests' of the modern world.[1] The idea of constructing a multipolar world order gained key metaphysical and political significance in the Russian public discourse during the period of Yevgeny Primakov's diplomacy (1996–98). It has subsequently turned into an official foreign policy doctrine with Vladimir Putin's accession to power.

Putin proceeded to clearly demarcate his normative position on the necessity of a multipolar world order in his 2007 speech at the Munich Security Conference. There, he branded the unipolar world as one of 'one master, one sovereign', in which the actions of the 'master' are often 'unilateral' and 'illegitimate'.[2] Russia's subsequent 'Foreign Policy Doctrines', issued in 2008, 2013, and 2016, restated Russia's normative commitment to the 'emergent' multipolar world order based on the 'principles of equality, mutual respect and mutually beneficial cooperation, as well as the norms of international law'.[3] This chapter examines the ideational and practical components of multipolarity as they are seen in Russia. The discussion begins by briefly introducing the existing models of world order and examining approaches to the multipolar world order. The chapter then focuses on the ideational and formal approach to the multipolar world order envisaged and promoted in Russia.

Existing models of world order

Five known models of world order have been proposed and partially implemented during the periods of modernity and post-modernity: the Westphalian system, the bipolar (Yalta–Potsdam) system, the unipolar (Malta) system, the non-polar system, and the multipolar system. A brief excursion into the first four systems will enable us to get a better grip on the final one.

The Westphalian system was formed at the end of the Thirty Years' War in Europe with the settlement of the Peace of Westphalia in 1648. The war aimed to break the erstwhile system of European empires, primarily the Holy Roman Empire that went hand in hand with the religious and political dictates of the papacy. The new system proclaimed the state as the supreme sovereign and reflected new societal realities of secularisation, enlightenment, and a rejection of religious universalism. This system survived until the end of the Second World War. It assumed legal equality among all the states in the international system, and by this assumption each state represented a separate pole of influence.

Multilateral arrangements represent a subversion of the Westphalian system. This arrangement not only emphasises the equality of international state actors in the world arena, but also assumes the rise of various international organisations of inter-state cooperation. Under multilateralism, all states are considered to have an equal status within those structures. The working of this system evokes criticism from many Russian policymakers and scholars, who often insist that the United States acts as a *de facto* leader among token equals, almost dominating various spheres of international activity. In its current state, they argue, multilateralism must be more accurately branded as *collective unilateralism* or *transatlantic multilateralism*, emphasising ideological monism and the political predominance of the liberal club of countries led by the United States.[4] Following the end of the Second World War, the Westphalian system remained *de jure*. Yet, *de facto*, the new system of international relations developed two poles of political influence with centres in Washington and Moscow and associated ideological blocs.[5] A group of non-allied countries emerged that did not make a clear choice to align with either capitalism or socialism. Their political preferences varied on the basis of the economic and political favours provided by the two main power centres. The 'third pole' of the world represented an arena of conflict between the two main powers, which could not engage in direct military confrontation due to the principles of mutually assured destruction.

Western literature on international relations branded this new system as bipolar.[6] Russian political discourse often refers to it as the Yalta–Potsdam system, emphasising a set of agreements reached at the end of the Second World War and the institutional structures that emerged in their wake.[7] The reference to the two founding international conferences held in Yalta and Potsdam accentuated the role of the Soviet Union as the alternative centre of political, economic, and military influence and served as a discursive reminder of the significance of the USSR (Russia) within the international scene.

With the dissolution of the Soviet pole of influence in 1991, the system of international relations experienced another significant transformation.[8] This formally took place at the US–USSR summit on 2–3 December 1989 between US President George H. W. Bush and Soviet General Secretary Mikhail Gorbachev. During this summit Bush and Gorbachev declared the end of the Cold War and agreed to a set of fundamental changes that were to take place in Europe. While no documents were signed at the summit, it set the foundations of the contemporary world order, in which the United States began to play the leading role. Russian observers often brand this new system the Malta arrangement instead of the term 'unipolar order' often deployed in the West. The 'Malta' term usually has pejorative connotations in contemporary Russian discourse as a sign of Russia's defeat in the Cold War.

The remaining pole led by the United States began to expand its influence towards geographic areas previously dominated by the Eastern bloc. The world now had one hegemonic centre of influence in the United States, while the rest of the world was viewed – according to Immanuel Wallerstein – as the semi-periphery and the periphery.[9] A number of American strategists developed theoretical justifications of the unipolar architecture of international affairs.[10] The premise was that the United States acts as the nucleus of global politics, setting the tone of what is happening in the rest of the world.[11] Similar to the bipolar arrangement, the unipolar world structure does not officially deny the *de jure* sovereignty of existing nation-states and their legal and political equality in the world's political scene. More importantly, the unipolar arrangement adheres somewhat to the bipolar world logic by officially upholding post-Second World War international agreements. These include the composition of the United Nations Security Council, the right of veto for the victors of the Second World War, the composition of the club of nuclear powers, and the remaining elements of the nuclear deterrent. Hence, the unipolar moment forms a peculiar symbiosis with the remnants of the Yalta–Potsdam order, which has not been comprehensively dismantled since the dissolution of the Soviet Union.

A non-polar world order conveys the idea that the world no longer has a clearly defined hegemon or clearly articulated poles of influence. A non-polar international system 'is characterized by numerous centers with meaningful power … no power dominates … Nor do concentrations of power revolve around two positions'.[12] The United States, as a nation-state, will not have clearly defined control over this process, giving way to an abstract world government that will be composed of non-state actors such as international organisations, non-governmental organisations, representatives of big business, as well as nation-states.[13] State sovereignty will be significantly reduced and states will resemble international organisations rather than meaningful outlets of power.[14] At the same time, it is hoped that, despite the rise of non-state hegemonic actors, the United States 'will long remain the largest single aggregation of power'.[15] This is because the largest share of leading world organisations – that were to assume the new leadership – have been built on US-devised principles.[16]

Yet, much of Western academic literature[17] has expressed concerns over the loss of leadership by the United States and its allied powers if that model were to be implemented. Many authors warned of multiple challenges testing humanity in the absence of a single power. For example, Niall Ferguson argued that non-polarity could 'turn out to mean an anarchic new Dark Age: an era of waning empires and religious fanaticism; of endemic plunder and pillage in the world's forgotten regions; of economic stagnation and civilization's retreat into a few fortified enclaves'.[18] Those authors proposed a means of counteracting the chaos that would inevitably involve American guidance and leadership. Richard Haass's proposition was to develop and maintain a larger military infrastructure that could deal with state failures across the world; to introduce the practice of pre-emptive strikes when threats become imminent; to strengthen home security; to promote world trade on the basis of the World Trade Organization (led and influenced by the United States); to deploy the means of soft power to build domestic consensus within states; and to introduce a multilateralism that would include non-state organisations.[19]

Much of the Western audience could accept those ideas as genuine concerns over the world's future and lamentations on the loss of American leadership. Russian observers, on the other hand, viewed this model as a logical continuation of the unipolar world order and an argument for a new, if only subtler, *type* of unipolarity. They argued that this model departs from the assumption that peace in such a model could be achieved only if most countries have adopted a liberal democratic (or invariably Western) way of development.

Political elites of states would become Westernised, capitalist, and liberal democratic regardless of their history, country, or origin, due to their socialisation in supranational structures predominantly run by the West. Alexander Dugin argued that this world model would adopt a new type of hegemony. Instead of the combination of economic, military, political, and intellectual hegemony, the model would deploy intellectual and soft-power hegemony.[20]

A multipolar world order

The academic literature has yet to develop a coherent theory on a multipolar world order. Benjamin Zala observes that scholars of international relations deploy the language of polarity as an analytical tool to discuss power structures of international relations,[21] to debate international stability,[22] and to focus on ordering in empirical analysis.[23] One distinct feature of the Russian approach to multipolarity is that it rests on a set of normative principles that in many ways challenge the previously discussed arrangements. First, the Russian understanding of multipolarity rejects the principles of cultural-ideological universalism that selects one particular political system or way of life as universally applicable and as a compulsory trajectory of human development.[24] Second, it envisages that the world could be run by a number of different centres of economic, military, and intellectual influence.[25] Third, such centres of power must be politically, economically, and intellectually independent and capable of resisting any hostile advances from other alliances.[26] From Russia's point of view, the shift in the number of power centres creates a new narrative of pluralism, or 'polyphony',[27] that contrasts the politics of the twentieth century with its posterity. Instead of states striving to impose their favoured 'universal' ideologies on the rest of the world, a normative language of plurality, multiplicity, and difference begs to be adopted.[28]

In the absence of a coherent theory of the multipolar world order, different models of multipolarity are considered legitimate. Russian thinkers invoke multiregionalism, *true* multilateralism, great power management, and balance of power systems to denote multipolarity.[29] These arrangements, however, expose some significant differences. Multiregionalism rests on the plurality of regional orders and largely echoes Russia's official stance on a 'regionalisation of global politics'.[30] It denotes a system of 'international order built around regional spheres of responsibility'.[31] This model assumes that superpowers have departed the global political arena, giving way to regional power centres.[32] Great power management or a 'concert of powers', promoted by a number of Russian realists,[33] implies a return to the more cooperative side of 'balance of power' diplomacy. Great powers ensure a 'greater manageability' of world politics. Vyacheslav Nikonov, Professor at Moscow State University and a State Duma Deputy, advocates this 'vision of multipolarity' and suggests that the new 'concert' will be performed by 'the US, Europe, Russia, Japan, India, China, and some other countries'.[34] This model of multipolarity is based on opposition to unilateralism (especially the collective unilateralism of the West) and is grounded in the logic of sovereign decisions of states.

A balance of power model represents a subversion of great power management signifying a competitive type of relationship between the great powers, or a conflictual one, when the balance breaks down.[35] *True* multilateralism is distinguished in the Russian discourse from the conventional concept of multilateralism deployed in the West, as discussed above. The Russian understanding of *true multilateralism* is grounded in the acceptance of all forms of alternative narratives within international organisations during the collective decision-making process. This would require a significant recasting of leading international institutions with a view to expanding membership towards weaker countries and grant greater decision-making powers to states who do not necessarily adopt a Western political narrative.

Russia's use of the multipolar world idea

A brief review of these visions of multipolarity indicates that, despite some discrepancies in practical nuances, the general Russian approach to the concept rests on a distinct ideational package. In what follows I examine Russia's approaches to ideological-cultural distinctness, equitable redistribution of power among world players, the concept of the nation-state, and the regionalisation of world politics. In discussing and implementing those issues in the practical policy realm, Russia deploys a combination of the existing approaches to multipolarity. The first two versions of multipolarity are most popular in Russia.

Ideological monism and cultural pluralism

A rejection of ideological universalism forms the basis of the Russian approach to the multipolar world structure. This position is often based on the thesis that universalism leads to new and more sophisticated forms of racism that, in the twentieth century, moved away from its primitive biological form towards cultural, civilisational, and moral guises. Many Russian analysts and political leaders (Sergey Karaganov, Nikonov, Dmitry Babich, Andranik Migranyan, Vladimir Yakunin and others) see the right of countries to choose a path of political development distinct from the pattern of Western constructivist rationalism as the cornerstone of their idealised multipolar world order. Yakunin argues that the neoliberal global world built on the Washington Consensus:

> necessitates the elimination of all borders between civilisations, and thus cultural differences as well, treating them as irritating obstacles to the expansion of free trade and the enlargement of common markets. The architects of this delusional planet-sized marketplace tend to overlook the fact that national borders provide people with distinct cultural identities, behavioural patterns, and strategies for living that preserve what is actually humane in humans – and the fact that we all need to cherish them.[36]

At the same time, it is essential to narrate an existing range of meaningfully alternative existential projects that could offer a different choice to the Western-centred path of development. More importantly, such projects must be just, as well as politically, culturally, and morally attractive to ensure free choice. Despite Russia's adherence to the general idea of a 'polyphony of narratives', it is significant that it does not offer any substantial ideological alternative to the contemporary Western world. This is also despite the fact that Russia's evolution has always rested on the role of a provider of a cultural-political alternative. This was first seen with Russia's embrace of Eastern Orthodox Christianity and its decisive rejection of Catholicism. Russia's distinct imperial organisation had a particular inland structure with a multicultural and multireligious composition buttressed by differing institutional arrangements across the imperial land. Crucially, Russia offered an option of 'alternative modernity' during the twentieth century in the shape of its communist modernisation and development. Contemporary Russia is tested with relentless debates on whether Russia forms part of European civilisation or whether it represents a distinct and independent cultural realm. In this context, Russia's claim to become an independent pole of influence could not be seriously substantiated unless it develops a clearly articulated and distinct political alternative.

On the one hand, a number of Russian thinkers argue that Russia's current path lies in the rejection of the postmodernist pattern adopted by the West at the close of modernity. Many of Russia's ideologues, such as Sergey Kurginyan, Karen Shakhnazarov, Alexander Panarin, Dugin and others, often argue that the Soviet Union challenged a different *type* of Western world – the type which then stood on the principles of classical modernity. They advance the claim that at the end of the twentieth century the situation began to change. A nation-state capitalism embedded in the matrix of modernity evolved towards a global capitalism rooted in the sociocultural paradigm of postmodernity. Kurginyan referred to this global capitalism as 'post-capitalism' and claimed that its cultural and ideological content was far removed from the ideas of democracy and equality, and is unacceptable to contemporary Russia.[37]

The gradual transition of the Western world from modernism to postmodernism was accompanied by significant shifts in the political structure of governance, the understanding of human anthropology, and patterns of 'universal' morality. In a January 2018 speech, Russian Foreign Minister Sergey Lavrov criticised 'pseudo-liberal morality' that is leading Europe to the 'rejection of its traditional cultural roots'. Lavrov stated that:

> Obviously, the revision of basic standards of morality, a permissive environment and tolerance reduced to an absurdity are doing irreparable damage to the moral health of people and depriving them of their cultural and civilisational roots. Thus, a number of EU [European Union] countries are banning religious paraphernalia and depriving parents of the right to bring up their children in the spirit of Christian morality ... I would like to recall that at one time the EU refused to include in its charter documents [sic] the idea that the European civilisation has Christian roots.[38]

The foreign minister continued that 'those who are ashamed of their moral roots cannot respect those of other religions. Likewise, the latter have no respect of the former.' Lavrov insisted that such conditions create a 'breeding ground for xenophobia and intolerance and opening the way to society's self-destruction'. He outlined Russia's mission to oppose this 'pseudo-liberal policy that encourages destructive models of behaviour'. Lavrov also claimed that more and more people around the world and in Europe, despite the resistance, are looking to Russia as 'a defender of traditional values'.[39] As it becomes clear, contemporary Russia sees its ideological-cultural mission as 'saving' Europe from the narcissistic politics of postmodernity and 'helping' Europe to remain European in the modernist sense of the word.[40] From this point of view, Boris Mezhuev insists that while Russia easily accepts some aspects of Western civilisation such as educational reform, economic neoliberalism, and political pluralism, it remains firm in its rejection of Western 'progressive' innovations in the spheres of family, faith, and state.[41]

On the other hand, Russian intellectuals admire the late Western project of modernity. Of particular importance are the ideas of Christian ethics, mainly in its puritan Protestant version, humanism, the nation-state, industrialism and economic growth, the idea of progress, and the inquisitive spirit of the Enlightenment. Many contemporary Russian ideologists insist that defending the ethical foundations of classical capitalism and modernity – once espoused by the West – represents Russia's ideological position. Mikhail Remizov argues that 'Russia and the postmodernist West espouse radically different values ... At the same time, Russia feels sympathetic towards the core American values of the mid-twentieth century.'[42] Remizov continues:

> Hillary Clinton and General De Gaulle would have significant ideological disagreements. De Gaulle would promote the nation state, reliance on traditional and national cultures, respect of civic and economic liberties and elements of economic dirigisme in large industries ... Hillary Clinton, on the other hand, represents the 'eco-feminist-multiculturalist' [sic] thinking embedded within clearly defined, culturally authoritarian, metaphysical boundaries. The ideological mutation of the Western world is clear and the post-World War Two West is not equal to today's West ideologically and culturally.[43]

One serious caveat of Russia's admiration of Western modernity is that this particular value package logically and historically led to the contemporary postmodern Europe that Russia claims to reject. Hence, a classically modern understanding of human social and cultural life does not guarantee that Russia will be spared from a similar trajectory to that adopted by the contemporary West. Mezhuev worries that Russia's intellectual, literary, and art scene is surprisingly vacuous and its further evolution will be able to assert whether Russia can offer a meaningful civilisational alternative to the West and whether it has some specific immunity to sociocultural trends emanating from Europe.[44] Some of Russia's left-wing thinkers propose combining the principles of Abrahamic morality with the economic ideas of equitable redistribution of income and the curbing of global corporate power around the world. But despite the general popularity of such ideas in Russian society, official Russian policy does not offer a substantial ideological alternative to contemporary Western ethics at the policy level. From this perspective, Russia does not have a clearly defined and meaningfully alternative ideological project. Currently, it stands at the conservative end of the spectrum, which, coupled with its neoliberal economic foundations, could logically lead towards the postmodern sociopolitical arrangement espoused by the West.

Equitable redistribution of power in the international arena

The Russian interpretation of multipolarity, especially for those focused on the idea of multiregionalism and *true* multilateralism, emphasises the equitability of world actors in their political, economic, and above all cultural evolution. Such an interpretation is very close to the official policy line, which has been enshrined in all of Russia's 'foreign policy concepts' since Putin's accession to power in 2000.[45] Russian intellectuals lament the unipolar world order and claim that it represents the result of the 'bloodless coup in international relations' that took place during the 1990s with the dissolution of the Soviet Union.[46] They propose to abolish the situation in which one country or a group of countries sets economic, legal, and normative rules for the rest of the world. The global community, they insist, has developed the need to adopt checks and balances in the international arena and to establish a set of international laws applicable for all. Humanity must develop societal laws of international conduct enforceable around the world. Every country must take part in establishing those rules; the supremacy of one country (or a group of countries) over others should not be permitted. Cultures must be respected and no other country, or group of countries, can claim superiority in the spheres of politics and culture. All countries must be able to decide which cultural, trading, and political union or alliance they would like to join and they must be able to choose their institutional frameworks on the basis of their history and culture.[47]

The idea of multiregionalism becomes one potential option that could fulfil this idealised multipolar world order with an equitable redistribution of influence. This system is more accurately described as the *dialogue of civilisations* – a term which has entered the Russian political lexicon. Yakunin, Head of the Department of State Governance in the Faculty of Political Science at Moscow State University, argues that the dialogue of civilisations advances the idea of 'unity in diversity', interdependence, and 'infrastructuralism'. He insists on communication between civil societies in different countries that do not necessarily share similar values, but are prepared to listen and interrogate each other's positions and engage in a constructive dialogue in order to build dialogical bridges between countries and peoples.[48] It is also important that this version of dialogue does not negate the idea of the nation-state as the main actor in international politics. To this end, such a concept could cater to the needs of the official Russian position in which the state in Russia is always seen as a vehicle of development, stability, and security. Indeed, Yakunin views civic inter-exchange as one important means of persuading state actors to embark on a constructive dialogue in the wider international arena of higher politics. He further claims that equitable dialogue between sovereign nation-states forms the base of civilisational dialogue.[49]

This generally normative approach sits somewhat in tension with practical ways of implementing multipolarity that, despite increasing the number of centres of influence, do not automatically dispense with the hierarchy between hegemonic and secondary states. Practical equitability of international actors still remains a distant goal, and a return to the old 'balance of power' language is a distinct possibility. It could be argued that Russia favours the *dialogue of civilisations* and the multiregional format of the multipolar world order practice from the point of view of a great power's political expediency. This type of arrangement grants Russia a special place across several regions such as Europe, Asia, Central Asia, and Eastern and Southern Europe, making Russia a serious world power.

Discussions at the Valdai Club in Russia suggest that Russia would benefit geostrategically from the multiregional version of the multipolar world order. As Samir Saran, a Valdai Club member, notes: 'There can be no connected Asia, no political Asia, no Asian century and no Asian order without Russia being at the center of that. There can be no Pacific or Arctic arrangement without Russia being an important voice in that. Russia is a continental and a maritime power, simultaneously.'[50] Andrey Makarychev and Viatcheslav Morozov argue that existing contradictions within the multipolarity discourse invariably result in the 'increasing prominence of GPM [great power management] … which is probably further away from multilateralism than any other model of multipolarity, at least if multilateralism is understood as being premised on the fundamental equality of all participants of the international system'.[51] Nikonov even insists on a return to the 'concert of powers' in the framework of potential multipolarity. He argues that the possibility of a 'deadly civilizational confrontation between South and North' could be avoided if the world keeps 'moving towards greater consolidation and governability, rather than increasing unilateral trends and chaos. That is, to the rather forgotten Concert of Powers that provided a century-long peace for Europe from 1815 to 1914.' He continued that the world might also be moving towards a 'Global Concert, the composition and format of which are yet to be identified'.[52]

At the same time, the softer diplomatic version of great power management could, in practice, give way to the much more conflictual balance of power system of polarity. Both the United States and Russia are rapidly resurrecting this system, which is more understandable to both sides due to their experience of the Cold War. The foreign policy strategy proposed by the former US President Donald Trump aimed to transition the United States from a position of global leadership and global regulation to one focused on securing more concrete national interests. Both the 2017 National Security Strategy and the 2018 National Defense Strategy are open about using *power* as a means of securing US national interests in every way possible. More importantly, the National Security Strategy states that 'after being dismissed as a phenomenon of an earlier century, great power competition has returned'.[53] Russia was also actively involved in the reconstruction of the old 'balance of power' system by focusing on reforming its army and strategic defence systems.[54]

Following nearly a decade of rearming military forces and working on an asymmetric response to the anti-missile defence system developed by the

United States across Russia's borders, Russia now stands as a formidable military opponent to the Western powers.[55] In October 2016, it protected its northern borders by deploying short-range Iskander (SS-26 Stone) ballistic missiles in the Kaliningrad region, the westernmost territory on the south-eastern coast of the Baltic Sea. Military bases planned in the Arctic Ocean and the Barents Sea will create obstacles to potential attacks from the north. The incorporation of Crimea into Russia ensured that the American Navy became largely powerless in the Black Sea, its potential neutralised by Crimean naval bases. Russia also secured its southern territories by deploying the Mediterranean Sea Syrian Tartus naval base, and Khmeimim and Idlib air bases that cover a large territory as far as Spain. The rapid development of the Russian Navy was called to achieve a strategic balance with the United States, whose fleet represents the most tangible threat to Russia. More importantly, the latest missiles, revealed in Putin's address to the Federal Assembly on 1 March 2018, render the American defence shield largely powerless and pose a significant threat to the US fleet. It is becoming clear that such policies represent a significant move away from the idea of an equitable redistribution of power and equality of all nations. Instead, we see the return of 'balance of power' politics, a potentially bipolar arrangement in the military sphere, and the Cold War pursuit of military deterrence and parity.[56]

The role of the nation-state

The role of the nation-state in the developing multipolar world order is contested both practically and theoretically. Some Russian intellectuals argue that, in contrast to previous historical periods, contemporary international alliances could seriously curb the sovereignty of their participant states. As an influential theoretical proponent of the multipolar world theory in Russia, Dugin argues that we could meaningfully discuss the sovereignty of a political-cultural-military *alliance* rather than the full sovereignty held by the states composing the alliance. Hence, he introduces the idea of *civilisational sovereignty* at the expense of state sovereignty as envisaged by the classical Westphalian system.[57]

At the same time, the impact of the shift from unipolarity (or bipolarity) to multipolarity on sovereignty of domestic political systems is contested. A case could be made that, in the contemporary political and economic international conditions, participation in a civilisational (or pole) alliance could exert a significant influence on the behaviour of the state in the domestic and international arenas. Some literature on international relations argues that the socialisation of secondary states by hegemonic nations plays a serious role in altering the political atmosphere at home, influencing norms, value orientations, and policy preferences.[58] Karl Deutsch and J. David Singer argue that:

> as a nation enters into the standard coalition it is much less of a free agent than it was while non-aligned. That is, its alliance partners now exercise an inhibiting effect – or perhaps even a veto – upon its freedom to interact with non-alliance nations.[59]

G. John Ikenberry and Charles Kupchan stress the role of international organisations erected by hegemonic states that lead the alliance: '[t]hrough frequent participation in the institutions … elites in secondary states are exposed to and may eventually embrace the norms and value orientations that those institutions embody'.[60] From this point of view, Dugin's idea of replacing state sovereignty with *civilisational sovereignty* (or pole sovereignty) does not seem entirely outlandish. The contemporary European Union embodies this logic.

At the same time, a substantial section of Western literature argues that, under multipolarity, quite different domestic systems are considered legitimate, thus exonerating states' flexibility of action. This is in contrast to unipolar or bipolar arrangements that require a strict ideological adherence of states to a chosen political system and an ideological line that buttresses it.[61] Indeed, in a multipolar world environment, smaller states obtain a more significant status due to their special international functions fostered by greater room for manoeuvre between the existing poles of influence.[62] Given that no hegemonic state exerts a commanding influence on the general international climate, the socialising effect under multipolar systems is markedly weaker than under unipolar or bipolar ones. This could partly explain the fact that there is more tolerance towards 'deviant' behaviour in domestic political systems.[63] Under multipolarity, hegemons would rather seek compliance via non-coercive means of persuasion, using soft power, media, and non-state actors. Hence, under the multipolar arrangement, ideological and political pressures exerted on secondary states by a hegemon become less significant. Taken from this point of view, multipolarity could be considered an argument for a strengthened role of the state.

This latter theoretical position falls in line with the position of Russian officials and intellectuals who ardently defend nation-state sovereignty. Russian officials view a strong state as a vehicle for order, stability, and continuous economic development. They would therefore be reluctant to accept any model of multipolarity that could curb the state. By deploying such an approach, Russia invokes a multiregional version of multipolarity. Lavrov often argues that state sovereignty and the ability to sustain the multiplicity of cultural and political forms based on sovereignty remains the cornerstone of international security and lasting peace.[64] In this light,

Russia's fundamental rhetorical position is the defence of the idea of the nation-state and the primacy of international law based on the Yalta–Potsdam system and the United Nations Charter. Russian intellectuals uphold the idea of state sovereignty as a means of preserving the cultural and political distinctness of various states, and as combating the uniformity of a Western-narrated global culture. Alexey Bogaturov argues that, in contrast to the 'collective unipolarity' advanced by the United States, the multipolar world arrangement represents 'a conglomerate of enclaves, interacting but not doomed to mutual assimilation'.[65] Hence, sovereignty must be sustained as an expedient instrument that could allow the idea of normative pluralism to capture the dominant discourse. Simultaneously, it is argued that countries should unite into cultural, political, and *civilisational* unions to advance the idea of *civilisational* diversity. These two processes – sustaining sovereignty and forming cultural unions – could occur in parallel, mutually reinforcing each other. Such an approach is seen in the ideology of the Eurasian Economic Union (EAEU), discussed later.

The main rationale behind the defence of the nation-state stems from the rejection of the unipolar world order and the US-led version of globalisation. Russian intellectuals such as Mikhail Khazin, Mikhail Delyagin, Kurginyan, Nikonov, Yakov Kedmi,[66] and others often argue that the unipolar world order is fraught with the dangers of restrictions on democracy and civil rights even in those countries that initially adopted the democratic political system. This stems from the idea that the unipolar world order is buttressed by global capital with its political and administrative hub located in the Western hemisphere, and its centre in the United States. A number of Western analysts have also discussed the emergence of a global economic elite that are surpassing the limitations previously imposed on them by nation-states and have extended their influence beyond national borders.[67] Hence, nation states, even those that host those corporations administratively, logistically, and financially, become an obstacle for the expansion of global capital.

Bearing these considerations in mind, the Russian political thinkers claim that it is too early to dispense with the idea of the nation-state.[68] First, a large number of countries in the developing world need to go through the process of modernisation, and the nation-state represents the most reliable context for industrialisation and modernisation. Second, somewhat in the Hegelian spirit, the nation-state is viewed as the most important guarantor of democracy, civil liberties, and human rights across the globe.[69] The state has an invariably national character and has national concerns at its heart, transmitting culture, historical narratives, language, and normative patterns of the community. Global corporations and organisations could not replace the nation-state in its functions, for these institutions pursue radically different existential goals. While securing profit is the prime motivator for business corporations, guaranteeing civic liberties, social economic rights, and individual freedoms is the purpose and *raison d'etre* of the nation-state. Similarly, supranational organisations that are often subject to the influence of global business pursue cosmopolitan goals relevant to supranational communities; they resolve private economic conflicts, in accordance with the Hegelian view on civil society.[70]

Third, only the nation-state can determine a country's national interests by taking both economic and non-economic factors into account. It is on this basis that the nation-state represents and defends those interests in the international arena. From this point of view, Russian public opinion-makers argue that the nation-state should not disappear at this stage of historical development. The state should resist the role of becoming a political appendix and the rubber stamp of global monopolies, as only the state can assure the rights and freedoms of its people.[71] Nikonov argues that 'sovereignty is a very important instrument of development', as external governance 'never results in economic prosperity but increases external debt, restricts strategic industries and leads to the flow of capital abroad'.[72] Russian commentators claim that Russia went through a severe decline in its domestic production and in its scientific and technological development during the 1990s, at a time when it lost its independence in foreign policy and *de facto* state sovereignty.[73]

It is important to conclude that Russia's approach to multipolarity has theoretical and practical dimensions. At the theoretical level, some thinkers imply that multipolarity could lead to a significant reduction of state sovereignty, both in the case of great power management politics or in the adoption of some forms of *civilisational* (or regional) sovereignty. At the practical level, a contemporary adherence to state sovereignty is necessary in that Russia realises that the abandonment of state sovereignty is unthinkable at this stage. Hence, Russia supports state sovereignty as a tool in constructing its military and political alliances and uses the idea of sovereignty as a precondition for alliance and pole formation. This could help Russia to either construct a fully fledged cultural-political pole of influence in the near future, or to divert back to bipolarity if sufficient resources could be accumulated.

Regionalisation and spheres of influence

Russia signals its adherence to the multipolar world architecture by participating in various economic alliances and in its work towards establishing the EAEU – a prospective pole of global political influence. It could be argued that the idea to form the union represented a response to global challenges posed by the political and economic domination of the West. The initiative originally came from Kazakh President Nursultan Nazarbayev in 1994. Nazarbayev argued in 2003 that the formation of the union represents a survival strategy in a rapidly changing global world. He claimed that in-depth integration with the rest of the global community could only take place if Eurasian states united and integrated in-depth themselves as a concerted effort.[74]

Contemporary globalisation has resulted in the creation of tightly knit economic clusters: the European Union, the North American Free Trade Agreement, the South American Mercosur, and others. There were only two ways to navigate this environment. One was to join one of those alliances, which was difficult due to the tough political, cultural, and value demands imposed on participants by existing members. The other option was to become a 'third world' cluster that provides resources and cheap labour to larger associations. The formation of the EAEU demonstrated a way in which participant countries were enabled to form a new pole of influence in the global landscape and to assure their independent economic development and modernisation.

It was important that the union's formation adhered to the two most important, albeit dualistic, principles. First, it did not aim to alter the cultural, political, religious, or value patterns of its member states. Second, there was an understanding that the union was built on the pre-existing Soviet (or Russian Imperial) cultural-political space, in which member states already shared some aspects of fate and history. In regard to the first point, Russian Foreign Minister Lavrov argued that Russia did not expect other states to sacrifice their prosperity for the sake of particular ideas or political doctrines, and that no country should try to fit into a particular developmental model which is considered optimal by other states.[75] The ideology of the EAEU proposed the integration of the post-Soviet space based on the idea of a plurality of cultural and political forms within the union, thus accepting the idea of domestic sovereignty.

Hence, at the practical level, the EAEU remains a political alliance of *sovereign* states. Concerning foreign policy issues, members pursue independent foreign policies and do not always tread the Russian line. For example, none of the member states recognise South Ossetia and Abkhazia as independent states. Union members also hold an independent line towards Ukraine and are often critical of Russian foreign policy in this sphere. Kazakhstan and Armenia habitually make positive political gestures towards the European Union, regardless of the Russian position. It is clear that the multi-vector nature of the foreign policies of participant states remains in place. Yet, diversity in foreign policy is also compensated by the member states' active participation in economic and institutional integration with Russia.

In regard to the second point, the EAEU offers integration on the basis of a common history and understanding of the political processes taking place in the contemporary world – an aspect that represents a theoretical dimension of multipolarity. The union often uses a metaphysical notion of the 'commonality of fate' of its constituent peoples: civilisational, geopolitical, and historical. The collective identity of the EAEU is built on the blueprints of the former Russian Empire and the Soviet Union, which welcomed a particularity of cultures, ethnic groups, and religions, but also kept to a specific form of collectivism that united these divergent peoples into a single political union.[76] Commonality of fate, altruism, and adherence to mutual history often determines the interest of the participant nations in the union.

Russia also pursues a multipolar line in the economic sphere, which it considers an important tool for challenging American domination. Within the conditions of the unipolar moment, Russia heavily relied on an overwhelmingly Eurocentric strategy in terms of economic alliances. The most recent political developments have determined the need for the diversification of its economic ties, with a turn towards the East. Russia hopes to reorient its economic strategies towards new markets that are free from the pressure of Western sanctions. These markets are located in states such as China, India, Iran, Israel, and South East Asia. China became Russia's leading trading partner in 2017–18. At the same time, investment cooperation between Russia and its new trading partners remains low.[77] Russia is lagging behind the European Union in terms of the number of its free trade agreements. Just one agreement was concluded with Vietnam, against the backdrop of the fourteen to fifteen free trade agreements that exist between Western countries and the 'rest of the world'. Nevertheless, the interest in forming a free trade agreement with Russia and the EAEU is strong, with serious political intentions coming from successful economic players such as Israel, Singapore, and South Korea.

Participation in the BRICS (Brazil, Russia, India, China, and South Africa) alliance is another multipolar economic initiative supported by Russia. More importantly, the BRICS have suggested the idea of BRICS+, which looks to expand partnerships between BRICS members with other states. The BRICS+ alliance adopts a multipolar approach to the economic and political integration of its member states. It is unique in the sense that its members are spread across the world geographically and participation in the alliance is not tied up with accession to a particular ideological or even territorial club. Each member can retain its unique cultural and political outlook while trading and cooperating successfully with other members. It could be argued that the BRICS+ concept represents an alternative technology for constructing global alliances.[78]

BRICS+ also has the chance to alter the unipolar moment within the existing international financial organisations of the Bretton Woods system. The alliance could increase its consolidated share of votes in the International Monetary Fund (IMF) by over 15 per cent, which would enable BRICS+ to block key decisions of the IMF. A similar situation is occurring at the World Bank and the World Trade Organization, which are usually dominated by American-centred officials. There are also important developments over cooperation between regional development banks formed by the BRICS+ economies. This could alter the strategic balance of international lending organisations and help finance the developing and developed economies. Of particular importance are the Eurasian Development Bank, the Development Bank of South Africa, the SAARC (South Asian Association for Regional Cooperation) Development Fund, the Mercosur Structural Convergence Fund, the China Development Bank, the China–ASEAN (Association of Southeast Asian Nations) Investment Cooperation Fund, and the New Development Bank.[79] Such developments have the potential to launch a process of 'alternative globalisation' that is more attuned to the multiregional world architecture.

More importantly, Russia also supports the idea of creating different currency zones – a step that could pose a serious challenge to the dollar-dominated Bretton Woods world economy. The most natural currency zones might be the dollar zone, which would encompass North America and Mexico, the eurozone covering the territory of the European Union and its closest trading partners, the yuan zone that would include some Asian and a number of African countries, and the Brazil real zone which could also emerge to include other countries in Latin America. Russia aims to create the rouble zone, which would encompass the EAEU and countries that would like to form a free trade agreement with it. While such plans have a future-oriented character and revolutionary changes are not expected, Russia proposes to take the first steps towards world currency diversification and institute trading in national currencies with its significant trading partners.

This primarily concerns Russia's trade with its EAEU partners. According to official reports of the Eurasian Development Bank, the share of the rouble in EAEU payments grew from 56 per cent to 75 per cent between 2013 and 2018, while the share of the dollar and the euro was reduced from 35 per cent to 19 per cent.[80] In polls of businesses conducted by the Eurasian Development Bank, 59 per cent of respondents thought that the share of national currencies in mutual trading would grow in the future, and only 17.4 per cent believed that domination by the US dollar would continue.[81] Russia is also negotiating a transfer to the rouble or national currency trading with Turkey, Egypt, Iran, India, China, and other BRICS+ countries. A full transition to national currencies still remains a distant goal due to the economic volatility of some of these currencies. However, some tectonic moves in this direction are clearly visible and the trend seems to be difficult to reverse. In general, BRICS+ serves as a platform for mutual payments and the expansion of the use of national currencies in trade and investment transactions, thus reducing the dependence on the dollar or euro. In addition, the BRICS+ countries have plans to establish and promote international financial centres via the listing of companies in the exchanges of the BRICS+ economies. Mutual currencies could become part of the gold and currency reserves of the respective Central Banks. The Eurasian Development Bank, the New Development Bank, Nord Hydro, and the International Investment Bank financed the construction of hydropower plants in Russia with credit opened in Russian roubles.

Finally, the Shanghai Cooperation Organisation (SCO) represents a step towards multipolarity in the political and, partly, the security spheres. Established in 2001 by China, Kazakhstan, Kyrgyzstan, Russia, Tajikistan, and Uzbekistan, the SCO is not a fully fledged military, economic, or cultural alliance. It occupies a middle ground between all these positions and serves as a union that helps to assure security and cooperation in the large Eurasian and Asian space. The organisation provides cultural and military avenues of cooperation between the participant nations, and recently China was able to bring the economic sphere into its dialogue.

It is important that China is seen as a new trading transition corridor (due to its Belt and Road Initiative) and its importance for Russia will grow significantly in the future. The focus is on transportation, and when transportation and energy links are involved, geopolitical issues are hard to avoid. China has already indicated that Syria will be a major hub at the far end of the Belt and Road Initiative. Hence, there will be an increase in Chinese funds channelled to Syria as part of the effort to reconstruct and develop the country, which will share cross-sections with Russian policy towards the Middle East.

The strategic partnership between Russia and China is the foundation of the SCO and in many ways the SCO was originally formed for Russia and China to manage their tensions in the region. However, the organisation is also seen as a push towards resisting the unipolar world moment led by the United States. China is considered to be the most important economic rival to the United States and faces a US military presence in the South China Sea. The United States also has a tense relationship with Iran, which is an observer in the SCO. To use Halford Mackinder's terminology, the organisation reflects a centuries-old conflict and a classical geopolitical dilemma about the 'heartland' and the 'sea'.[82] Given that the SCO is composed of the 'heartland countries', it presents a political and economic counterweight to the sea powers.

Conclusion

The multipolar world order is becoming an important concept in the international relations of the twenty-first century. With this concept, the very idea of global leadership and hegemony has begun to be redefined. Despite there being no coherent theory of the multipolar world architecture, the passing of the unipolar moment and the emergence of a new order with multiple centres of power has become a reality. The new multipolar order could materialise in different models and forms, depending on the strategies and wishes of international community actors. What is clear at this stage, however, is that the idea of a changing world order evokes concerns in the political elites of countries that have relied heavily on the now diminishing US leadership and unipolarity. Simultaneously, it gives hope to those who wish to become new claimants to the share of the world's hegemony pie.

This chapter focused on Russia's understanding of the newly emerging multipolar world order at both philosophical and practical levels. It has been argued that Russia has a normative vision of multipolarity that relies on the ideas of cultural diversity, civilisational distinctness of the world's regions, and independence of countries and civilisations in their political choices. The discussion showed that at the practical level, Russia's view on multipolarity balances between the ideas of multiregionalism and great power management, both of which exonerate the role of the nation-state and state sovereignty in international politics. The future choice of the multipolar world order, however, remains open.

Notes

1 Ministry of Foreign Affairs of the Russian Federation, 'Foreign policy concept of the Russian Federation (approved by President of the Russian Federation Vladimir Putin on November 30, 2016)', 1 December 2016, www.mid.ru/en/foreign_policy/official_documents/-/asset_publisher/CptICkB6BZ29/content/id/2542248 (accessed 24 October 2019).
2 Vladimir Putin, 'Speech and the following discussion at the Munich Conference on Security Policy', 10 February 2007, http://en.kremlin.ru/events/president/transcripts/24034 (accessed 22 October 2019).
3 Ministry of Foreign Affairs of the Russian Federation, 'Foreign policy concept of the Russian Federation'.
4 Andrey Makarychev and Viatcheslav Morozov, 'Multilateralism, multipolarity, and beyond: a menu of Russia's policy strategies', *Global Governance*, 17:3 (2011), 353–73, at 358; Leonid Ivashov, *Geopolitika Russkoi Tsivilizatsii* (Moscow: Institut Russkoi Tsivilizatsii, 2015), pp. 775–7; Ministry of Foreign Affairs of the

Russian Federation, 'Foreign policy concept of the Russian Federation'; Alexander Dugin, *Teoriya Mnogopolyarnogo Mira* (Moscow: Evraziiskoe Dvizhenie, 2013).

5 Robin Edmonds, 'Yalta and Potsdam: forty years afterwards', *International Affairs*, 62:2 (1986), 197–216.

6 Kenneth Waltz, *Theory of International Politics* (Reading, MA: Addison-Wesley, 1979); Karl W. Deutsch and J. David Singer, 'Multipolar power systems and international stability', *World Politics*, 16:3 (1964), 390–406.

7 Alexander Dugin, *The Fourth Political Theory* (London: Arktos, 2012); Ivashov, *Geopolitika Russkoi Tsivilizatsii*, p. 676; Viacheslav Nikonov, 'Nazad k kontsertu' [Back to the concert], *Global Affairs*, 6 (7 December 2017), https://globalaffairs.ru/number/Nazad-k-Kontcertu-19191 (accessed 22 October 2019).

8 Charles Krauthammer, 'The unipolar moment', *Foreign Affairs*, 70:1 (1990/91), 23–33.

9 Immanuel Wallerstein, *Geopolitics and Geoculture: Essays on the Changing World-System* (Cambridge: Cambridge University Press, 1991). See also John Keane, *Global Civil Society?* (Cambridge: Cambridge University Press, 2003).

10 Robert D. Kaplan, *Imperial Grunts: On the Ground with the American Military, from Mongolia to the Philippines to Iraq and Beyond* (New York: Vintage, 2006); Michael Mastanduno, 'System maker and privilege taker: US power and the international political economy', *World Politics*, 61:1 (2009), 121–54; John J. Mearsheimer, *The Tragedy of Great Power Politics* (New York: W. W. Norton, 2001); G. John Ikenberry, *Liberal Leviathan: The Origins, Crisis, and Transformation of the American World Order* (Princeton, NJ: Princeton University Press, 2011); Francis Fukuyama, *State Building: Governance and World Order in the Twenty-First Century* (London: Profile Books Ltd, 2004).

11 Mearsheimer, *Tragedy of Great Power Politics*, pp. 34–5.

12 Richard Haass, 'The age of nonpolarity: what will follow US dominance', *Foreign Affairs*, 87:3 (2008), 44–56, at 44–5.

13 Dugin, *Teoriya Mnogopolyarnogo Mira*, p. 25.

14 Ernst B. Haas, *The Uniting of Europe: Political, Social, and Economic Forces, 1950–1957* (Stanford, CA: Stanford University Press, 1958), pp. 213–14.

15 Haass, 'The age of nonpolarity', 46.

16 Randall Germain, 'The dollar and the world economy: *long durée* thinking', paper prepared for workshop 'Becoming Hegemonic: Hegemonic and Counter-Hegemonic Strategies', Berlin, 27 August 2018.

17 Haass, 'The age of nonpolarity'; Niall Ferguson, 'A world without power', *Foreign Policy*, 143 (2004), 32–9.

18 Ferguson, 'A world without power', p. 34.

19 Haass, 'The age of nonpolarity'.

20 Dugin, *Teoriya Mnogopolyarnogo Mira*.

21 Waltz, *Theory of International Politics*; Kenneth Waltz, 'The stability of a bipolar world', *Daedalus*, 93:3 (1964), 881–909.

22 Deutsch and Singer, 'Multipolar power systems'.

23 Benjamin Zala, 'Polarity analysis and collective perceptions of power', *Journal of Global Security Studies*, 2:1 (2017), 2–17, at 3–4.

24 Hans Morgenthau, *Politics Among Nations: The Struggle for Power and Peace* (New York: Alfred Knopp, 1948); E. H. Carr, *The Twenty Years' Crisis 1919–1939* (London: Palgrave Macmillan, 2001); Henry Kissinger, *World Order: Reflections on the Character of Nations and the Course of History* (London: Penguin Books, 2014); Anatol Lieven and John Hulsman, *Ethical Realism: A Vision for America's Role in the World* (New York: Pantheon Books, 2007); Henry Nau and Deepa Ollapally, *Worldviews of Aspiring Powers: Domestic Foreign Policy Debates in China, India, Iran, Japan, and Russia* (Oxford: Oxford University Press, 2012).

25 Chantal Mouffe, 'Democracy in a multipolar world', *Millennium: Journal of International Studies*, 37:3 (2009), 549–61; Shmuel Noah Eisenstadt (ed.), *Multiple Modernities* (London: Transaction Publishers, 2002); Adrian Pabst, 'Euro-Atlantic and Eurasian security in a multipolar world', *American Foreign Policy Interests*, 33:1 (2011), 26–40.

26 Amitav Acharya, 'Can Asia lead? Power ambitions and global governance in the twenty-first century', *International Affairs*, 87:4 (2011), 851–69; C. Dale Walton, *Geopolitics and the Great Powers in the Twenty-First Century: Multipolarity and the Revolution in Strategic Perspective* (Abingdon: Routledge, 2007); Chantal Mouffe, 'Schmitt's vision of a multipolar world order', *South Atlantic Quarterly*, 104:2 (2005), 245–51; Charles A. Kupchan, 'The false promise of unipolarity: constraints on the exercise of American power', *Cambridge Review of International Affairs*, 24:2 (2011), 165–73.

27 Daria Kazarinova, 'Dialogue for a new architecture of macro-regional security: from the clash of narratives to a secure greater Eurasia', in Andrei Malashenko, Vladimir Popov, and Peter Schultz (eds), *Making Multilateralism Work: Enhancing Dialogue on Peace, Security and Development* (Berlin: Dialogue of Civilisations Institute, 2018), pp. 179–89, at p. 181.

28 Vadim Tsymbursky, *Ostrov Rossiya: Geopoliticheskie I Khronopoliticheskie Raboty: 1993–2006* (Moscow: Evropa, 2007); Ministry of Foreign Affairs of the Russian Federation, 'Foreign policy concept of the Russian Federation'.

29 Makarychev and Morozov, 'Multilateralism, multipolarity, and beyond', p. 357.

30 Yevgenyi Primakov, 'A world without superpowers', *Global Affairs*, 3 (2 September 2003), https://globalaffairs.ru/number/n_1560 (accessed 22 October 2019); Kazarinova, 'Dialogue for a new architecture'.

31 Andrew Hurrell, 'One world? Many worlds? The place of regions in the study of international society', *International Affairs*, 83:1 (2017), 127–46, at 128.

32 Primakov, 'A world without superpowers'.

33 Nikonov, 'Nazad k kontsertu'.

34 *Ibid.*

35 Haass, 'The age of nonpolarity', 45.

36 Vladimir Yakunin, 'The world after 2016: Imagining possible futures', DOC Research Institute, 14 June 2017, https://doc-research.org/2017/06/world-2016-imagining-future-development/ (accessed 22 October 2019).

37 Vladimir Soloviev interviews Sergey Kurginyan, *Vecher s Vladimirom Soloviovym*, 16 April 2018, www.youtube.com/watch?v=ZYz0e340l8w&t=1s (accessed 27 September 2018).

38 'Foreign Minister Sergey Lavrov's remarks at the opening ceremony of the 26th International Educational Christmas Readings', Moscow, 24 January 2018, www.mid.ru/en/press_service/video/-/asset_publisher/i6t41cq3VWP6/content/id/3033884 (accessed 21 February 2018).

39 *Ibid.*

40 Yulia Sineokaya, 'Nietzsche pomog russkim intellektualam obresti svobodu dukha', *Theory and Practice* [website], 14 December 2014, https://theoryandpractice.ru/posts/9905-nietzsche-interview (accessed 22 October 2019).

41 Boris Mezhuev, 'Intellektualnyi klass i sovremennoe protivorechie epokhi', *Russkaya Ideya*, 6 June 2018, https://politconservatism.ru/thinking/intellektualnyj-klass-i-osnovnoe-protivorechie-epohi (accessed 22 October 2019).

42 *Vecher s Solovyovym*, 'Efir ot 1 Fevralya 2018', 1 February 2018, www.youtube.com/watch?v=poIZUkkiT9U (accessed 1 March 2018).

43 Remizov in *ibid.*

44 Mezhuev, 'Intellektualnyi klass i sovremennoe protivorechie epokhi'.

45 Ministry of Foreign Affairs of the Russian Federation, 'Foreign policy concept of the Russian Federation'.

46 Alexey Bogaturov, 'Sindrom pogloshcheniya v mirovoi politike', *Pro et Contra*, 4:4 (1999), 28–48, at 28; Kazarinova, 'Dialogue for a new architecture'; Yakov Kedmi and Yevgeny Satanovsky, 'Balans sil v mire', *Dialogi in Rossiya 24*, 1 September 2017, www.youtube.com/watch?v=7WTcQY6Vuxo (accessed 14 May 2021).

47 Ministry of Foreign Affairs of the Russian Federation, 'Foreign policy concept of the Russian Federation'.

48 Vladimir Yakunin, 'Moving from dialogue to action: changing the world through civic councils', DOC Research Institute, 19 October 2017, https://doc-research.org/de/2017/10/moving-dialogue-action-changing-world-civic-councils/ (accessed 22 October 2019).

49 *Ibid.*

50 Samir Saran, 'In a pluralist Asia-centric world order, Russia has a crucial role to play', Valdai Discussion Club, 2 October 2018, http://valdaiclub.com/a/highlights/in-a-pluralist-asian-centric-world-order-russia/ (accessed 22 October 2019).

51 Makarychev and Morozov, 'Multilateralism, multipolarity, and beyond', 370.

52 Nikonov, 'Nazad k kontsertu'.

53 *National Security Strategy of the United States of America, December 2017*, p. 27, https://www.hsdl.org/?abstract&did=806478 (accessed 14 May 2021); Department of Defense, USA, *Summary of the 2018 National Defense Strategy of the United States of America*, https://admin.govexec.com/media/20180118173223431.pdf (accessed 22 May 2018).

54 Alexander Belkin, 'Civil–military relations in Russia after 9/11', *European Security*, 12:3–4 (2003), 1–19; Zoltan Barany, 'The politics of Russia's elusive defense reform', *Political Science Quarterly*, 121:4 (2006/07), 597–627; Margarete Klein, 'Towards a "new look" of the Russian armed forces? Organizational and personnel changes', in Roger N. McDermott, Bertil Nygren, and Carolina Vendil Pallin (eds), *The Russian Armed Forces in Transition: Economic, Geopolitical and*

Institutional Uncertainties (Abingdon: Routledge, 2012), pp. 29–48; Dmitry Gorenburg, *The Russian Military under Sergei Shoigu: Will the Reform Continue?* PONARS Eurasia Policy Memo No. 253 (Washington, DC: Elliott School of International Affairs, George Washington University, 2013); Makarychev and Morozov, 'Multilateralism, multipolarity, and beyond'.

55 Alec Luhn and Roland Oliphant, 'Vladimir Putin claims Russia has developed nuclear weapons "invulnerable" to US missile defence', *The Telegraph*, 1 March 2018.

56 The idea of parity is not in Russia's vision. As mentioned earlier, Russia's military budget is dwarfed by that of the US.

57 Dugin, *Teoriya Mnogopolyarnogo Mira.*

58 Waltz, *Theory of International Politics*, pp. 127–8; G. John Ikenberry and Charles A. Kupchan, 'Socialization and hegemonic power', *International Organization*, 44:3 (1990), 283–315; Elana Wilson Rowe and Stilana Trojessen, *Multilateral Dimensions in Russian Foreign Policy* (London: Routledge, 2009), p. 2.

59 Deutsch and Singer, 'Multipolar power systems', 392.

60 Ikenberry and Kupchan, 'Socialization and hegemonic power', 292.

61 Raimo Vayrynen, 'Bipolarity, multipolarity, and domestic political systems', *Journal of Peace Research*, 32:3 (1995), 361–71.

62 Deutsch and Singer, 'Multipolar power systems', 394.

63 Vayrynen, 'Bipolarity, multipolarity, and domestic political systems', 362–3.

64 'Vystuplenie Sergeya Lavrova v Gosdume', *RT*, 14 October 2015, https://russian.rt.com/article/123511 (accessed 22 May 2018).

65 Bogaturov, 'Sindrom pogloshcheniya v mirovoi politike', 40.

66 Although Yakov Kedmi is an Israeli political activist, public speaker, intellectual, and former head of the Nativ intelligence service, he is a native Russian speaker (being Soviet-born), a frequent guest on Russia's analytical programmes on television and radio, and a frequent contributor to Russia's printed press.

67 Christopher Lasch, *The Revolt of the Elites and the Betrayal of Democracy* (London: W. W. Norton, 1995); David Harvey, *A Brief History of Neoliberalism* (New York: Oxford University Press, 2005); Noam Chomsky, *Profit Over People: Neoliberalism and Global Order* (New York: Seven Stories Press, 1998); Karl Polanyi, *The Great Transformation: The Political and Economic Origins of Our Time* (New York: Farrar and Rinehart, 1944); Agnes Cornell, Jorgen Moller, and Svend-Rik Skaaning, 'The real lessons of the interwar years', *Journal of Democracy*, 28:3 (2017), 14–28.

68 Vladimir Soloviev interviews Sergey Kurginyan, *Vecher s Vladimirom Soloviovym.*

69 John Keane, *Democracy and Civil Society* (London: Verso, 1988), pp. 52–3; Z. A. Pelczynski, 'Introduction: the significance of Hegel's separation of the state and civil society', in Z. A. Pelczynski (ed.), *The State and Civil Society: Studies in Hegel's Political Philosophy* (Cambridge: Cambridge University Press, 1984), pp. 1–13, at p. 11; Jean Cohen and Andrew Arato, *Civil Society and Political Theory* (Cambridge, MA: MIT Press, 1992), pp. 91–102.

70 Noberto Bobbio, 'Gramsci and the concept of civil society', in John Keane (ed.), *Civil Society and the State: New European Perspective* (London: Verso,

1998), pp. 73–99, at pp. 79, 81–2; Cohen and Arato, *Civil Society and Political Theory*, pp. 91–102.

71 Kedmi and Satanovsky, 'Balans sil v mire'.

72 Vyacheslav Nikonov and Ariel Cohen, *Poedinok*, 23 January 2017, www.youtube.com/watch?v=vv_1WKlIus46 (accessed 14 May 2021).

73 Alexander Lukin, *The Political Culture of the Russian 'Democrats'* (Oxford: Oxford University Press, 2000), pp. 47–8, 294; John Gray, *False Dawn: The Delusions of Global Capitalism* (London: Granta Publications, 1998).

74 Alexander S. Panarin, 'Budet li sozdan evraziiskii soyuz?', *Chto Delat?*, 4 March 2003, www.youtube.com/watch?v=-6o8clYchKg (accessed 6 March 2018).

75 'Vystuplenie Sergeya Lavrova v Gosdume'.

76 Panarin, 'Budet li sozdan evraziiskii soyuz?'

77 Yaroslav Lissovolik, 'Russia's economic modernization: a long-term perspective', Valdai Discussion Club, 28 February 2018, www.valdaiclub.com/a/highlights/russia-s-economic-modernization/ (accessed 6 March 2018).

78 Yaroslav Lissovolik, 'BRICS-plus: alternative globalization in the making?', Valdai Papers No. 69, July 2017, http://valdaiclub.com/a/valdai-papers/valdai-paper-69/ (accessed 21 October 2019).

79 *Ibid.*

80 Yaroslav Lissovolik, *Natsionalnye valyuty vo vzaimoraschetakh v ramkakh EAES: Prepyatstviya i persperktivy*, Evraziiskii Bank Razvitiya Report No. 48 (Almaty, Kazakhstan: Eurasian Development Bank, January 2018); Dmitry Titov, 'Raschety v natsionalnykh valyutakh stran EAES budut vnedryatsia postepenno', *Ekonomika i Zhizn*, 11 January 2018; Dmitry Korshunov, 'Dolya rublya v raschetakh EAES rastet, nesmotrya na riski novogo krizisa', *Prime* [website], 9 January 2018, https://1prime.ru/finance/20180109/828322561.html (accessed 12 March 2018).

81 'Rubl gotovyat k mirovoi ekspansii', *RIA Novosti*, 22 January 2018.

82 Halford Mackinder, 'The geographical pivot of history', *Geographical Journal*, 23:4 (1904), 421–37; Walton, *Geopolitics and the Great Powers*.

Part II

The unipole and its allies

5

Does the United States face a multipolar future? Washington's response through the lens of technology

James Johnson

Does the United States still harbour ambitions to regain its (albeit fleeting) unipolar status? Or is it instead resigned to an existence as simply one of a number of great powers in a multipolar era?[1] In what ways is the increasingly multipolar strategic environment encouraging new forms of competition that may threaten stability? Alternatively, will the increasingly competitive US–China relationship dominate world politics, creating what would therefore be a new bipolarity? International Relations (IR) scholars have long recognised the central role that technological innovation plays in power transitions, the balance of power, and international politics and security more broadly.[2] IR scholars of various stripes have also begun to reflect on the nuanced relationship between advances in technology, the rise of new powers and political and military prominence in the international order, and responses to these trends by dominant powers.[3]

While scholars have demonstrated the salience of technological innovation and, more recently, illuminated how dominant and rising powers interact in this arena, much less literature exists on the consequences of technological change, and in particular the notion of a return to multipolarity.[4] Robert Gilpin argued that while major advances in technology allow new nations to rise to political pre-eminence, over the long term technological know-how and 'inventiveness' diffuses to other countries.[5] More recently, scholars have considered the technology and innovation arena as a particular kind of great power interaction, directly affecting not just the nature of the power transitions but also the challenges and constraints placed on rising powers as they jostle to ensure their rise.[6]

This chapter contextualises these broader questions with US responses to recent trends in artificial intelligence (AI), and the distribution of power in the international order more broadly.[7] Despite the recent surge of articles in the popular press and trade journals on the potential transformative impact of AI (the so-called 'Fourth Industrial Revolution'), there has been little in the way of rigorous scholarship on the consequences of these developments for existing power dynamics between great and rising powers. Specifically, this chapter unpacks the key drivers of US national security policy in response to the AI capabilities of rising powers.[8] It also considers how the resultant decentralisation and diffusion of power might empower different (state and non-state) actors, and how this diffusion could influence the distribution of power between states.[9]

In the past decade, researchers have achieved major milestones in the development of AI and related technologies (quantum computing, big data, the 'internet of things', miniaturisation, and robotics and autonomy)[10] significantly faster than the projections of experts in the field. In 2014, for example, the AI expert who designed the world's best Go-playing (or AlphaGo) program predicted that it would be another ten years before a computer could defeat a human Go champion. Researchers at Google's DeepMind achieved this technological feat just one year later. Since at least the Second World War, partially autonomous systems have been used in military technology, but recent advances in machine learning and AI represent a fundamental turning point in the use of cognitive solutions and automation to enhance 'battlespace awareness'.[11]

There are several ways to frame this discussion within the broader context of the US response – resisting the notion, embracing it, or eschewing it – to the notion of multipolarity associated with this incipient technological phenomenon. The most compelling narratives include, first, the US as the dominant power in AI and the fallacy of the narrative centred on multipolarity and the rise of the rest.[12] Second, and juxtaposed, there is a sense of alarm building in the US defence community spurred by rising powers' rapid development of AI-enabled technologies, and thus a mounting sense of urgency (or 'innovation imperative') that the US may be unable to sustain its first-mover advantage in this increasingly diffused and competitive arena.[13] Third, faced with the inexorable shift away from unipolarity and towards multipolarity more generally, Washington has begun to accept its reduced status in the emerging technological multipolar order.[14]

Connecting these three narratives is the following research puzzle: is Sino-US bilateral AI competition the key driving force behind the 'AI revolution'? Or is there a genuine sense that the nature of this innovation-driven race is fundamentally more widely distributed, to middle and lower powers, and to non-state entities? From a US perspective, the former proposition would intimate that we can speak of an emerging bipolar order in AI, and the latter would support the 'new multipolarity' thesis. This chapter critically unpacks these interconnected trends and themes and presents a nuanced account of the challenge posed to the US by the rise of the rest in AI.

The chapter proceeds as follows. First, it summarises the response by US decision-makers and analysts – 'denialists', 'accepters', and 'resistors' – to the debate about a US decline and the rise of the narrative of an imminent shift to a multipolar order. Second, it sets up the debate over the rapid diffusion and proliferation of AI capabilities through an exploration of those that view harnessing these capabilities as a key aspect of efforts to maintain Washington's unipolar dominance. It outlines a range of US opinions surrounding the impact of AI on future warfare, the military balance, and national security more broadly.[15] It also examines the potential threat scenarios that could emerge from the several proven transformative innovations in AI in the hands of rising revisionist and revanchist powers, thereby threatening the durability of US military superiority and the unipolar order that it underpins.

Third, the chapter examines the perception of the rise of a bipolar order divided between Washington and Beijing. Again using the lens of high-end technological innovation, it analyses the credibility of the popular idea that the US has been caught off guard by China's accomplishments in the development of AI technologies (or the US' 'Sputnik moment'), and that as a result the United States risks losing its first-mover advantages in the adoption of AI on the future battlefield.[16]

Fourth and finally, in response to calls from within the US to take action to sustain its primacy in the emerging global AI race, the chapter investigates the nature of this particular 'arms race' in the context of predictions of a shift to a multipolar order – above all, the commercial driving forces and dual-use features of this dynamic, which intonates a much more diffused and multipolar reality – as opposed to a bipolar one. It argues that the rapid acquisition and diffusion of AI amongst great and rising powers will fundamentally influence the future distribution of power, and in a manner that will be likely to trigger security dilemmas and strategic rivalry between states.[17]

The prospect of multipolarity and the US response

In the post-Cold War era, a preoccupation of US policymakers and analysts has been the nature and implications of US unipolarity. This discourse has centred on two key questions: How long will unipolarity endure? And is the pursuit of hegemony a viable and worthwhile grand strategic objective for the US? The preservation of the US liberal hegemonic role as unipole has been the overarching grand strategic goal of every post-Cold War administration from George H. W. Bush to Barack Obama.[18] Having outlined the prominent strands and voices on how the US should and can respond to the notion of decline and the rise of a multipolar order, the analysis that follows uses AI as a lens to explore how the US is positioning itself vis-à-vis China – preparing for bipolarity with China, or reluctantly accepting multipolarity? The major reactions (both official and non-official) to the notion of US decline and a shift to a multipolar order can be categorised into three broad strands of thought: 'denialists', 'accepters', and 'resistors'.

Denialists and the preservation of Pax Americana

The 'denialists' represent the views of a diverse (albeit shrinking) band of US policymakers and analysts (official and non-official) who argue that, despite the 'great recession' of 2008, unipolarity is a durable reality in world politics, and thus talk of any meaningful decline in US power is overstated. Even in the face of overwhelming evidence to the contrary, unipolarity still exists and remains durable.[19] This optimistic view is premised on two central ideas: the economic and military power gap between the US and its rivals is insurmountable, and the 'benevolent' nature of US hegemony means that no other state would want to challenge the dominant position of the US.[20] Arguing against a 'rising tide of opinion' that depicts unipolarity quickly giving way to multipolarity, Stephen Brooks and William Wohlforth argue that '[T]oday's global order reflects the unique position of the United States as the sole superpower that alone among states has the capability to sustain a worldwide network of alliances and organize major politico-military operations in multiple key regions.'[21]

Even in the event that unipolarity were to end, therefore, the US would remain the pivotal power in world politics. In other words, despite the absence of US economics and military might to buttress the post-Second World War 'liberal order', *Pax Americana* will endure even if US unipolarity does not.[22] This view characterised the George W. Bush administrations' unilateralist and neoconservative approach to foreign policy (e.g. military intervention in Iraq and Afghanistan associated with the 'global war on terror').[23] Despite being more closely associated with the 'resistors' camp discussed further below, elements of the Donald Trump administration's foreign policy – especially its preference for unilateralism and scepticism about alliance entanglements – fall into this category.

Accepters and the era of US relative decline

The 'accepters' camp is represented by those advocating US retrenchment or forms of 'offshore balancing' to manage the inevitable 'rise of the rest' (notably China), and more broadly acknowledges the limits of US power imposed by the realities of multipolarity. At the core of this thesis is that after several decades of US primacy in world politics, we are now living in an era of US decline, measured in terms relative to economic and military capacity. According to some, this fundamental (and arguably irreversible) erosion and diffusion of power should therefore finally put to rest the caveats and contrarian analysis associated with the denial camp.[24] Years of US attention being devoted to wars of choice in Afghanistan and Iraq in the early twenty-first century coincided with the dramatic economic rise of new powers, particularly in Asia. While strategically questionable economic wars in the Middle East and Central Asia were not the root cause of the shift in the balance of power, they compounded a process that was already under way. For Graham Allison, 'Even if American attention had not been focused elsewhere, Washington would have struggled to defy the laws of economic gravity.'[25] As a result of this erosion, it would be strategic folly for US leaders to continue to pursue (even benevolent) hegemonic designs, without the requisite capacities to fulfil these aspirations, or to 'rage against the dying of the light' of American primacy.

At the heart of this approach lies the relative decline of the US vis-à-vis China, and the implications for the US of being displaced as global hegemon. Many in this camp would argue that this great power transition pattern is well established, but the geopolitical significance is nonetheless striking. That is, China's claims of a 'peaceful rise' aside, the emergence of new great powers in the international system has invariably had destabilising geopolitical outcomes. As rising powers gain in economic power their geopolitical ambitions increase, and they are inclined to convert this new-found wealth (and status) into military power.[26] Rising powers invariably seek spheres of influence (or hegemony) in the regions in which they are situated.[27] The accepters approach has also been embraced by US scholars from the realist school, who argue in favour of 'offshore balancing' as a prescription to fix the erosion of US power.[28] President Obama's prudent and relatively circumspect foreign policy has been considered by some as consistent with the accepters' arguments regarding the exercise of America's diminishing power.[29] Many in this camp argue that accommodating the rising power (and therefore rising ambitions) of new powers will require large-scale changes in the way foreign policy and grand strategy is approached in Washington. Lyle Goldstein writes of the 'painful psychological adjustment' required of American decision-makers to meet states such as China 'halfway'.[30] Others argue that the realities of the change in the balance of power that accompanies a shift in polarity will effectively do the work for them. In this view, the rise of a multipolar order is out of the hands of the United States, and therefore 'the unipolar system seems to have been short-lived, which means the United States will once again have to worry about other great powers'.[31]

Resistors and the 'rage against the dying of the light' of American primacy

This final approach shares the accepters' sense of inevitably (i.e. of the relative decline of US power), but interprets the root cause of this trend very differently, and thus advocates a diametrically opposed strategic solution to meet this challenge. Though the resistors are concerned about the implications for the US of the rise of near-peer competitors – a concern they share with the accepters – they believe that the US should counter this challenge by doubling down on its defence of US primacy, eschewing the limits of US power imposed by the re-emergence of multipolarity.

Moreover, this camp view the erosion of US power as a direct result of weak leadership, and therefore despite the costs, Washington should not be afraid to exercise its power to reverse the course of this trend. President Donald Trump's brand of realism was an occasional ally to the resister camp in the traditional US foreign policy elite. The hardening of the administration's stance in its relations with China and Russia represented a victory for conservative resisters in the Trump administration – led by Trump's then national security advisor, John Bolton.[32] Bolton criticised Trump in his recent memoir, for example, for restricting information within the United States about the coronavirus 'for fear of adversely affecting the elusive definitive trade deal with China, or offending the ever-so-sensitive Xi'.[33] Bolton argued that restricting the information made little sense, given China's own role in concealing the origins and spread of the disease. That said, Trump's erratic behaviour and an inclination to prioritise his coalition of domestic supporters in foreign policy issues, allowed him to be a nationalist on one issue, a realist resister on another, and an internationalist on yet another, without resolving the underlying ideological contradictions that this *chameleon* approach to policymaking creates.[34]

Denying multipolarity: maintaining America's unipolar edge through the promise of AI?

Central to the narratives about multipolarity developed by those identified in the previous section as the 'denialists' and 'resisters' camps is the argument that the US lead in technological innovation is still as yet unmatched by any rising challenger. For the denialists, the American technology and research sectors outmatch their equivalents in any other rising power and therefore simply must be maintained and resourced at roughly current levels in order for unipolarity to hold. For example, Brooks and Wohlforth argue that the data that shows rising powers increasing their technological inputs (R&D spending, the number of science and technology doctorates being awarded by universities etc.) only tells half the story.[35] For them, this needs to be matched by an understanding of the size of the technology gap with the United States as well as an assessment of how quickly these inputs can be converted to meaningful technology outputs. Unipolarity will be bolstered, the argument goes, given that 'America's unique combination of massive scale and technological prowess will be a long-term feature of the distribution of capabilities'.[36] For the resisters, the gap between the United States and aspiring powers is less pronounced and narrowing, and therefore the issue of resourcing is vital. For Robert Hormats, the risk of technological decline vis-à-vis other powers, and China in particular, is already well under way. The trend is reversable according to Hormats, but to do so the United States 'must develop a nationwide, multi-generational strategy and commit sizable resources'.[37]

Recent IR scholarship has posited that rising powers' pursuit of innovation is most likely to raise security concerns for the dominant state when the rising powers' behaviour is perceived as an attempt to undermine the existing order – rules, norms, and governing institutions – particularly if the emergent order conflicts with the dominant state's national security interests.[38] World leaders have been quick to recognise the transformative potential of AI as a critical component of national security.[39] In large part driven by the perceived challenges posed by rising revisionist and revanchist powers (especially China and Russia),[40] the US Defense Department (DoD) released a 'National Artificial Intelligence Research and Development Strategic Plan' – one of a series of studies on AI machine learning – on the potential for AI to reinvigorate US military dominance.[41] This report echoed the determination of the 'resisters' to sustain US technological primacy by out-innovating potential peer (or near-peer) competitors, who seek to impose multipolarity. In the context of managing the potential flashpoints in the Taiwan Straits, the South China Seas, and Ukraine, then US Secretary of Defense Ashton Carter stated that Russia and China are the US' 'most stressing competitors' and continue to 'advance military system[s] that seek to threaten our [US] advantages in specific areas' (including AI) and in 'ways of wars that seek to achieve their objectives rapidly, before they hope, we [the US] can respond'.[42]

Even if AI-augmented weapons and systems are unable to produce better decisions than humans, militaries that use AI will doubtless gain significant advantages on the battlefield (e.g. remote-sensing, situational-awareness, and battlefield-manoeuvre), compared to those who depend on human judgement alone, particularly in operating environments that demand endurance and rapid decision-making across multiple combat zones. The US intelligence community, for example, is actively pursuing several publicly documented AI research projects to reduce the 'human-factors burden', increase actionable military intelligence, and enhance military decision-making, and ultimately to predict future attacks and national security threats.[43]

China and Russia have developed a range of military-use AI technologies as part of a broader strategic effort to exploit perceived US military vulnerabilities.[44] In a quest to become a 'science and technology superpower', and catalysed by AlphaGo's victory (or China's 'Sputnik moment'), Beijing launched a national-level AI-innovation agenda for 'civil–military fusion' – or US Defense Advanced Research Projects Agency (DARPA) with Chinese characteristics.[45] Russia has a target of 30 per cent of its entire military force structure to be robotic by 2025. In short, national-level objectives and initiatives demonstrate recognition by the global security community of the transformative (or military-technical revolution) potential of AI for states' national security and strategic calculus.[46]

For those concerned with resisting narratives of the 'inevitable drift' towards multipolarity, highlighting the potential threats to US military dominance posed by AI-enhanced capabilities has been high on the agenda in recent years.[47] These security challenges have tended to be grouped under three broad categories: digital security (e.g. spear phishing, speech synthesis, impersonation, automated hacking, and data poisoning),[48] physical security (e.g. micro-drones in swarm attacks), and political security (e.g. surveillance, deception, and coercion), especially in the context of authoritarian states. It is too early to predict what AI programs will enable which capabilities, or how these dynamics might influence the offensive or defensive balance, but the general trajectory of this disruptive technology is clear.[49] Moreover, the effects of these challenges are likely to be exacerbated by a multipolar order.

US analysts and policymakers falling broadly into the 'resisters' camp outlined above have suggested a range of possible responses to these emerging security threats to preserve US technological leadership, which harnesses US natural advantages to push back against the rise of a multipolar order. These national security policy recommendations, *inter alia*, include: funding and leading AI simulated war games and red-teaming creative thinking exercises; leveraging its world-class think tank community, academics, AI experts, computer scientists, and strategic thinkers to assess the implications of AI for a range of security scenarios and devising a long-term AI strategic agenda to meet these challenges; prioritising DoD AI-based research and development to leverage its low-cost and force multiplier effects (i.e. autonomy and robotics) to mitigate potential vulnerabilities and risks; investing in a commanding position in the nascent development of 'counter-AI' capabilities;

seeking increased funding for AI-related research, and supporting and engaging university programmes to ensure adequate numbers of AI talent to collaborate with the government; and funding research and development in reliable fail-safe and safety technology for AI systems – especially military AI applications and tools.

AI will probably have a similar (or possibly greater) impact on the augmentation and diffusion of military power as cyberspace has already had.[50] Just as the low cost of cyber capabilities has given offence the upper hand in cyberspace,[51] so the proliferation of cheap weaponised autonomous systems means that future drone attacks (e.g. for targeted assassinations) could prove even more difficult to attribute, and thus defend against.[52] A related research question, albeit outside the scope of this study, is how and in what ways could the increasingly multipolar strategic environment intensify competition for AI-enabled capabilities in ways that threaten stability?[53] Rapid advances in AI could, even if these capabilities are unproven, blur the lines between conventional and nuclear capabilities and doctrines in ways that are liable to stoke tensions, undermine deterrence, and cause arms race instability and inadvertent escalation – as in the historical case of missile defence technology.[54]

The US Sputnik moment in AI: the growing narrative of bipolar competition

As AI military applications have grown in scale, sophistication, and lethality, many in the US defence community have become increasingly alarmed about the implications of this trend for international competition and national security.[55] In his opening comments at 'The Dawn of AI' hearing, 'resister camper' Senator Ted Cruz stated, 'ceding leadership in developing artificial intelligence to China, Russia, and other foreign governments will not only place the United States at a technological disadvantage, but it could have *grave implications for national security*'.[56] Similarly, Director of US National Intelligence Daniel Coates recently opined: 'The implications of our adversaries' abilities to use AI are *potentially profound and broad*.'[57] Given the anticipated national security value that US strategic competitors (especially China and Russia) ascribe to AI military applications, several defence analysts have characterised the inexorable pace and magnitude of AI technology as a 'Sputnik moment' that could trigger a global AI arms race, and change the character (and even nature) of warfare.[58]

The prospect of losing the first-mover advantages in AI adoption has prompted Pentagon leaders to openly question whether the US will be able to sustain the upper hand on the future battlefield; this is explicitly envisioned in recent US DoD AI-related initiatives including the 'Third Offset Strategy', the 'Multi-Domain Battle' operational concept, and various initiatives developed by DoD's DIUx, DARPA, Strategic Capabilities Office, and the newly established Joint Artificial Intelligence Center.[59] These initiatives demonstrate the perceived gravity of the challenge posed to US national security by other states' (especially China's) pursuit of AI capabilities to enhance their military power. In response to Chinese strategic interests in AI, for example, DoD's DIUx prepared a report proposing greater scrutiny and restrictions on Chinese investment in Silicon Valley companies.[60]

The US alarmist tone and draconian policy responses to the perceived threat posed by China's bid for technological leadership reveals the following. When we compare the public narratives surrounding the 'new multipolarity' thesis with what is actually happening, two things materialise: the nature of the emerging great power competition in AI suggests that a shift to Sino-US bipolarity (rather than multipolarity) is more likely in the short to medium term; and even in the event that China surpasses the US in AI (many experts consider this to be a strong possibility),[61] it still trails the US in several qualitative measures that coalesce to preserve the US technological leadership (e.g. the US has the world's largest intelligence budget, most popular hardware, software, and technology companies, and the most advanced capabilities in both cyber offence and cyber defence).[62]

China is, by some margin, Washington's closest peer-competitor in the global AI arena. Beijing's 2017 'Next Generation AI Development Plan' identified AI as a core 'strategic technology' and 'focus of international competition'. China's official goal is to 'seize the strategic initiative' (especially vis-à-vis the US), and achieve 'world leading levels' of AI investment by 2030 – targeting in excess of US$150 billion in government investment.[63] Beijing has leveraged lower barriers of entry to data collection in China to assemble a vast database to train AI systems. China is on track to possess 30 per cent of the world's share of data by 2030.[64] State-directed Chinese investment in the US AI market has also become increasingly active, and in several instances Chinese investment has competed head-on with that of the Pentagon.[65] In 2017, for example, a Chinese state-run company, Haiyin Capital, outmanoeuvred the US Air Force's efforts to acquire AI software developed by Neurala.[66] Incidences such as these are indicative of wider US concerns relating to China's proclivity for industrial espionage in its race to catch up (and overtake) the United States in several strategically significant advanced technological fields, including AI.[67]

In 2017, Chinese President Xi Jinping explicitly called for the acceleration of the military 'intelligentisation' agenda, to better prepare China for future warfare against a near-peer adversary, namely the United States.[68] Although Chinese think tanks and academic discourse are generally poor at disseminating their content, evidence from selected open sources suggests a strong link between China's political agenda related to the 'digital revolution', Chinese expert opinion, and the prevailing public debate surrounding the rejuvenation of the Chinese nation as a great power.[69] This high-profile, state-led agenda has reinforced an emerging consensus in the US – in particular in the 'resister' and 'accepter' camps – that the US risks being displaced as global hegemon by China, either in a bipolar or multipolar world order. The evidence suggests a strong link between the pursuit of AI leadership and China's broader geopolitical objectives. This link has, in turn, reinforced the narrative in the US defence community that China views this technological transformation as an opportunity to strengthen its claim on the leadership (and eventual dominance) of the emerging technological revolution, having missed out on the previous waves.[70]

President Xi has stated that AI, 'big data', cloud storage, cyberspace, and quantum communications are amongst the 'liveliest and most promising areas for civil-military fusion', and towards this end, Xi has pledged additional state support and resources.[71] President Xi's 'One Belt One Road', and the virtual dimension of the 'digital Silk Road', are high-level efforts designed to ensure that the mechanisms, coordination, and support for this agenda will become increasingly normalised.[72] In contrast, the increasingly strained relationship between the White House and Silicon Valley during the Trump administration will likely present additional challenges for the Biden administration in this critical strategic partnership.[73]

Following a high-profile backlash from Google employees, for example, the company announced that it would discontinue its work with the Pentagon on Project Maven.[74] Several analysts have noted the growing gap between the rhetoric and the research momentum (especially in AI and robotics) and the paucity of resources put towards making the US military more networked and integrated.[75] Moreover, the apparent mismatch (even dissonance) between the rapid pace of commercial innovation in AI and the lagging timescales and assumptions that underpin DoD's existing procurement processes and practices could exacerbate the scale and scope of these bilateral competitive pressures.

China's pursuit of AI (especially dual-use capabilities) will fuel the perception (accurate or otherwise) in Washington that Beijing is *intent* on exploiting this strategically critical technology to fulfil its broader revisionist goals.[76] Despite a brief pause in the development of the US' AI strategic road map, the White House announced the creation of a new committee of AI experts to advise it on policy choices.[77] In 2017, following the recommendation of the Committee on Foreign Investment in the United States, President Trump blocked a Chinese firm from acquiring Lattice Semiconductor, a company that manufactures chips critical in the operation of AI applications.[78] This behaviour typifies a broader concern that synergies created by China's civil-military fusion strategy could allow the technology, expertise, and intellectual property shared between American and Chinese commercial entities to be transferred to the People's Liberation Army.[79]

While most external analysts consider that China's centralised approach to the development of AI affords it unique advantages over the US, others posit that Beijing's AI strategy is far from perfect. Some analysts, for example, have characterised Beijing's funding management as inherently inefficient. These analysts note that China's state apparatus is inherently corrupt, and that this approach tends to encourage overinvestment in particular projects favoured by Beijing, which may exceed market demand.[80] Moreover, although China had already surpassed the US in the quantity of AI-related research papers produced between 2011 and 2015, the quality of these papers ranks far below US academic institutions.[81]

More than just a two-horse race in AI: a slow drift towards multipolar diffusion

As the most powerful nation-states and leaders in the development of AI, the competitive tensions between the United States and China have often evoked comparisons with the Cold War-era US–Soviet space race. In response to the global AI arms race, and to sustain US superiority and first-mover advantages in AI, John Allen and Amir Husain posit that the US must push further and faster to avoid losing the lead to China (and to a lesser degree Russia) in the development of AI.[82] While these depictions accurately reflect the *nature* of the emerging global AI battlefield, the *character* of this particular arms race suggests a much more diffused and multipolar reality, compared to the distinctly bipolar space race. Specifically, the commercial driving forces underlying AI technology (hardware, software, and research and development), together with the intrinsic dual-use character of AI innovations, reduces the usefulness of the space race analogy. The particular problem set associated with the Cold War-era bipolar structure of power – a pernicious obsession with the other side's military capabilities – is far less intense in the context of contemporary AI.[83] Moreover, where primarily commercial forces drive military innovation, technology tends to mature and diffuse at a faster pace compared to technologies with only a military utility, such as stealth technology.[84]

As literature on the diffusion on military technology demonstrates, how states react to and assimilate innovations can have profound implications for the global order, strategic stability, and the likelihood of war.[85] Both the 'resister' and 'accepter' camps discussed above are keenly focused on this.

For the former, the argument is that the United States must pay close attention not only to maintaining its own technological edge but also to matching the breakthroughs of other powers when they occur. For the latter, the argument instead is that the management of great power stability under conditions of multipolarity will require close attention to the technological balance of power. The rate and nature of diffusion, therefore, is a critical determinate of the durability of the relative advantages of being the first mover, which decelerates the faster innovations are adopted.[86] Thus, as the costs and availability of computing power (an essential ingredient for AI machine learning software) decrease, so technically advanced rising powers (i.e. Russia and India) will likely pull away from those nations who are more reliant on mimicry and espionage.

This trend will be accelerated if either the costs or complexity of AI algorithms increase, allowing AI innovation leaders to maximise their competitive advantages.[87] Furthermore, in cases where military AI innovations are primarily driven by commercial (and especially dual-use) imperatives, the impact of states' relative power advantages is likely to be eroded over time – as others mobilise their own commercial sector and prepare to catch up. IR power transition theory also recognises that economic resources are one of the key foundations of military power, especially in the context of a declining hegemon. That is, as the US' economic relative power declines, concomitantly its military primacy will also shrink.[88] Over time this trend is likely to lead to the diffusion of AI to technically advanced small and middle-sized powers (e.g. South Korea, Singapore, Israel, France, and Australia),[89] and non-state entities will become pioneers in cutting-edge dual-use AI and key influencers shaping future security, economics, and global norms in AI, as they already have in robotics.[90]

Despite the growing sense that the nature of the AI revolution has the potential to accelerate a shift towards multipolarity, the pace and trajectory of this transformation does not come without caveats and will probably be constrained by several factors. If military AI applications were based exclusively on military-based research and development, it would be more difficult and costly for other powers to successfully emulate.[91] Moreover, for AI applications that do not have clear commercial drivers, or require military-grade software development and integration (i.e. for classified use), the first-mover advantages are likely to be substantial, and potentially unassailable.[92]

The pace of military-use AI diffusion to other states and non-state entities could also be constrained by three major aspects related to this phenomenon: hardware constraints (i.e. physical processors); the algorithmic complexity inherent to Deep learning; and the resources and know-how to effectively deploy AI code.[93] In aggregate, these constraints could make it almost impossible for a new entrant to deploy modular AI with the same power and force that a country like the US or China might be able to use given the requisite resources, data sets, and technological infrastructure.[94] Military-led innovations could, therefore, potentially concentrate and consolidate leadership in this nascent field amongst the existing military superpowers (i.e. China, Russia, and the United States), and revive the prospect of bipolar competition.[95] For now, it remains unclear how specific AI applications might influence military power, or whether and in what form these innovations translate into operational concepts and doctrine.[96]

Conclusion

This chapter has made the following central arguments. First, although disagreement exists about the pace and trajectory of AI innovations and their impact on national security and great power rivalry, a consensus within the US defence community has formed intimating that the potential impact of AI on the future distribution of power and military balance is likely to be transformational if not revolutionary, especially autonomous swarming technology and machine learning applications. These assessments have in large part been framed in the context of the perceived challenges posed by rising revisionist and revanchist powers (especially China and Russia) to the prevailing US-led order – i.e. rules, norms, and governing institutions.

Second, the rapid proliferation and diffusion of AI capabilities has occurred concomitant with a sense that the US has dropped the ball in the development of this disruptive technology. Even with the perception that the US leadership in this emerging strategic arena was under attack from the rising powers (especially China), the implications for international security would surely be profound. In response to the emergent sense of alacrity within the US defence community, the Pentagon has authored several AI-related programmes designed to sustain the US upper hand on the future digitised battlefield. Moreover, wider US national security concerns relating to China's behaviour in trying to catch up and overtake the US in several core technological fields (including AI) have prompted the US to adopt increasingly wide-ranging and draconian responses. Against the backdrop of deteriorating US–China relations, these harsh responses could further decouple bilateral relations between these two poles, and in turn hasten the trend towards multipolar policies and political structures within the international order.

Third, and related, in the development of AI, evocations of the Cold War-era space race do not accurately capture the nature of the evolving global AI phenomenon. Rather, compared to bipolar features of the US–Soviet struggle, this innovation arms race intimates much more multipolar characteristics. Above all, the dual-use and commercial drivers of the AI revolution are likely to narrow the technological gap separating great powers (US and China) from other rising powers. In turn, these rising powers will become key influencers in shaping future security, economics, and global norms in AI.

Finally, while the pace of AI diffusion amongst great and rising powers will ultimately determine the effect of AI on the future balance of power, the aggressive pursuit of AI (especially dual-use) tools, against the backdrop of a multipolar political landscape, is nonetheless likely to trigger security dilemmas and stoke broader competitive tensions between states. With respect to Sino-US strategic competition, as China reaches parity with (and possibly surpasses) the US in AI, future landmarks and breakthroughs in this emerging strategic domain will increasingly be viewed by the US through the lens of national security, and responses will be shaped and informed by broader US–China geopolitical confrontation. The route back to multipolarity (or bipolarity) is a road fraught with danger and uncertainties. With two or (more likely) multiple claimants to primacy, increased strategic competition, distrust, and the potential for great power conflict is likely to make its way back onto the world stage.

Several future research questions that merit further research flow from this study. First, if the distribution of capabilities among great and rising powers is evolving, with small and medium-sized powers more independent of poles, what behaviour might we expect from powers in the new multipolar order? Second, and closely related, will medium and small powers less dependent on the US for their security be more (or less) inclined to reach out to one another and form new bonds, or instead grow to fear one another? And how might the speed of this transition influence this outcome? Third, how might the increasingly multipolar strategic environment affect competition for AI-enabled capabilities in ways that threaten stability?

Notes

1 'Multipolarity' in this context implies that no single state is unambiguously in the lead (or polar) in the international order. In contrast, 'bipolarity' implies much less ambiguity in the stratification of power surrounding two poles. William C. Wohlforth, 'Unipolarity, status competition, and great power war', in G. John Ikenberry, Michael Mastanduno, and William C. Wohlforth (eds), *International Relations Theory and the Consequences of Unipolarity* (Cambridge: Cambridge University Press, 2011), pp. 33–65.

2 A. F. K. Organski and Jacek Kugler, *The War Ledger* (Chicago: University of Chicago Press, 1980); Robert Gilpin, *War and Change in World Politics* (New York: Cambridge University Press, 1981).

3 Robert Gilpin, *US Power and the Multinational Corporation: The Political Economy of Foreign Direct Investment* (New York: Basic Books, 1975), p. 67.
4 Daniel Drezner, 'State structure, technological leadership and the maintenance of hegemony', *Review of International Studies*, 27:1 (2001), 3–25; Mark Zachary Taylor, *The Politics of Innovation: Why Some Countries are Better than Others at Science and Technology* (Oxford: Oxford University Press, 2016); Andrew Kennedy, 'Slouching tiger, roaring dragon: comparing India and China as late innovators', *Review of International Political Economy*, 23:2 (2016), 1–28; Joel W. Simmons, *The Politics of Technological Progress* (Cambridge: Cambridge University Press, 2016).
5 Gilpin, *US Power and the Multinational Corporation*, p. 67.
6 Andrew Kennedy and Darren Lim, 'The innovation imperative: technology and US–China rivalry in the twenty-first century', *International Affairs*, 94:3 (2018), 553–72, at 557.
7 The many elements in which a great power (or pole) should excel include population, territory, natural resources, economic capacity, military might, technological prowess, and managerial competence. Simmons, *The Politics of Technological Prowess*, p. 37.
8 The key forces driving this evolution include the exponential growth in computing performance; expanded data sets; advances in the implementation of machine-learning techniques and algorithms (especially in the field of deep neural networks); and above all, the rapid expansion of commercial interest and investment in AI. Greg Allen and Taniel Chan, *Artificial Intelligence and National Security* (Cambridge, MA: Belfer Centre for Science and International Affairs, 2017).
9 Sections of this chapter are adapted from James Johnson, 'The end of military-techno *Pax Americana*? Washington's strategic responses to Chinese AI-enabled military technology', *Pacific Review*, 34:3 (2021), 351–78, https://doi.org/10.1080/09512748.2019.1676299 (accessed 30 April 2021).
10 AI refers to computer systems capable of performing tasks normally requiring human intelligence, such as visual perception, speech recognition, and decision-making. These systems have the potential to solve tasks requiring human-like perception, cognition, planning, learning, communication, or physical action.
11 The US Department of Defense defines 'battlespace awareness' as a capability area where unmanned systems in all domains have the ability to contribute significantly into the future to conduct intelligence, surveillance, and reconnaissance and environment collection-related tasks.
12 The decentralisation of AI could also bring challenges to the US in the leadership of this technology from states traditionally friendly to the US (and even US allies), especially in the case of dual-use technologies that are driven by commercial forces but have potential military effects.
13 'Innovation imperative' refers to the need to acquire and develop new technologies in order to overcome the structural challenges facing middle-income states and sustain the US' dominant position. Kennedy and Lim, 'The innovation imperative', 553–72.

14 Emerging technologies, broadly defined, are technologies that possess the potential to disrupt society, politics, economics, and national security. Although the uses for cyber capabilities and weapons continue to evolve, cyberspace is arguably no longer 'emerging'.
15 James Johnson, 'Artificial intelligence and future warfare: implications for international security', *Defense & Security Analysis*, 35:2 (2019), 147–69.
16 Johnson, 'The end of military-techno *Pax Americana*?'
17 Recent scholarship has noted that agreement on the measurement of the relative distribution of power between states remains elusive. 'Polarity' as defined by the distribution of capabilities can be imminent or latent in nature. Barry R. Posen, 'From unipolarity to multipolarity: transition in sight?', in Ikenberry et al. (eds), *International Relations Theory and the Consequences of Unipolarity*, 317–41. See the Conclusion to this volume for further discussion.
18 Christopher Layne, 'This time it's real: the end of unipolarity and the *Pax Americana*', *International Studies Quarterly*, 56:1 (2012), 203–12.
19 Stephen Brooks and William Wohlforth, 'American primacy in perspective', *Foreign Affairs*, 81:4 (2002), 20–33; Fareed Zakaria, *The Post-American World* (New York: W. W. Norton, 2008).
20 William C. Wohlforth, 'US strategy in a unipolar world', in G. John Ikenberry (ed.), *America Unrivaled: The Future of the Balance of Power* (Ithaca, NY: Cornell University Press, 2002), pp. 98–121; Stephen W. Walt, *The Origins of Alliances* (Ithaca, NY: Cornell University Press, 1997); Stephen W. Walt, *Taming American Power: The Global Response to US Primacy* (New York: W. W. Norton, 2005).
21 Stephen G. Brooks and William C. Wohlforth, *America Abroad: The United States' Global Role in the 21st Century* (New York: Oxford University Press, 2016), p. 190.
22 Layne, 'This time it's real', 1.
23 Adam Quinn, 'The art of declining politely: Obama's prudent presidency and the waning of American power', *International Affairs*, 87:4 (2011), 803–24.
24 *Ibid.*
25 Graham Allison, *Destined for War: Can America and China Escape Thucydides's Trap?* (Boston and New York: Houghton Mifflin Harcourt, 2017), p. 8.
26 Zakaria, *The Post-American World*.
27 John J. Mearsheimer, *The Tragedy of Great Power Politics* (New York: W. W. Norton, 2001).
28 As an offshore balancer, the US would disengage (or retreat) from its military commitments in Europe, Japan, and South Korea. Thus, the overriding objectives of an offshore balancing strategy would be to insulate the US from future great power wars, and to maximise its relative power position in the international system. Christopher Layne, 'From preponderance to offshore balancing: America's future grand strategy', *International Security*, 22:1 (1997), 86–124, at 112; Barry R. Posen, *Restraint: A New Foundation for US Grand Strategy* (Ithaca, NY: Cornell University Press, 2014).
29 Quinn, 'The art of declining politely'.

30 Lyle J. Goldstein, *Meeting China Halfway: How to Defuse the Emerging US–China Rivalry* (Washington, DC: Georgetown University Press, 2015), p. 364.
31 John J. Mearsheimer, *The Great Delusion: Liberal Dreams and International Realities* (New Haven and London: Yale University Press, 2018), p. 228.
32 White House, *National Security Strategy of the United States of America*, December 2017, https://trumpwhitehouse.archives.gov/wp-content/uploads/2017/12/NSS-Final-12-18-2017-0905.pdf (accessed 14 May 2021).
33 Dan Diamond, 'Bolton casts light on Trump's deference to China on coronavirus', *Politico*, 24 June 2020, www.politico.com/news/2020/06/24/bolton-trump-china-coronavirus-338647 (accessed 30 June 2020).
34 Josh Rogin, 'Trump's only foreign policy doctrine is Trumpism', *Washington Post*, 25 October 2018.
35 Brooks and Wohlforth, *America Abroad*, pp. 23–4.
36 *Ibid.*, p. 31.
37 Robert D. Hormats, 'US risks falling behind China on technology and innovation, if we don't reset our priorities', *The Hill*, 14 July 2019, https://thehill.com/opinion/technology/452694-us-risks-falling-behind-china-on-technology-and-innovation-if-we-dont-reset-our-priorities (accessed 20 August 2019).
38 Kennedy and Lim, 'The innovation imperative', 559.
39 Robert O. Work, 'Remarks by Defense Deputy Secretary Robert Work at the CNAS Inaugural National Security Forum', Speech, Washington, DC, 14 December 2015.
40 Office of the Secretary of Defense, *Annual Report to Congress: Military and Security Developments Involving the People's Republic of China, 2017* (Washington, DC: US Department of Defense, 2017), https://dod.defense.gov/Portals/1/Documents/pubs/2017_China_Military_Power_Report.PDF (accessed 20 August 2019).
41 National Science and Technology Council, *The National Artificial Intelligence Research and Development Strategic Plan* (Washington, DC: Executive Office of the President of the United States, 2016).
42 Ash Carter, 'Remarks by Secretary Carter on the Budget at the Economic Club of Washington, DC', 2 February 2016, www.defense.gov/News/Transcripts/Transcript-View/Article/648901/remarks-bysecretary-carter-on-the-budget-at-the-economic-club-of-washington-dc/ (accessed 20 August 2019).
43 Patrick Tucker, 'What the CIA's tech director wants from AI', *Defense One* [website], 6 September 2017, https://cdn.defenseone.com/b/defenseone/interstitial.html?v=8.22.2&rf=https%3A%2F%2Fwww.defenseone.com%2Ftechnology%2F2017%2F09%2Fcia-technology-director-artificial-intelligence%2F140801%2F (accessed 20 August 2019).
44 In addition to AI, China and Russia have also developed other technologically advanced (and potentially disruptive) weapons such as cyberwarfare tools, stealth and counter-stealth technologies, counter-space, missile defence, and guided precision munitions.
45 State Council Information Office of the People's Republic of China, 'State Council notice on the issuance of the new generation AI development plan', 20 July

2017, www.gov.cn/zhengce/content/2017–07/20/content_5211996.htm (accessed 20 August 2019).

46 Military-technical revolution has been associated with periods of sharp, discontinuous change that render obsolete or subordinate existing military regimes, or the most common means for conducting war.

47 Miles Brundage, Shahar Avin, Jack Clark, et al., *The Malicious Use of Artificial Intelligence: Forecasting, Prevention, and Mitigation* (Oxford: Oxford University, 2018), https://arxiv.org/pdf/1802.07228.pdf (accessed 20 August 2019).

48 These AI vulnerabilities are, however, distinct from traditional software vulnerabilities (e.g. buffer overflows), and demonstrate that while AI systems may exceed human performance, they often fail in unpredictable ways in which a human never would.

49 Michael Horowitz, Paul Scharre, and Alex Velez-Green, *A Stable Nuclear Future? The Impact of Automation, Autonomy, and Artificial Intelligence* (Philadelphia, PA: University of Pennsylvania, 2017).

50 'Cyberspace' was enabled by three core technologies: digital computing, internet networking, and cryptography. See Peter W. Singer and Allan Friedman, *Cybersecurity and Cyberwar: What Everyone Needs to Know* (New York: Oxford University Press, 2014), p. 13.

51 'Cyber weapons' can be best defined as computer programs designed to compromise the integrity (or availability) of data in an adversary's information technology network for military purposes. Joseph J. Nye, 'Deterrence and dissuasion in cyberspace', *International Security*, 41:3 (2017), 44–71; and James Johnson, 'The AI–cyber nexus: implications for military escalation, deterrence and strategic stability', *Journal of Cyber Policy*, 4:3 (2019), 442–60.

52 The ability of states to attribute a drone attack will depend in part on how homogeneous drone technology becomes, and in particular the use of these weapons by non-state actors.

53 James Johnson, 'Artificial intelligence: a threat to strategic stability', *Strategic Studies Quarterly*, 14:1 (2020), 16–39, www.jstor.org/stable/26891882 (accessed 30 April 2021).

54 Paul Bracken, 'The intersection of cyber and nuclear war', *The Strategy Bridge* [website], 17 January 2017, https://thestrategybridge.org/the-bridge/2017/1/17/the-intersection-of-cyber-and-nuclear-war (accessed 20 August 2019).

55 Daniel S. Hoadley and Nathan J. Lucas, *Artificial Intelligence and National Security* (Washington, DC: Congressional Research Service, 2017), https://fas.org/sgp/crs/natsec/R45178.pdf, p. 2 (accessed 10 August 2019).

56 *Ibid.*, p. 17, emphasis added.

57 *Ibid.*, emphasis added.

58 James Johnson, 'Artificial intelligence in nuclear warfare: a perfect storm of instability?', *Washington Quarterly*, 43:2 (2020), 197–211.

59 Hoadley and Lucas, *Artificial Intelligence and National Security*.

60 Tom Simonite, 'Defense Secretary James Mattis envies Silicon Valley's AI ascent', *Wired* [website], 8 November 2017, www.wired.com/story/james-mattis-artificial-intelligence-diux/ (accessed 20 August 2019).

61 Kai-Fu Lee, *AI Superpowers: China, Silicon Valley, and the New World Order* (New York: Houghton Mifflin Harcourt, 2018).

62 Having the largest and most advanced digital technology industry is a significant advantage for the US. The current relationship between the government and Silicon Valley (including several AI research institutions) is, however, tense and combative. Reconciling the competing commercial and national security factions will remain a challenge for the US. Allen and Chan, *Artificial Intelligence and National Security*, p. 4.

63 State Council Information Office of the People's Republic of China, 'State Council notice'.

64 Will Knight, 'China's AI awakening', *MIT Technology Review*, 10 October 2017, www.technologyreview.com/s/609038/chinas-ai-awakening/ (accessed 20 August 2019). In contrast, between 2012 and 2017, US DoD expenditure on AI-related contracts was relatively flat. Govini, *Department of Defense Artificial Intelligence, Big Data, and Cloud Taxonomy* (Arlington, VA and San Francisco, CA: Govini), 3 December 2017, https://en.calameo.com/read/0000097792ddb787a9198 (accessed 14 May 2021).

65 Chinese venture capital investment in US AI companies between 2010 and 2017 totalled approximately US$1.3 billion. Elsa B. Kania, *Battlefield Singularity: Artificial Intelligence, Military Revolution, and China's Future Military Power* (Washington, DC: Center for a New American Security, 2017).

66 Paul Mozur and Jane Perlez, 'China bets on sensitive US start-ups, worrying the Pentagon', *New York Times*, 22 March 2017.

67 He Yujia, *How China is Preparing for an AI-Powered Future*, Wilson Brief (Washington, DC: Wilson Center, 2017).

68 'Xi Jinping's report at the 19th Chinese Communist Party National Congress', *Xinhua*, 27 October 2017, www.china.com.cn/19da/2017-10/27/content_41805113_3.htm (accessed 20 August 2019).

69 'Opinions on strengthening the construction of a new type of think tank with Chinese characteristics', *Xinhua*, 21 January 2015, www.xinhuanet.com/zgjx/2015-01/21/c_133934292.htm (accessed 20 August 2019).

70 For example, in April 2018 the Chinese People's Political Consultative Conference convened a symposium to support government engagement with AI leaders from academia and industry. The debate focused on the gap between the degree of AI development in China compared to the US, and was supportive of a market-orientated strategy with strong state backing. François Godement, Marcin Przychodniak, Katja Drinhausen, Adam Knight, Elsa B. Kania, and Angela Stanzel, 'The China dream goes digital: Technology in the age of Xi', in *China Analysis* (Paris: European Council on Foreign Relations, 2018), pp. 1–5.

71 For example, in collaboration with Baidu, Beijing established a 'National Engineering Laboratory of Deep Learning Technology' initiative. Robin Li, '"China brain" project seeks military funding as Baidu makes artificial intelligence plans', *South China Morning Post*, 3 March 2015.

72 China's recent five-year plan reportedly committed over US$100 billion to AI. Moreover, as China moves forward with its One Belt One Road-related projects

that extend to potentially more than eighty countries, AI would become an integral part of these international infrastructure projects. Wenyuan Wu, 'China's "digital silk road": pitfalls among high hopes', *The Diplomat*, 3 November 2017, https://thediplomat.com/2017/11/chinas-digital-silk-road-pitfalls-among-high-hopes/ (accessed 20 August 2019).

73 For example, when Google acquired DeepMind it specifically prohibited the use of its research for military purposes. Loren DeJonge Schulman, Alexandra Sander, and Madeline Christian, *The Rocky Relationship between Washington and Silicon Valley: Clearing the Path to Improved Collaboration* (Washington, DC: Center for a New American Security, 2015).

74 Jeremy White, 'Google pledges not to work on weapons after Project Maven backlash', *The Independent*, 7 June 2018.

75 Harry B. Harris Jr, Robert B. Brown, Scott H. Swift, and Richard D. Berry, 'The integrated joint force: a lethal solution for ensuring military preeminence', *Strategy Bridge* [website], 2 March 2018, https://thestrategybridge.org/the-bridge/2018/3/2/the-integrated-joint-force-a-lethal-solution-for-ensuring-military-preeminence (accessed 20 August 2019).

76 The historical record demonstrates that the cause of the rising powers' dissatisfaction with the status quo is often difficult to connect to the costs and benefits associated with the prevailing order, and much of the evidence suggests that recognition and status are key motivators. Wohlforth, 'US strategy in a unipolar world'.

77 Aaron Boyd, 'White House announces select committee of federal AI experts', *Nextgov* [website], 10 May 2018, www.nextgov.com/emerging-tech/2018/05/white-house-announces-select-committee-federal-ai-experts/148123/ (accessed 20 August 2019).

78 Ana Swanson, 'Trump blocks China-backed bid to buy US chip maker', *New York Times*, 13 September 2017.

79 Carolyn Bartholomew and Dennis Shea, *US–China Economic and Security Review Commission: 2017 Annual Report* (Washington, DC: US–China Economic and Security Review Commission, 2017), p. 507.

80 He, *How China is Preparing*.

81 Simon Baker, 'Which countries and universities are leading on AI research?' *Times Higher Education*, World University Rankings, 22 May 2017, www.timeshighereducation.com/data-bites/which-countries-and-universities-are-leading-ai-research (accessed 20 August 2019).

82 John R. Allen and Amir Husain, 'The next space race is artificial intelligence', *Foreign Policy*, 3 November 2017, http://foreignpolicy.com/2017/2011/2003/the-next-space-race-is-artificial-intelligence-and-america-is-losing-to-china/ (accessed 20 August 2019).

83 It has been argued that in the more stratified hierarchy that exists under bipolarity, where two poles have a clear preponderance of power, middle and small states are less likely to experience status dissonance and dissatisfaction associated with a multipolar order. Wohlforth, 'US strategy in a unipolar world'.

84 According to the adoption capacity theory, military capabilities based on hardware diffuse more slowly than those based primarily on software, which results in a greater advantage for the first adopter of a given capability – especially when the unit cost of that capability is relatively high. Michael C. Horowitz, *The Diffusion of Military Power: Causes and Consequences for International Politics* (Princeton, NJ: Princeton University Press, 2010).

85 James Johnson, 'Delegating Strategic Decision-Making to Machines: Dr. Strangelove Redux?', *Journal of Strategic Studies* (2020), published online, https://doi.org/10.1080/01402390.2020.1759038 (accessed 30 April 2021); and Gregory D. Koblentz, *Strategic Stability in the Second Nuclear Age*, Council Special Report No. 71 (New York: Council on Foreign Relations Press, 2014).

86 Samuel Bendett, 'Russia is poised to surprise the US in battlefield robotics', *Defense One* [website], 25 January 2018, www.defenseone.com/ideas/2018/01/russia-poised-surprise-us-battlefield-robotics/145439/ (accessed 20 August 2019).

87 The hardware costs and computer power associated with complex software required to support 'narrow AI' applications are potentially significant – the more complex the algorithm required to train AI applications, the more computational power is needed. Robert D. Hof, 'Deep learning', *MIT Technology Review*, 23 April 2013, www.technologyreview.com/technology/deep-learning/ (accessed 14 May 2021).

88 Organski and Kugler, *The War Ledger*; Gilpin, *War and Change in World Politics*.

89 For example, South Korea has developed a semi-autonomous weapon system to protect the demilitarised zone from North Korean aggression (the SGR-A1), Singapore's 'AI Singapore' is a commercially driven US$110 million effort to support AI R&D, and both France and the United Kingdom have announced major public–private AI-related initiatives. Itai Barsade and Michael C. Horowitz, 'Artificial intelligence beyond the superpowers', *Bulletin of the Atomic Scientists*, 16 August 2018, https://thebulletin.org/2018/08/the-ai-arms-race-and-the-rest-of-the-world/ (accessed 20 August 2019).

90 Analysts argue that small and medium powers can leverage the intersection of AI and robotics to overcome some of the social and economic problems caused by small populations. Mick Ryan, 'Building a future: integrated human–machine military organization', *Strategy Bridge* [website], 11 December 2017, https://thestrategybridge.org/the-bridge/2017/12/11/building-a-future-integrated-human-machine-military-organization (accessed 20 August 2019).

91 Andrea Gilli and Mauro Gilli, 'The diffusion of drone warfare? Industrial, organizational and infrastructural constraints', *Security Studies*, 25:1 (2016), 50–84.

92 The historical record has demonstrated that great military powers often struggle to adopt and assimilate new technologies into military organisations, and disruptive technological adaptations frequently result in significant organisational and creativity-stifling pressures.

93 Kareem Ayoub and Kenneth Payne, 'Strategy in the age of artificial intelligence', *Journal of Strategic Studies*, 39:5–6 (2016), 793–819, at 809.

94 *Ibid.*

95 This notion of bipolar competition could be accentuated in the case of 'general' AI (or 'superintelligence'), as opposed to 'narrow'-use AI. In theory, a leader in general AI technology might lock in advantages gained by the development of this technology so large that others are unable to catch up. Nick Bostrom, *Superintelligence: Paths, Dangers, Strategies* (Oxford: Oxford University Press, 2014).

96 Mary L. Cummings, *Artificial Intelligence and the Future of Warfare*, Research paper (London: Chatham House, 2017), www.chathamhouse.org/publication/artificial-intelligence-and-future-warfare (accessed 20 August 2019).

6

Japan and the dangers of multipolarisation

H. D. P. Envall

How does Japan understand its place in the international order? And how do its policymakers then respond to challenges presented by that order to the country's national interests? Japan has an established discourse on *international order* (*kokusai chitsujo*), as well as a literature which focuses on questions of *multipolarisation* (*takyokuka*). This encompasses both scholarly research in International Relations (IR) and more policy-oriented analysis.[1] An important characteristic of the Japanese understandings of order and polarity, therefore, is the particular manner in which crossover between the scholarly and practitioner realms occurs and how this, in turn, shapes the interplay between the explanatory and normative dimensions of Japan's approach to international order.

Indeed, Japan has a strong tradition of seeking to understand the trajectory of the 'objective' international order. It is a tradition that might be described as 'foreign policy' rather than 'IR', and one centred on two broad questions. First, what does the changing international order mean for Japan? And second, how should Japan respond? With one very major exception – the tragedy of the Greater East Asian Co-Prosperity Sphere – Japan has not historically sought to establish itself as a pole in its own right. Rather, it has focused on finding ways to adapt to, maintain autonomy in, and gain prestige from the given international order. Thus, the explanatory and normative sides of the Japanese discourse have been closely intertwined, with one informing the other.

The interplay between these dimensions is evident in Japanese strategic thinking since the early Cold War. Japan's answers to these normative questions remained consistent throughout the Cold War and into the 1990s – a preference for an American-led order, whether based around a bipolar, unipolar, or multipolar structure. Bipolarity from the 1950s, US primacy within a more multipolar structure in Asia from the 1970s, and unipolarity from the 1990s: all these reinforced Japan's preference for US power in the

Asia-Pacific even as these conditions created incentives for Japan to push the regional order in different directions. At the same time, the explanatory side of Japan's discourse has continued to inform Japan's strategic thinking. Both scholars and practitioners perceive the regional order as moving towards multipolarity, with associated dangers for Japan. Such assessments tend to focus on Japan's shrinking role, China's rise (as a threatening new pole), and the possibility of American decline. Normatively, Japan's response has been to buttress American unipolarity, as illustrated by Japan's strong support for US President Barack Obama's 'pivot' to Asia. Japan's aim, in this respect, has been to shape the form of multipolarity that might emerge and so minimise the potential dangers.

This chapter considers these issues in four stages. First, it outlines the development of Japan's thinking about international order. This encompasses both the scholarly as well as the practitioner community. Second, it then explains the manner in which Japan has addressed order issues in the Asia-Pacific through the Cold War. Third, it looks at how Japan is engaging with the current shift in regional order brought about by the rise of China and (relative) American decline. In concluding, it considers the likely implications of Donald J. Trump's term as US president on how Japan approaches international order and manages the dangers of multipolarity.

Japan's IR traditions

Japan's preference in terms of IR scholarship in the post-war period has been for policy-oriented and Japan-focused normative work. At the same time, however, Japanese scholarship has been heavily influenced by Western academic trends. In describing this Western influence, Kuniyuki Nishimura characterises Japanese IR as 'an imported discipline'.[2] Yet, as Nishimura shows in his study on the interpretation of E. H. Carr's works in Japan, the ways in which ideas are imported and understood are likely to depend heavily on the circumstances and perceptions of those adopting the ideas.[3] Indeed, Japan has developed a set of questions and approaches that, although heavily influenced by Western practice, unsurprisingly reflect Japanese perspectives. To paraphrase Amitav Acharya and Barry Buzan, like other states outside the English-language IR tradition, Japanese scholars have been chiefly interested in theories which help them understand Japan's own interests.[4]

Western influence on Japanese IR scholars is reflected in the broad traditions of IR that have emerged in Japan. A key example has been the German-inspired *Staatslehre* (*kokkagaku*, or the study of the state) tradition of political science.[5] This tradition offers a method for studying international developments so far as they 'affect Japan's foreign relations'.[6] Heavily historical and focused on the role of institutional contexts, it has a strong area-studies flavour, with scholars focusing on Chinese, Thai, or other specific national areas of research.[7] In addition to the *Staatslehre* approach, Takashi Inoguchi also identifies Marxism, historicism, and finally an American approach as key traditions in Japanese IR.[8] Others employ variations on these approaches. Writing in the 1960s, for instance, Tadashi Kawata and Saburō Ninomiya examined Japanese IR in the post-war period in terms of three broad approaches: international political science, international relations, and international political history.[9]

Unsurprisingly in light of the wider Japanese political environment, pacifist ideas played a prominent role in Japanese IR debates during the Cold War. A key debate of the 1960s and 1970s took place between scholars such as Yoshikazu Sakamoto, who argued that Japan should adopt a position of neutrality in the new bipolar international environment, and those such as Masataka Kōsaka, who adopted elements of realism that took account of the region's shifting balance of power.[10] Such separate approaches, as Inoguchi argues, are 'evident in Japan's IR studies even today and ... coexist fairly amicably without many efforts made toward integration'.[11]

Japanese IR, then, has been a relatively segmented discipline – especially from the 1970s onwards – located more in the humanities than the social sciences and concerned with historical as much as contemporary questions.[12] The links to government and foreign policy debates in some of these traditions have meant that normative questions about good policy have been prominent. Indeed, Inoguchi identifies three major research questions that have preoccupied Japanese research since the Second World War. All have a strongly normative focus. They pay attention, in turn, to: Japan's foreign policy leading up to and during the Second World War in terms of what went wrong; the types of international institutions or arrangements required to establish peace and stability in world politics; and Japan's contemporary foreign policy in terms of what is lacking in the country's approach to foreign affairs and why.[13]

Japanese IR and polarity

On issues of international order and polarity, Japanese scholars have been especially interested in questions relating to multipolarisation. Compared to the European experience, this reflects the more complex nature of polarity in Asia during the Cold War. As Akihiko Tanaka contends, this was largely because of the 'looming presence of China'. Indeed, Tanaka argues that Asia's Cold War experience 'cannot be compressed into a simple bipolar confrontation'.[14]

Writing in the 1970s, Kinhide Mushakōji examined major polarity issues at a key juncture where the Asia-Pacific shifted from a bipolar to a more multipolar order. Making use of the writings of Morton Kaplan and Richard Rosecrance, Mushakōji explored international system transitions from a bipolar order (*sōkyoku taisei* or *nikyoku taisei*) to a multipolar order (*takyoku taisei*) in a process of multipolarisation.[15] Accordingly, he sought to explain the conditions under which such multipolarisation – which he termed 'multipolarisation within bipolarity' or 'bi-multipolarity' (*sōkyoku nai takyokuka*) – might occur and what form such a process might take.[16] Tōru Yano similarly focused on the changing structure of international systems from bipolarity to multipolarity, looking especially at the operation of a subordinate system, such as a subregion like South East Asia, in response to changes brought about by great powers in the dominant system.[17] In the 1980s, Yoshinobu Yamamoto sought to explore system stability in international politics, by examining the relationships between structural shifts in power and overall system stability (i.e. where wars would not occur). His work considered this relationship across bipolar, unipolar, and multipolar systems.[18]

Early post-Cold War Japanese scholarship aimed to understand the implications of the demise of the Cold War system and the rise of globalisation. Writing in the late 1990s, scholars such as Yūzō Yabuno and Yoshitaka Ikeda assessed how the international system was moving beyond the traditional nation-state level of analysis, to include new global actors such as non-governmental organisations, coalitions, and multilateral institutions. Yabuno termed this new structure a 'global' rather than 'international' system. Ikeda, likewise, highlighted how the system was being challenged both from above and below. In his view, two simultaneous trends were occurring in global politics – fragmentation and integration – pointing to the need for a clearer two layered model of IR.[19] Likewise, Seiji Endō considered the potential effects of increasing globalisation on world order (*sekai chitsujo*), as distinct from the international Westphalian order, and the potential for tensions to emerge between these two elements of world politics.[20] In particular, he explored the idea of a post-Westphalian order and how it was necessary for political science to better understand new types of interaction between the state, markets, civil societies, and other actors.

In the post-Cold War period, a significant focus of Japanese IR has been on notions of American primacy and, by implication, the idea of a unipolar order (*tankyoku taisei* or *ikkyoku taisei*). Japanese IR scholars have offered a different perspective on the otherwise US-centric debates around US primacy in global affairs. Inoguchi has examined the notion of 'regional bipolarity under global unipolarity'. His work follows a logic similar to that of Mushakōji's bi-multipolarity in placing the emerging Sino-American rivalry following the Third Taiwan Strait Crisis within the wider context of global US primacy.[21] Looking more specifically at the US, Tatsuya Nishida has examined US policy under the presidency of George W. Bush in terms of how such policies influence US primacy. Nishida's argument is that the maintenance of unipolar order requires the hegemon to both constrain its unilateralism while continuing to provide international public goods.[22]

Contemporary Japanese work on international or world order in the post-Cold War period is influenced, at least in part, by the English School.[23] Hideaki Shinoda has looked into the establishment of international society (*kokusai shakai*) and sought to understand the international order on which it is based. In particular, he has adopted the position that it is possible to know the shape of order set up in international society by understanding the norms and values espoused by that society 'as a whole'.[24] Shinoda follows other Japanese scholars working in this field, such as Hidemi Suganami, who has explored 'domestic analogy' arguments in IR. Such arguments consider the benefits of transferring domestic political order principles to the world order.[25] Other scholars, such as Testuya Sakai, have looked at the evolution of thinking on international orders across pre-war, wartime, and post-war periods in Japan. Sakai highlights the influence of Japan's transition from 'imperial' to international order in terms of its subsequent IR thinking.[26]

Some contemporary Japanese scholars have sought to combine power-balance thinking with the English School's wider conceptualisation of order. Akio Takahara has argued that international order, because of its normative dimension, does not change merely because of an altered power distribution. He cites Japan's brief rise and failed international order as an example of power distributions shifting without leaving a significant impact on international order as a normative concept. Instead, change in international order, Takahara argues, moves from the extent to which rising revisionist powers seek to change the order and promote new values and norms of their own. In Japan, what this means for normative order in East Asia, in light of China's rise, is a key question for both theory and policy.[27]

Indeed, Japanese scholarship has focused on the policy implications of power and order redistributions. According to Inoguchi, Japanese policymakers focus firstly on the likely shifts in power distribution before considering how to address any potentially negative implications for Japan. He thus characterises Japanese policymakers as 'order-takers' rather than 'order-makers'. Japan, he suggests, has sought to 'cope with uncertainty by riding high on the wave of US unipolarity'.[28]

As a result, Japan is unsurprisingly preoccupied with the 'rise of China' (*chūgoku no taitō*) and the associated 'China risk'.[29] Yoshihide Soeya has outlined China's growing territorial assertiveness in the Asia-Pacific region since the Cold War, especially after the US reduced its regional presence, such as by withdrawing from the Philippines. He notes that China accepted US hegemony in the region under a separate coexistence or 'same bed, different dreams' (*dōshōimu*) approach, arguing that the '"same bed" is the American-led international order'.[30] Yet he also suggests that, in terms of its long-term outlook, China has not let go of its 'sense of discomfort and resistance' to the US-led order.[31]

Japanese scholars such as Tanaka have also considered how China's rise is influencing the structure of the international system.[32] Making use of power transition analysis, especially by A. F. K. Organski, Tanaka argues that the likelihood of conflict between the US and China is not high and that, accordingly, 'the chances of a peaceful transition are great'.[33] Nonetheless, even with a peaceful transition, he suggests, it is reasonable to expect that a more Chinese-centred international order is likely to be more advantageous to China and correspondingly disadvantageous to the interests of other countries. Given its historical and territorial differences with China, Japan can easily be imagined as one of these countries. Indeed, Shin Kawashima has argued that Japan has a 'special place' (*tokushu na ichi*) in Chinese foreign policy as the sole major power from the G7 in its immediate neighbourhood.[34] Given China's view of the regional order and its difficult relationship with Japan, bilateral cooperation between the two appears much less realistic.

Japan's Cold War: from bipolarity to multipolarity

On the policy front, Japan's early Cold War approach was clearly reshaped by its changed circumstances following the Second World War. Defeat to the US and subsequent US-led occupation meant that Japan could no longer establish itself as an independent pole in the international system, but instead had to return to its practices of adapting to regional power shifts. Japan's position in this newly emerging international order was unsurprisingly influenced most by the US. At the same time, however, because the Soviet Union and China sought to contest America's primacy in the Asia-Pacific after the Second World War, Japan aimed to establish a clear national strategy that ensured some national security in the context of a contested rather than harmonious regional order – that is, Asia's emerging bipolarity.

The strategy that emerged was influenced most by Japan's early post-war Prime Minister Shigeru Yoshida and thus came to be known as the 'Yoshida Doctrine'. Operating from a weak position, Yoshida essentially pursued a strategy that would achieve a grand bargain with the US while also finding a domestic political balance between conservatives who supported rearmament and progressives who argued for unarmed neutrality. Even as scholars continued to debate these positions through the 1960s and 1970s, as noted earlier, the Japanese government had decided clearly where Japan would sit in the new bipolar structure of the Cold War. Consequently, Yoshida accepted US hegemony in return for security guarantee – a formal alliance. The quid pro quo was Japan's acceptance of US military bases on Japanese territory.[35]

By aligning itself so closely with the US in the Cold War order, Japan made the management of its relations with the other poles of the Asia-Pacific – the Soviet Union and China – more difficult. The messy end to Japan's Second World War was particularly apparent in Japan's Cold War relations with the Soviet Union. The Soviets only entered the war against Japan in August 1945 and then occupied Sakhalin, the Kuril Islands, and Japan's Northern Territories (Hoppō Ryōdo) or South Kuril Islands. It also captured around 600,000 Japanese soldiers, whom it sent to prison camps. These decisions caused major damage to subsequent bilateral relations. Not only did the two countries now share an unresolved territorial dispute, but subsequent Soviet conduct contributed, as Kazuhiko Togo explains, to Japan's 'sense of injustice and wounded feelings', absent from many of Japan's other post-war relationships.[36]

Such antagonisms were exacerbated by the emerging bipolarity of the Cold War. When Japan signed the San Francisco Peace Treaty in September 1951, with the Korean War under way in the background, the US would not allow amendments proposed by the Soviet Union. In response, the Soviets refused to sign the treaty, arguing that it was part of a wider preparation on the part of the US for a new conflict in East Asia.[37] This hardening of positions then complicated subsequent attempts by Tokyo to negotiate a separate peace with Moscow. Negotiations took place between 1955 and 1956, but broke down over the issue of how many islands to return. The US and then Japan hardened their positions and, in the end, only a minimal Soviet-Japanese agreement ending their state of war was achieved.[38] Such tensions would impede better Soviet–Japanese relations for the remainder of the Cold War. When Japan began to participate more fully in the US–Japan alliance through the 1970s and 1980s, for instance, it did so in part because of the threat it saw in Soviet missile deployments to Asia.[39] Indeed, the differences between the two sides persisted beyond the collapse of the Soviet Union as a Cold War pole and now complicate Japan's relations with Russia in the emerging multipolar Asia-Pacific.[40]

Japan's relations with China (the People's Republic) were similarly complicated by emerging bipolarity in Asia in the late 1940s and early 1950s. Tokyo's capacity to re-engage Beijing was constrained, in particular, by the American stance on China following the communist victory in the

Chinese Civil War, subsequent Sino-Soviet strategic alignment, and the Korean War. This is not to suggest that Japan did not pursue a more independent stance where possible. In seeking to circumscribe the constraints imposed by the bipolar conditions of the early Cold War, Japan adopted its policy of *seikei bunri* (separating economics and politics), which allowed it to open indirect relations with China on trade. Indeed, the two sides re-established trading relations not long after the end of the Second World War.[41]

Nonetheless, America's decision to recognise Taiwan (the Republic of China) ahead of communist China forced Japan to follow suit. Yoshida had favoured a more open approach to China, by normalising relations with a view to splitting Beijing from Moscow. A similar line was also pushed by Prime Minister Ichirō Hatoyama. Yet American insistence overwhelmed such attempts at independence and, especially after Kishi became prime minister, Japan fell into line on the American side of the new bipolar order.[42]

From the 1970s, the US under the administration of President Richard Nixon began to reorient its own strategic posture towards China. America's sudden shift proved a painful experience for the Japanese government. In July 1971, when Nixon announced that he would visit Beijing the following year, the Japanese government received only a one-hour warning, with Prime Minister Eisaku Satō learning of the news just minutes before it became public. This was despite US Secretary of State William Rogers reassuring Japan that 'close contact would be maintained regarding the China issue'.[43] The 'betrayal', as Matake Kamiya describes it, meant that some Japanese worried that the US was shifting away from Japan and towards China, and that a new multipolar environment in Asia would disadvantage Japan.[44] Japanese scholarly attention on multipolarisation, noted earlier, corresponded to this shift.

China's subsequent participation in international politics provides some substantial evidence in support of Japan's 'non-strategic' approach. Under the leadership of Deng Xiaoping, China opened up its economy and became a more reliable player in regional affairs. Sino-Japanese economic relations grew substantially over the remainder of the Cold War, with trade growing from around US$1.1 billion in 1972 to nearly US$20 billion in 1988.[45] Relations between Japan, China, and the US – and thus the regional order in the Asia-Pacific – became more stable.[46]

Japan's new relationship with China did have its challenges, however. In the lead-up to the signing of the Peace and Friendship Treaty in 1978, armed Chinese fishing vessels entered the waters around the Senkaku/Diaoyu Islands, administered by Japan but also claimed by China. China's assertiveness at this time was a response to suggestions from conservatives in Japan that the status of the islands should be dealt with as part of the normalisation process. In the end, rather than let the negotiations fail, Deng suggested that the two sides should concentrate on joint resource development and postpone any negotiations over the islands' sovereignty until another time.[47]

Japan's post-Cold War globalism and uni-multipolarity

For a brief period at the end of the Cold War, some in Japan – but more accurately, many outside Japan – saw the country as an emerging, or potential, new pole in the international order.[48] In the late 1970s, American scholars such as Ezra Vogel had recognised Japan's increasing economic power and its potential implications for the US.[49] By the late 1980s, Japan's growing economic influence led Vogel to talk of the international trade order 'moving toward a Pax Nipponica'.[50] In Japan, greater economic confidence led to a more robust attitude in some quarters about the post-Cold War order and Japan's likely place in it. In 1989, nationalist politician Shintarō Ishihara, together with the founder of Japanese electronics company Sony, Akio Morita, published *'No' to Ieru Nihon* [The Japan that Can Say 'No'].[51] Ishihara described Japan as an 'economic and high-tech superpower' and argued that it had the 'power to say no to the United States'.[52] He further contended that the twenty-first century would 'be a tripolar world – the United States, Japan, and Europe'.[53] Given what he saw as the increasing importance of economic capability in underpinning national power, Ishihara viewed China and the Soviet Union as 'losers in economic power'.[54]

In reality, Japan was ill-prepared to deal with the ending of the Cold War and its implications for international polarity. On the one hand, Japan's economy began to struggle just as politicians such as Ishihara were trumpeting its virtues. The collapse of share market and property bubbles across 1990–91 and subsequent 'lost decades' of economic stagnation undermined Japan's position as an economic superpower.[55] This would later be weakened further by China's economic rise. On the other hand, the events of the 1991 Gulf War and the return to pre-eminence of the US led to a new political debate in Japan concerning how the country might better adapt to the new international order based around US primacy.[56]

The Gulf War exposed the limitations of the Yoshida Doctrine for dealing with the challenges of a new post-Cold War order. In what came to be known as Japan's 'Gulf War trauma',[57] the US heavily criticised Japan for being unable to do more than provide 'checkbook diplomacy' in support of the American-led coalition as it pushed Iraq out of Kuwait.[58] Even as Japan was able to contribute US$14 billion to the war effort, the government led by Prime Minister Toshiki Kaifu found itself split over how to respond in terms of offering support beyond the financial. After acrimonious debate, it duly failed to pass the legislation needed to even allow for a relatively low-key contribution, the dispatch of Japanese minesweepers to the Persian Gulf.

Kaifu's Gulf War failure helped set off a wider debate over Japan's future international role. At its heart, the debate has been concerned with the idea of Japan transforming itself into a 'normal nation' or *futsū no kuni*. Andrew Oros views this debate as one focused on security 'identity' as well as 'practice'; in other words, it has revolved around questions of what might be 'normal' for a country such as Japan in the twenty-first century.[59] As a proposed new security identity, however, the idea of 'normal' in this case assumes that what had gone before – primarily the tenets of the Yoshida Doctrine along with wider concepts of pacifism and anti-militarism – no longer function, and indeed have become 'abnormal' in the context of the post-Cold War international order.[60]

Initially, the debate took on a globalist outlook, with a strong emphasis on what Japan should be doing as a more active contributor to the international community and the United Nations. A major contributor in the early 1990s was the political figure Ichirō Ozawa, then a leading politician in the ruling Liberal Democratic Party (LDP). Ozawa contended that Japan had to 'become a "normal nation"', and defined a normal nation in terms of two important features.[61] First, a normal nation was a country that willingly shouldered 'those responsibilities regarded as natural in the international community'. It would not, he added, 'refuse such burdens on account of domestic political difficulties' (i.e. as the Kaifu government had done). Second, a normal nation would 'cooperate fully with other nations in their efforts to build prosperous and stable lives for their people'. Japan would have to 'satisfy these two conditions' if it were to 'go beyond simply creating and distributing domestic wealth and become what the world community recognizes as a "normal nation"'.[62]

Ozawa's characterisation of normal, however, rested on two ideas. First, he assumed that such a thing as 'normal nation' existed in international affairs, even though it is not clear what a typical nation might look like in security affairs. In the early 1990s, at the height of US unipolarity and the 'end of history', Ozawa's idea of 'normal' was most obviously shaped by US global dominance.[63] Second, he saw the decline of ideology in international relations as creating an opportunity to develop a new international 'security edifice' which, in his view, would be centred on the United Nations (UN).[64] According to this argument, Japan should seek to strengthen the UN framework and reform its institutions, especially the Security Council; it should also seek to cooperate with the US to ensure that it remained engaged in the UN process. Indeed, as a vision for international order and a certain form of polarity, Ozawa's thinking is not dissimilar to the idea of uni-multipolarity described by Samuel Huntington.[65]

Despite locating his idea of normalcy within the context of international community, Ozawa had made his argument mostly with a view to Japan itself. Much of Ozawa's key work, *Blueprint for a New Japan*, was focused on domestic reform in Japan and the development of a more coherent foreign policy.[66] Ozawa's thinking, therefore, fits within the Japanese tradition of adapting to either an international order that is already established or one that is perceived to be emerging. His idea of normal was less about redefining the international order and more about redefining Japan's role in that order. As Oros argues, 'the question is not what is "normal" in the abstract, but what is considered normal by Japan, and by Japanese'.[67]

Ozawa's vision was to be undermined, however, by subsequent events. First, the security situation in Northeast Asia, despite the collapse of the Soviet Union and the supposed acceptance of US primacy by China, remained unstable. The North Korean nuclear crisis of 1993–94 and the Taiwan Strait Crisis of 1996 pushed the Japanese government to reinvigorate its alliance with the US rather than pursue a more independent, UN-centric foreign policy.[68] Second, the nuclear tests conducted in 1998 by India and Pakistan revealed the limits of Japanese influence in the UN system. Given its historical experience of nuclear weapons, Japan reacted strongly. At the time a non-permanent Security Council member, it sought to have an emergency Council meeting opened and pushed for a resolution condemning the nuclear tests. Japan argued for a strong international response, froze grants and loans to Pakistan and India, and sought to have other international actors criticise the tests as well.[69] Yet Tokyo's actions had little impact, other than to expose weaknesses in its own diplomacy. Domestically, the episode undermined globalists' arguments about the utility of a multilateral UN-based order. Combined with instability in Northeast Asia and the 'war on terror' after 2001, these failures pushed Japan away from policies based on multipolarity or uni-multipolarity and back towards a more orthodox reliance on American unipolarity.[70]

Revisionism, Asianism, and Indo-Pacific multipolarity

What followed the globalism of Ozawa was a more realist assessment of international order and Japan's role in that order. Led by Prime Minister Jun'ichirō Koizumi, the LDP government sought to introduce a revisionist vision of Japanese security. This vision emphasised the importance of Japan's alliance with the US over multilateralism and sought to revise Japan's security institutions to allow the country to play a more active role in international affairs. According to Christopher Hughes and Ellis Krauss, Koizumi 'smashed long-standing taboos and created the conditions for ending Japan's foreign and security policy inertia'.[71] As part of Japan's contribution to the 'war on terror', for instance, the Koizumi government passed legislation for anti-terrorism efforts, including sending Japanese naval forces to the Indian Ocean to provide support to the US, which was then involved in the conflict in Afghanistan. Subsequently, Japan sent the Ground Self-Defense Forces to contribute to humanitarian activities as part of the US engagement in Iraq.[72]

Compared to Ozawa's thinking, Koizumi's idea of a normal Japan was directed at the country's capacity to manage a more threatening security environment. Rather than take a liberal institutionalist approach, Koizumi focused on Japan's internal security capabilities and the country's capacity to cooperate with the US. Although Koizumi sought to maintain some independence from the US over foreign policy initiatives, such as on Iraq and North Korea, he also set out a pattern of increasingly close US–Japanese cooperation. He pushed for the further development of ballistic missile defence systems, as well as further rationalisation of US bases in Japan, and an improvement in interoperability between the two allies.[73] Publicly, Koizumi cultivated a closer relationship with President George W. Bush.

Koizumi's revisionist agenda, and that of his successor Shinzō Abe, reflected in part the international climate at the height of the 'war on terror'. Growing American unilateralism in an international order already seen as unipolar meant that allies and partners such as Japan were under greater pressure to 'do more' as part of a 'coalition of the willing'. In Tokyo, there emerged a strong view that greater 'risk sharing' was now required to maintain the alliance.[74]

By the late 2000s, however, the international environment and Japan's own outlook and preferences began to shift. First, as the US struggled to extract itself from Afghanistan and Iraq, Japanese perceptions of American power became more negative. Meanwhile, difficulties over America's military presence in Japan began to weaken alliance solidarity.[75] Second, the global financial crisis weakened American power and undermined the idea of a unipolar international order. How to manage in a post-American economic order now became a key question for Japanese policymakers.[76] Third, the Japanese public began to lose confidence in the ruling LDP and the political leadership of Koizumi's successors. Abe, for instance, resigned in September 2007 after only twelve months as prime minister.[77]

Japan was therefore ready for a historic change of government in late 2009. Led by the Democratic Party of Japan (DPJ) and Prime Minister Yukio Hatoyama, the new government pursued not only a significant break in Japanese politics but also a reorientation of Japan's approach to regional order. In response to the apparent shift in the global economic order ushered in by the global financial crisis, the DPJ sought to establish Japan as a 'bridge between China and the US'.[78] Japan would move away from the US to pursue closer relationships with partners in Asia, especially China. Hatoyama's vision for a new regional order was based on the idea of *yūai* (fraternity) and a new 'Asianist' outlook on regional engagement.[79] Hatoyama saw Japan's national interests as better served by being part of Asia than by sticking with 'US-led globalism'. This would be especially important, he argued, as the world 'was becoming increasingly multipolar'.[80] Japan 'aspired to be within Asia', operating on a policy based around 'open regional cooperation'.[81]

But this new strategy proved fragile and was quickly abandoned after Hatoyama's resignation as prime minister in June 2010.[82] Hatoyama's ambition was undermined in two ways. The key institutional pillar of his *yūai* vision was the establishment of an East Asian Community (EAC) intended to bring about 'mutual trust with China, South Korea, and other Asian countries'.[83] Yet the idea proved problematic. There was initial confusion over America's role.[84] China was also sceptical, viewing the EAC as an attempt by Japan to establish a 'Japan-led order' in the region.[85] More broadly, Hatoyama's Asianism was undermined by growing regional tensions from 2010 onwards, including the worsening of Sino-Japanese relations due to the territorial dispute over the Senkaku/Diaoyu Islands as well as growing tensions on the Korean peninsula. In response, Hatoyama's successors reverted to foreign policy orthodoxy in the form of greater dependence on the US alliance. They also began to reform Japan's own security posture, aware that US unipolarity was no longer a given, but would be increasingly challenged by China.[86]

Still, major change only got under way after the DPJ's election loss to an LDP-led coalition in September 2012. Led once again by Abe, Japan became more active in countering China's growing influence and minimising the dilution of US primacy. From 2012, Japanese analysts and policymakers clearly perceived China as adopting a 'creeping expansionism' aimed at intimidating other regional players through 'coercive behavior' (*iatsuteki na furumai*).[87] For Japan, this was occurring not just in territorial disputes but also in terms of wider strategic competition. A common view was that China demonstrated 'little room for compromise' on contentious issues.[88] It was, moreover, undermining key aspects of the established international order on its way to creating a new, undesirable (from Japan's perspective) multipolarity. Indeed, China's promotion of the Belt and Road Initiative from 2013 was viewed by Japan as a challenge to the established trade, investment, and development order. Its refusal to acknowledge the 2016 ruling by the Permanent Court of Arbitration against its territorial claims in the South China Sea was seen in Japan as a threat to international law.[89]

To address what it saw as the emergence of a coercive Chinese-dominated regional order, the Abe government promoted a broader vision of a rules-based order, which came to be known as the 'Free and Open Indo-Pacific' or FOIP. With FOIP, as well as creating a rules-based order, Japan aimed to develop greater regional connectivity and build regional resiliency via capacity building.[90] The expressed intention was to construct a regional order that allowed for China's rise but also counterbalanced China when it engaged in creeping expansionism or coercive behaviour.[91] The region within FOIP, moreover, was not Asia or the Asia-Pacific. Rather, FOIP entailed an expansion of the region to cover an 'Indo-Pacific' linking together the Pacific and Indian Oceans in what Abe described as the 'confluence of the two seas'.[92] Under Abe, Japan actively promoted this vision around the region. It engaged multilaterally with regional entities such as the Association of Southeast Asian Nations and bilaterally with countries such as India and Australia. But perhaps most significantly, it engaged minilaterally by helping to reinvigorate the Quadrilateral Security Dialogue or 'Quad' with India, Australia, and the US.[93]

In addition to FOIP, Abe also sought to transform Japan's own foreign and security policies. In what has been called the 'Abe Doctrine', the Abe government sought to boost Japan's defence capabilities, its alliance with the United States, and its regional diplomacy. It established a National Security Council and issued a National Security Strategy in 2013, with a view to the country making a 'proactive contribution to peace' (*sekkyokuteki hewiwashugi* or 'proactive pacifism').[94] It also loosened earlier restrictions on Japan's right to collective self-defence (CSD) – that is, having the right to defend an ally – by 'reinterpreting' Article 9 of the Constitution in 2014 and passing an array of security legislation in 2015.[95] The government also worked closely with the US to revise the two countries' joint security guidelines in 2015 in order to make the alliance more flexible, give Japan a more active role, and integrate the alliance into regional security frameworks such as the Quad.[96]

Conclusion: Japan and the dangers of Asia's new multipolarisation

Japan's approach has clearly been focused on identifying the shifting patterns of international order and seeking to adapt effectively to these changes. Japanese scholars have often adopted a strongly normative outlook regarding the region and Japan's place within it. This is well illustrated by Inoguchi's assessment of the three key questions that have dominated the Japanese discourse.[97] Linking academics to policymakers has been an awareness of the shifting balance of power and polarity in the Asia-Pacific and its likely impact on Japan's own position in the region, especially the dangers posed by multipolarisation or *takyokuka*. During the Cold War, considerable attention was paid to the shift to multipolarity from bipolarity. During the post-Cold War period, attention has moved to a different form of *takyokuka* – this time, the potential shift from US-led unipolarity to a new, potentially Chinese-dominated, multipolarity.

Japanese policymakers have long paid close attention to the risks in *takyokuka*. They have, as Pyle notes, been determined and persistent in their 'attentiveness to power' and in their 'fundamental realism' and readiness to accommodate themselves to the 'conditions of the external world'.[98] Such a characterisation strongly echoes Inoguchi's assessment of Japan as 'order-takers' rather than 'order-makers'.[99] Indeed, as this chapter indicates, Japan's adaptiveness is evident throughout the Cold War. Japan was able to adapt to rising bipolarity in the 1950s as well as to the multipolarisation of the 1970s, maximising trade and diplomatic opportunities along the way. Since the Cold War, Japan has sought to rethink its formerly low-key international role to take a more 'normal' approach to international affairs within a unipolar context. Since 2012, it has sought to hedge against the risks to the international order stemming from America's decline and China's rise.

This is not to suggest that Japan has always succeeded in its efforts at accommodation. At times, it has even found maintaining its American relationship difficult, as illustrated by the troubled periods after the Gulf War and during the Hatoyama-led government of 2009–10. Japan's approach to China has also been beset by difficulties over the past two decades. Nor is it to argue that Japanese political figures have always refrained from trying to 'make' rather than just 'take' the regional order. When leading political and corporate figures such as Ishihara and Morita began talking of Japan as a new economic superpower in the late 1980s, it seemed that Japan might establish itself as a central pole in a new trade-focused international order. Notwithstanding such difficulties or the odd temptation to make a new order, however, Japan has largely stuck with and benefited from its order-taking strategy.

Even if Japan has successfully responded to the dangers of *takyokuka* in the past, can the same be said of the future? The Trump presidency posed major challenges for Japan. Still, the Abe government demonstrated adroit diplomacy towards Trump. Abe in particular actively promoted Japanese views to Trump, especially on the importance of the alliance, the US–Japan trading relationship, and the wider security and economic order underpinning America's role in the region. He also sought to instil in the mind of the US president Japan's interests in strategic issues of mutual concern, such as relations with China, the idea of the 'Indo-Pacific', and the tensions over

North Korea. Overall, Abe was able to limit the damage that Trump inflicted on US–Japan relations during his four years as president.[100]

However skilled its diplomacy, Japan still faces two deeper challenges further exposed, and indeed exacerbated, by Trump. These stem from the uncertainty around America's likely future role in the Asia-Pacific order – whether maintaining the order (as a central pole), destabilising it (as a unilateral interventionist), or disengaging from it (as an isolationist). Although these challenges have been apparent for some time, and have long been debated in Japan, Trump's erratic diplomacy brought to the fore serious questions for America's allies as to the long-term reliability of the US as a strategic partner in a more contested multipolar order.[101] Such problems were further worsened, moreover, by Trump's continued attacks on some of the key principles that have underpinned the US-led order, notably a commitment to shared rules and institutions.[102]

Paradoxically, in his careless and often aggressive rhetoric, Trump heightened both abandonment and entrapment fears for Japan. On the one hand, Trump eroded allies' confidence in America's commitment to the region. If the US were to abandon its allies' interests in the North Korean nuclear issue, for instance, this would force Japan to begin pursuing more independent hedging strategies.[103] On the other hand, Trump stoked fears of entrapment in Japan, for instance by suggesting that the US should intervene unilaterally in the region's various disputes. Japan's fear was that, so soon after it had loosened its own defence restrictions by reinterpreting CSD, it would find itself drawn into a conflict precipitated by the US.[104]

Abandonment and entrapment fears will persist beyond Trump and so will inevitably create alliance frictions between the government of Abe's successor, Yoshihide Suga, and the new US President Joe Biden. Japan cannot easily 'pivot' away from its strategy of supporting the US-led order to counter the dangers of multipolarisation. The 'pivot in Asia', as Japan's 'diversification of external balancing' has been described, may constitute an early form of hedging against US decline.[105] However, it was originally envisaged as a way to supplement US power by increasing Japan's international role and helping to integrate the cooperative efforts of US allies and partners around the region. Japan's aim, until now, has been to buttress US power, not find a substitute for it.[106] Indeed, Abe's FOIP vision should be viewed in this light. After all, for Japan, as with other partners to the US, there is no realistic replacement for the US in an increasingly contested, multipolar region.

How, then, might Japan respond to the dangers of multipolarity and declining US power in the coming years? Japan may hope to persuade the Biden administration of the value of its alliances and partnerships in the

Asia-Pacific (especially with Japan), and return to the *status quo ante* of the alliance. Again, FOIP offers an obvious mechanism for pursuing this goal, and Japan will also probably promote the Quad. The Biden administration is likely to be more receptive to these ideas; however, it may be constrained in what it can do on much regional order-building, especially on trade.[107] Japan still has the alternative option – of moving towards a more autonomous and independent strategic posture. It could establish itself, if not as a new pole in a regional order, then at least as a counterweight to growing Chinese influence.[108] But such a posture would involve substantial costs, fly in the face of past incrementalism in Japan's security policymaking, and may also be beyond Japan's capacity. A properly independent deterrence capability, for example, would require Japan to reconsider its hitherto 'nuclear allergy' and develop its own nuclear weapons.[109] Whatever its response, the country faces a more contested and challenging multipolar regional order. The era of dependence on US hegemony, under either bipolar or unipolar conditions, is passing. For Japan, the dangers of multipolarity await.

Notes

1 On international order, see for example Hideaki Shinoda, *Kokusai Shakai no Chitsujo* [The Order of International Society] (Tokyo: Tōkyō Daigaku Shuppankai, 2007); Tetsuya Sakai, *Kindai Nihon no Kokusai Chitsujoron* [The Political Discourse of International Order in Contemporary Japan] (Tokyo: Iwanami Shoten, 2007); Taizō Miyagi, 'Shinkōkoku taitō to kokusai chitsujo no hensen' [The rise of emerging states and the changes in the international order], *Kokusai Seiji* [International Relations], 183 (2016), 1–14; Atsushi Ishida, 'Joron kokusai chitsujo to kokunai chitsujo no kyōshin' [Reciprocal reconfiguration of international and domestic orders], *Kokusai Seiji* [International Relations], 147 (2007), 1–10; Kazuhiko Noguchi, 'Tankyoku sekai no kokusai seiji riron: riarizumu, Eikokugakuha, fukuzatsukei' [International relations theory of unipolar world: realism, the English School, and a complex system], *Kokusai Seiji* [International Relations], 184 (2016), 157–65. On regional order in Asia, see Takeshi Yuzawa 'Higashi Asjia no takokukan seido to chīki chitsujo no tenbō: genjō iji sōchi toshite no chīki seido no yakuwari' [Multilateral institutions and the prospects for regional order in East Asia: the role of regional institutions as mechanisms for maintaining the status quo], *Kokusai Seiji* [International Relations], 158 (2009), 10–24. On multipolarisation, see for example Kinhide Mushakōji, '"Takyokuka" no riron: hitotsu no keishika no kokoromi' [A theory of 'multipolarization': a formal attempt], *Kokusai Seiji* [International Relations], 48 (1973), 1–11 or Tōru Yano, 'Takyokuka to "jūzoku taikei" jōkyō no hen'yō: Chiiki Shugi to no kanren – kokusai shakai no tōgō to kōzō' [Multi-polarization of the international system and transformation of regional

subordinate systems: prospects for regionalism in South East Asia – integration and change in international society], *Kokusai Seiji* [International Relations], 48 (1973), 12–29. More recently, an assessment that international politics is moving towards multipolarity underpins Soeya's recommendations that Japan adopt a more 'middle power' approach to diplomacy. See Yoshihide Soeya, *Nihon no 'Midoru Pawā' Gaikō: Sengo Nihon no Sentaku to Kōsō* [Japan's 'Middle Power' Diplomacy: Postwar Japan's Choices and Conceptions] (Tokyo: Chikuma Shinsho, 2005). For recent work on the changing order and Japan, see also Yoshihide Soeya, 'Chūyō toshite no "Kujō, Anpo Taisei"' ['Article 9 and the US–Japan security system' as a middle way], in Yoshihide Soeya (ed.), *Chitsujo Hendō to Nihon Gaikō: Kakudai to Shūshuku no 70 Nen* [Order, Change and Japanese Diplomacy: 70 Years of Expansion and Reduction] (Tokyo: Keiō Gujuku Daigaku Shuppankai, 2016), pp. 3–28, at pp. 25–6.

2 Kuniyuki Nishimura, 'Nihon no kokusai seijigaku keisei ni okeru no "yunyū": E. H. Carr no shoki no juyō kara' ['Importing' theories in the creation of Japanese international studies: insights from the early readings of E. H. Carr], *Kokusai Seiji* [International Relations], 175 (2014), 41–55, at 41.

3 *Ibid.*, 41–2.

4 Amitav Acharya and Barry Buzan, 'Why is there no non-Western international relations theory? An introduction', in Amitav Acharya and Barry Buzan (eds), *Non-Western International Relations Theory: Perspectives on and Beyond Asia* (London: Routledge, 2010), pp. 1–25, at p. 3.

5 Tadashi Kawata and Saburō Ninomiya, 'The development of the study of international relations in Japan', *Developing Economies*, 2:2 (1964), 190–204, at 190.

6 Takashi Inoguchi, 'Are there any theories of international relations in Japan?', *International Relations of the Asia-Pacific*, 7:3 (2007), 369–90, at 372.

7 Kosuke Shimizu, *Why There is No Non-Western IR Theory in Japan? Genealogy of Japan's Cultural IR, and the Study of Regional History*, Working Paper Series, Studies on Multicultural Societies, No. 32 (Kyoto: Afrasian Research Centre, Ryukoku University, 2016), p. 3.

8 Inoguchi, 'Are there any theories', 371–4. See also Takashi Inoguchi and Paul Bacon, 'The study of international relations in Japan: towards a more international discipline', *International Relations of the Asia-Pacific*, 1:1 (2001), 1–20, at 11–13.

9 Kawata and Ninomiya, 'The development of the study of international relations', 199–202.

10 Kazuya Yamamoto, 'International relations studies and theories in Japan: a trajectory shaped by war, pacifism, and globalization', *International Relations of the Asia-Pacific*, 11:2 (2011), 259–78, at 263–4; Koji Murata, 'The evolution of Japanese studies or international relations', *Japanese Journal of Political Science*, 11:3 (2010), 355–65, at 357–8; Inoguchi, 'Are there any theories', 376; Yoshihiko Nakamoto, 'Japanese realism and its contribution to international relations theory', *Issues & Studies*, 33:2 (1997), 65–96, at 68–70. See also Yoshikazu Sakamoto, 'Chūritsu Nihon no bōei kōsō: nichibei anpo taisei ni

kawaru mono' [The defense policy of Japan as a neutral state], *Sekai* [World], 164:8 (1959), 31–47; Masataka Kōsaka, 'Genjitsu shugisha no heiwaron' [A realist's argument for peace], *Chūō Kōron* [Central Review], 78:903 (1963), 38–49.

11 Inoguchi, 'Are there any theories', 373.

12 On the diversification of Japanese IR from the 1970s onwards, see Yamamoto, 'International relations studies', 261; Akihiko Tanaka, 'Joshō: kokusai seiji riron no saikōchiku' [Introduction: reconstructing international relations theory], *Kokusai Seiji* [International Relations], 124 (2000), 1–10, at 3–4. For a study of historical IR questions, see Jon Uon Ryū, Takahiko Tanaka, and Yūichi Hosoya (eds), *Nihon no Kokusai Seijigaku: Rekishi no naka no Kokusai Seiji* [Japanese Studies of International Politics: Historical Approaches to International Politics] (Tokyo: Japan Association of International Relations, 2009).

13 Inoguchi, 'Are there any theories', 375.

14 Akihiko Tanaka, *Japan in Asia: Post-Cold-War Diplomacy*, trans. Jean Connell Hoff, 2nd edn (Tokyo: Japan Publishing Industry Foundation for Culture, 2017), p. 1.

15 Mushakōji, '"Takyokuka" no riron', 1–11. Mushakōji draws in particular from Richard N. Rosecrance, 'Bipolarity, multipolarity, and the future', *Journal of Conflict Resolution*, 10:3 (1966), 314–27.

16 Mushakōji, '"Takyokuka" no riron', 5.

17 Yano, 'Takyokuka to "jūzoku taikei" jōkyō no hen'yō'.

18 Yoshinobu Yamamoto, 'Kokusai shisutemu no dōtai to antei' [The dynamics and stability of the international system], *Kokusai Seiji* [International Relations], 82 (1986), 7–25, L5.

19 Yūzō Yabuno, 'Gurōbaru shisutemu no hen'yō' [The transformation of the global system], *Kokusai Seiji* [International Relations], 111 (1996), 1–4, L5; Yoshitaka Ikeda, 'Gurōbaru shisutemu no sansō kōzō ron no hihanteki kentō nisokōzō no kanōsei' [Critical analysis of the 'three-layered structure model of the global system': the possibility of a two-layered structure model], *Kokusai Seiji* [International Relations], 111 (1996), 115–28, L15–L16.

20 Seiji Endō, 'Posuto Uesutofaria no sekai chitsujo e no apurōchi' [An approach to the post-Westphalian world order], in Makoto Kobayashi and Seiji Endō (eds), *Gurōbaru Poritikusu: Sekai no Sakōzōka to Atarashii Seiji Gaku* [Global Politics: Global Restructuring and the New Political Studies] (Tokyo: Yūshindō Kōbunsha, 2000), pp. 27–48.

21 Takashi Inoguchi, 'Japan's foreign policy under US unipolarity: coping with uncertainty and swallowing some bitterness', *Asian Journal of Political Science*, 6:2 (1998), 1–20, at 18.

22 Tatsuya Nishida, 'Kinkō riron (baranshingu seorii) kara mita beikoku ikkyoku taisei' [Unipolar system in the post-cold war period: a perspective from balancing theories], *Kokusai Seiji* [International Relations], 150 (2007), 35–51, L8–L9.

23 For a recent review on the work of the English School, see Noguchi, 'Tankyoku sekai no kokusai seiji riron'.

24 Shinoda, *Kokusai Shakai no Chitsujo*, p. v.

25 See, for instance, Hidemi Suganami, *On the Causes of War* (Oxford: Clarendon Press, 1996); Hidemi Suganami, 'The international society perspective on world politics reconsidered', *International Relations of the Asia-Pacific*, 2:1 (2002), 1–28; Hidemi Suganami, *The Domestic Analogy and World Order Proposals* (Cambridge: Cambridge University Press, 1989); Hideaki Shinoda, *Re-examining Sovereignty: From Classical Theory to the Golden Age* (Houndmills, Basingstoke: Macmillan Press, 2000).
26 Sakai, *Kindai Nihon no Kokusai Chitsujoron*, p. 10.
27 Akio Takahara, 'Joron: Higashi Ajia chitsujoron no shomondai' [Introduction: issues in the discussion on the new East Asian order], *Kokusai Seiji* [International Relations], 158 (2009), 1–9, especially 1–3.
28 Inoguchi, 'Japan's foreign policy', 15, 19.
29 Shin Kawashima (ed.), *Chaina Risuku* [China Risk] (Tokyo: Iwanami Shoten, 2015).
30 Soeya, *Nihon no 'Midoru Pawā' Gaikō*, p. 172.
31 *Ibid.*
32 Akihiko Tanaka, 'Pawā toranjisshon to kokusai seiji no hen'yō: Chūgoku taitō no eikyō' [Power transition and change in international politics: the impact of China's rise], *Kokusai Mondai* [International Affairs], 604 (2011), 5–14.
33 *Ibid.*, 11. See also A. F. K. Organski, *World Politics* (New York: Alfred A. Knopf, 1958).
34 Shin Kawashima, 'Chugoku to iu mondai gun' [An assortment of problems called China], in Kawashima (ed.), *Chaina Risuku* [China Risk], pp. 1–15, at p. 13.
35 On the debates over the Yoshida Doctrine, see Yoshihide Soeya, 'Yoshida Rosen to Yoshida Dokutorin' [The Yoshida Way and the Yoshida Doctrine], *Kokusai Seiji* [International Relations], 151 (2008), 1–17.
36 Kazuhiko Togo, *Japan's Foreign Policy, 1945–2003: The Quest for a Proactive Policy*, 2nd edn (Leiden: Brill, 2005), p. 231.
37 Kimie Hara, *Japanese–Soviet/Russian Relations since 1945: A Difficult Peace* (London: Routledge, 1998), p. 18.
38 Michael Schaller, *Altered States: The United States and Japan since the Occupation* (New York: Oxford University Press, 1997), pp. 114–23. See also Kimie Hara, '50 years from San Francisco: reexamining the peace treaty and Japan's territorial problems', *Pacific Affairs*, 74:3 (2001), 361–82.
39 H. D. P. Envall, *Japanese Diplomacy: The Role of Leadership* (Albany, NY: State University of New York Press, 2015), p. 150. On Japanese defence capabilities for responding to threats during this period, notably those presented by the Soviet Union, see Masashi Nishihara, 'Expanding Japan's credible defense role', *International Security*, 8:3 (1983/84), 180–205, at 185–89.
40 'Abe, Putin post-summit comments reveal different priorities', *The Mainichi*, 28 April 2017.
41 Linus Hagström, *Japan's China Policy: A Relational Power Analysis* (London: Routledge, 2005), pp. 78–9.

42 C. W. Braddick, *Japan and the Sino-Soviet Alliance, 1950–1964: In the Shadow of the Monolith* (Houndmills, Basingstoke: Palgrave Macmillan, 2004), pp. 13–36.
43 Junnosuke Masumi, *Contemporary Politics in Japan*, trans. Lonny E. Carlile (Berkeley, CA: University of California Press, 1995), p. 109.
44 Matake Kamiya, 'Japanese politics and Asia-Pacific policy', in Ezra F. Vogel, Yuan Ming, and Tanaka Akihiko (eds), *The Golden Age of the US–China–Japan Triangle, 1972–1989* (Cambridge, MA: Harvard University Press, 2002), pp. 52–75, at p. 59.
45 Hitoshi Tanaka, 'Japan and China at a crossroads', *East Asia Insights*, 1:2 (2006), 1–5, at 1.
46 Tsuneo Watanabe, 'Japan's security strategy toward the rise of China: from a friendship paradigm to a mix of engagement and hedging', Tokyo Foundation for Policy Research [website], 6 April 2015, www.tokyofoundation.org/en/articles/2015/security-strategy-toward-rise-of-china (accessed 30 April 2021).
47 James Manicom, *Bridging Troubled Waters: China, Japan, and Maritime Order in the East China Sea* (Washington, DC: Georgetown University Press, 2014), pp. 45–6.
48 Such thinking persisted well into the 1990s. See Inoguchi, 'Japan's foreign policy', 15.
49 Ezra F. Vogel, *Japan as Number One: Lessons for America* (Cambridge, MA: Harvard University Press, 1979).
50 Ezra F. Vogel, 'Pax Nipponica?', *Foreign Affairs*, 64:4 (1986), 752–67, at 767.
51 Morita Akio and Ishihara Shintarō, *'No' to Ieru Nihon: Shin Nichibei Kankei no Hōsaku* [The Japan that Can Say 'No': Plan for a New Japan–US Relationship] (Tokyo: Kōbunsha, 1989).
52 Shintaro Ishihara, *The Japan that Can Say No: Why Japan will be First Among Equals*, trans. Frank Baldwin (New York: Simon & Schuster, 1991), pp. 25, 43.
53 *Ibid.*, p. 125.
54 *Ibid.*, p. 124.
55 See Kobayashi Keiichiro, 'The two "lost decades" and macroeconomics: changing economic policies', in Yoichi Funabashi and Barak Kushner (eds), *Examining Japan's Lost Decades* (London: Routledge, 2015), pp. 37–55.
56 H. D. P. Envall, 'Clashing expectations: strategic thinking and alliance mismanagement in Japan', in Yoichiro Sato and Tan See Seng (eds), *United States Engagement in the Asia Pacific: Perspectives from Asia* (Amherst, NY: Cambria Press, 2015), pp. 61–88, at p. 68.
57 Yoichiro Sato, 'Three norms of collective defense and Japan's overseas troop dispatches', in Yoichiro Sato and Keiko Hirata (eds), *Norms, Interests, and Power in Japanese Foreign Policy* (New York: Palgrave Macmillan, 2008), pp. 93–108, at p. 94.
58 Michael J. Green, *Japan's Reluctant Realism: Foreign Policy Challenges in an Era of Uncertain Power* (New York: Palgrave, 2001), p. 17. See also H. D. P. Envall, 'Japan: from passive partner to active ally', in Michael Wesley (ed.),

Global Allies: Comparing US Alliances in the 21st Century (Canberra: ANU Press, 2017), pp. 15–30, at p. 20.

59 Andrew L. Oros, *Normalizing Japan: Politics, Identity and the Evolution of Security Practice* (Stanford, CA: Stanford University Press, 2008), p. 2.

60 See Yoshihide Soeya, 'A "normal" middle power: interpreting changes in Japanese security policy in the 1990s and after', in Yoshihide Soeya, Masayuki Tadokoro, and David A. Welch (eds), *Japan as a 'Normal Country'?: A Nation in Search of Its Place the World* (Toronto: University of Toronto Press, 2011), pp. 72–97, at p. 72.

61 Ichirō Ozawa, *Blueprint for a New Japan: The Rethinking of a Nation*, trans. Louisa Rubinfien (Tokyo: Kodansha International, 1994), p. 94.

62 *Ibid.*, pp. 94–5. See also Envall, *Japanese Diplomacy*, pp. 77–8.

63 Francis Fukuyama, 'The end of history?', *The National Interest*, 16 (1989), 3–18.

64 Ozawa, *Blueprint for a New Japan*, p. 114.

65 Samuel P. Huntington, 'The lonely superpower', *Foreign Affairs*, 78:2 (1999), 35–49, at 36.

66 Ozawa, *Blueprint for a New Japan*, pp. 132–3.

67 Oros, *Normalizing Japan*, p. 3.

68 On the alliance reforms, see Matake Kamiya, 'Reforming the US–Japan alliance: what should be done?', in G. John Ikenberry and Takashi Inoguchi (eds), *Reinventing the Alliance: US–Japan Security Partnership in an Era of Change* (New York: Palgrave Macmillan, 2003), pp. 91–116, at pp. 92–6.

69 Satu Limaye, 'Tokyo's dynamic diplomacy: Japan and the subcontinent's nuclear tests', *Contemporary Southeast Asia*, 22:2 (2000), 322–39, at 332–5. See also H. D. P. Envall, 'Japan's India engagement: from different worlds to strategic partners', in Ian Hall (ed.), *The Engagement of India: Strategies and Responses* (Washington, DC: Georgetown University Press, 2014), pp. 39–59, at pp. 44–6; Takeshi Yuzawa, *Japan's Security Policy and the ASEAN Regional Forum: The Search for Multilateral Security in the Asia-Pacific* (London: Routledge, 2007), pp. 124–6.

70 Envall, 'Japan', p. 21.

71 Christopher W. Hughes and Ellis S. Krauss, 'Japan's new security agenda', *Survival*, 49:2 (2007), 157–76, at 157. See also H. D. P. Envall, 'Transforming security politics: Koizumi Jun'ichiro and the Gaullist tradition in Japan', *Electronic Journal of Contemporary Japanese Studies*, 8:2 (2008) [published online], www.japanesestudies.org.uk/articles/2008/Envall.html (accessed 30 March 2021); H. D. P. Envall, 'Exceptions that make the rule? Koizumi Jun'ichirō and political leadership in Japan', *Japanese Studies*, 28:2 (2008), 227–42, at 235–6.

72 Richard J. Samuels, *Securing Japan: Tokyo's Grand Strategy and the Future of East Asia* (Ithaca, NY: Cornell University Press, 2007), pp. 94–9. See also Tomohito Shinoda, *Koizumi Diplomacy: Japan's Kantei Approach to Foreign and Defense Affairs* (Seattle, WA: University of Washington Press, 2007), pp. 86–98, 113–32.

73 Envall, 'Transforming security politics'. See also Christopher W. Hughes, *Japan's Remilitarisation* (London: Routledge, 2009), pp. 91–8.

74 Samuels, *Securing Japan*, pp. 82–3. See also Christopher W. Hughes, 'Japan's security policy, the US–Japan alliance, and the "war on terror": incrementalism confirmed or radical leap?', *Australian Journal of International Affairs*, 58:4 (2004), 427–45.

75 On Okinawa, see H. D. P. Envall and Kerri Ng, 'The Okinawa "effect" in US–Japan alliance politics', *Asian Security*, 11:3 (2015), 225–41, at 231. There was growing criticism of the alliance in Japan during this period. For example, see Tsuyoshi Sunohara, 'The anatomy of Japan's shifting security orientation', *Washington Quarterly*, 33:4 (2010), 39–57.

76 See Akira Kojima, 'Japan's economy and the global financial crisis', *Asia-Pacific Review*, 16:2 (2009), 15–25, at 23–4; Ko Hirano, 'China wary of Hatoyama's "East Asian community"', *Japan Times Online*, 3 October 2009; H. D. P. Envall and Kiichi Fujiwara, 'Japan's misfiring security hedge: discovering the limits of middle-power internationalism and strategic convergence', in William T. Tow and Rikki Kersten (eds), *Bilateral Perspectives on Regional Security: Australia, Japan and the Asia-Pacific Region* (Houndmills, Basingstoke: Palgrave Macmillan, 2012), pp. 60–76, at pp. 63–4.

77 H. D. P. Envall, 'Abe's fall: leadership and expectations in Japanese politics', *Asian Journal of Political Science*, 19:2 (2011), 149–60, at 158–62.

78 Takashi Yokota, 'The real Yukio Hatoyama; Japan's new prime minister could be Asia's first "third way" leader', *Newsweek*, 28 September 2009.

79 Daniel Sneider, 'The new Asianism: Japanese foreign policy under the Democratic Party of Japan', *Asia Policy*, 12 (2011), 99–129.

80 Yukio Hatoyama, 'Japan's new commitment to Asia: toward the realization of an East Asian community', Address by Prime Minister of Japan, Singapore, 15 November 2009, http://japan.kantei.go.jp/hatoyama/statement/200911/15singapore_e.html (accessed 30 March 2021).

81 Yukio Hatoyama, 'Policy speech by Prime Minister Yukio Hatoyama at the 174th Session of the Diet', 29 January 2010, http://japan.kantei.go.jp/hatoyama/statement/201001/29siseihousin_e.html (accessed 30 March 2021); Hatoyama, 'Japan's new commitment to Asia'. See also Christopher W. Hughes, 'The Democratic Party of Japan's new (but failing) grand security strategy: from "reluctant realism" to "resentful realism"?', *Journal of Japanese Studies*, 38:1 (2012), 109–40, at 115; H. D. P. Envall, 'Underplaying the "Okinawa card": how Japan negotiates its alliance with the United States', *Australian Journal of International Affairs*, 67:4 (2013), 383–402, at 391.

82 Envall and Fujiwara, 'Japan's misfiring security hedge', pp. 62–71.

83 Democratic Party of Japan, 'Manifesto: The Democratic Party of Japan's Platform for Government', 18 August 2009, p. 28, www.dpj.or.jp/english/manifesto/manifesto2009.pdf (accessed 30 March 2021).

84 Ryo Sahashi, 'The DPJ government's failed foreign policy: a case of politician-led government gone wrong', in Ryo Sahashi and James Gannon (eds), *Looking for Leadership: The Dilemma of Political Leadership in Japan* (Tokyo: Japan

Center for International Exchange, 2015), pp. 131–58, at pp. 142–3. Envall, 'Clashing expectations', p. 72.

85 Hirano, 'China wary of Hatoyama's "East Asian community"'. See also Envall and Fujiwara, 'Japan's misfiring security hedge', pp. 66–7.

86 Envall, 'Clashing expectations', pp. 75–6.

87 Masashi Nishihara, 'Japan should stand firm on the Senkaku Islands dispute', *AJISS Commentary*, 164 (6 November 2012); '"Seiji no genba", Nichū Reisen (3): Yasukuni ni genin surikaeru' ['Politics on site', the Sino-Japanese Cold War, part 3: Sidestepping Yasukuni as a cause], *Yomiuri Shinbun* [Yomiuri Newspaper], 6 February 2014.

88 National Institute for Defense Studies, *NIDS China Security Report 2013* (Tokyo: National Institute for Defense Studies, 2014), p. 2.

89 Kei Koga, 'Japan's "Indo-Pacific" question: countering China or shaping a new regional order?', *International Affairs*, 96:1 (2020), 49–73, at 55–6.

90 Kei Koga, 'Japan's "Free and Open Indo-Pacific" strategy: Tokyo's tactical hedging and the implications for ASEAN', *Contemporary Southeast Asia*, 41:2 (2019), 286–313, at 298; Tomohiko Satake and Ryo Sahashi, 'The rise of China and Japan's "vision" for Free and Open Indo-Pacific', *Journal of Contemporary China*, 30:127 (2021), 18–35, at 22–3, https://doi.org/10.1080/10670564.2020.1766907 (accessed 30 March 2021); H. D. P. Envall, 'The Pacific Islands in Japan's "Free and Open Indo-Pacific": from "slow and steady" to strategic engagement?', *Security Challenges*, 16:1 (2020), 65–77, at 70–1.

91 Envall, 'The Pacific Islands',70. See also Tomohiko Satake, 'Japan's "Free and Open Indo-Pacific Strategy" and its implication for ASEAN', *Southeast Asian Affairs*, 2019 (2019), 69–82, at 73–4.

92 Shinzo Abe, 'Confluence of the two seas', speech at the Parliament of the Republic of India, 22 August 2007, www.mofa.go.jp/region/asia-paci/pmv0708/speech-2.html (accessed 30 March 2021).

93 See Satake, Japan's "Free and Open Indo-Pacific Strategy"',77–8; Koga, 'Japan's "Indo-Pacific" question', 58–9; H. D. P. Envall, *The Quadrilateral Security Dialogue: Towards an Indo-Pacific Order?* Policy Report (Singapore: S. Rajaratnam School of International Studies, September 2019).

94 Government of Japan, 'National Security Strategy', 17 December 2013, p. 1, http://japan.kantei.go.jp/96_abe/documents/2013/__icsFiles/afieldfile/2013/12/18/NSS.pdf (accessed 14 May 2021). See also H. D. P. Envall, 'Japan's "pivot" perspective: reassurance, restructuring, and the rebalance', *Security Challenges*, 12:3 (2016), 5–19, at 15.

95 H. D. P. Envall, 'The "Abe doctrine": Japan's new regional realism', *International Relations of the Asia-Pacific*, 20:1 (2020), 31–59, at 43. See also Daisuke Akimoto, *The Abe Doctrine: Japan's Proactive Pacifism and Security Strategy* (Singapore: Palgrave Macmillan, 2018).

96 Tomohiko Satake, 'The new guidelines for Japan–US defense cooperation and an expanding Japanese security role', *Asian Politics & Policy*, 8:1 (2016), 27–38, at 28; Envall, 'The "Abe doctrine"',43–6.

97 Inoguchi, 'Are there any theories', 375.

98 Kenneth B. Pyle, *Japan Rising: The Resurgence of Japanese Power and Purpose* (New York: Public Affairs, 2007), p. 42.
99 Inoguchi, 'Japan's foreign policy', 15.
100 Gaku Shimada, 'Abe's fourth arrow – diplomacy', *Nikkei Asian Review*, 26 January 2018; H. D. P. Envall, 'Can Japan's golden golf diplomacy win over Donald Trump?', in *The Trump Administration's First 100 Days: What Should Asia Do?* (Canberra: ANU College of Asia & the Pacific, 2017), pp. 16–17; H. D. P. Envall, 'Has Shinzo Abe left a lasting legacy?', *Inside Story*, 1 September 2020, https://insidestory.org.au/has-shinzo-abe-left-a-lasting-legacy/ (accessed 30 March 2021).
101 See Shogo Suzuki and Corey Wallace, 'Examining Japan's response to geopolitical vulnerability', *International Affairs*, 94:4 (2018), 711–34, at 718.
102 Daniel W. Drezner, 'Who is to blame for the state of the rules-based liberal order?', *Washington Post*, 5 June 2018.
103 Brendan Taylor and H. D. P. Envall, 'A nuclear arms race in Northeast Asia?', in *Nuclear Asia*, Paradigm Shift no. 2 (Canberra: ANU College of Asia & the Pacific, Summer 2017–18), pp. 19–24, at p. 24.
104 Thomas Wright, 'Trump's 19th century foreign policy', *Politico Magazine*, 20 January 2016, www.politico.com/magazine/story/2016/01/donald-trump-foreign-policy-213546?o=0 (accessed 30 March 2021).
105 Richard J. Samuels and Corey Wallace, 'Introduction: Japan's pivot in Asia', *International Affairs*, 94:4 (2018), 703–10, at 708.
106 Envall, 'The "Abe doctrine"', 14–15.
107 'Prospects dim for early US return to TPP despite Biden win', *Japan Times*, 9 November 2020, www.japantimes.co.jp/news/2020/11/09/business/us-return-tpp-joe-biden/ (accessed 30 March 2021).
108 H. D. P. Envall, 'What kind of Japan? Tokyo's strategic options in a contested Asia', *Survival*, 61:4 (2019), 117–30, at 121–2; Samuels and Wallace, 'Introduction', 709–10; Kenneth B. Pyle, 'Japan's return to great power politics: Abe's restoration', *Asia Policy*, 13:2 (2018), 69–90, at 88.
109 Taylor and Envall, 'A nuclear arms race in Northeast Asia?' p. 23; Richard A. Bitzinger, 'Does Japan really want nuclear weapons?', *Asia Times*, 8 September 2017.

7

The uses and abuses of the polarity discourse in UK foreign and defence politics

David Blagden

Britain's unfolding debate on 'multipolarity' reflects the country's own tortured concerns with power and status.[1] On the one hand, the United Kingdom (UK) is deeply invested in the club goods provided by the Western hegemonic order that US unipolarity delivered after the Cold War. American power – infused with the ideational but buttressed by the material – has delivered security and prosperity for Britain since 1945 in a way that could easily not have occurred under slightly different circumstances,[2] and that US relative power advantage increased even further in 1990. On the other hand, Britain has its own enduring obsession with national 'greatness': a politically contested, but undeniably present, understanding of a special national 'role' in the world. Since Britain is evidently not an economic or military superpower, but nonetheless wishes to be considered influential, this produces a hankering for a conception of 'greatness' understood in terms beyond relative material capacity alone. And on still another hand – to contrive a three-armed metaphor – Britain's strategic and broader political context is such that there is no common understanding of what 'polarity' actually *means*. So, while the term has recently found a place in official documents and discourse that it did not previously enjoy, it is also deployed as a political speech-act: to mean different things by different actors depending on their policies, preferences, and proclivities.

The chapter proceeds as follows. First, it surveys the strategic backdrop, in the form of a brief history of the UK's priorities and associated force posture that the US-dominated 'unipolar moment' enabled.[3] Second, it discusses Britain's new-found eagerness for discussions of 'multipolarity' – along with various related terms, such as 'peer adversary' – and the confusion that surrounds their invocation. Third, it considers Britain's own obsessions with 'great powerness' and the policy contradictions that this engenders. Fourth, it assesses how the relative power shifts that are afoot in the wider world might affect the UK's strategic environment; shifts that – domestic political actors' hand-wringing about Britain's own greatness or otherwise aside – are already affecting UK security policy debates. In closing, it offers some recommendations for British strategy in a multipolar age.

The chapter concludes that while Britain has not been a systemic 'pole' since 1945 and is unlikely to ever be one again, the country remains an important major power in the Euro-Atlantic region (conceived broadly to include the Mediterranean, South Atlantic, and High North). The UK also retains some residual capacity for – and interest in – modest strategic involvement in the non-Atlantic world. However, a lack of clarity over what multipolarity actually means, coupled with Britain's own ideational obsession with an international 'role', risks precluding the prudent national strategy required to defend and advance UK security and prosperity in the environment of multiple diffused power centres now emerging. As such, Britain's discourse of (multi)polarity and relative power is not just some academic curiosity for scholars of International Relations (IR). In fact, it has very real consequences for both Britons and the many allies that benefit from UK security commitments.

The backstory: UK posture through unipolarity and its twilight

The collapse of the Soviet Union over the years 1989–91 removed the sole power capable of meaningful opposition to US global preponderance. Of course, the Soviet economy was in deep trouble long before the late 1980s; the USSR was only a 'pole' in terms of the size of its military forces, rather than any long-spent industrial prowess, by the time Mikhail Gorbachev attempted his ill-fated programme of domestic reform.[4] Nonetheless, the sudden disappearance of the closest thing that Washington faced to a 'peer-competitor' freed the now-unipolar United States and its rich, capable allies – Britain foremost among them – to tackle foreign policy priorities beyond the previously all-consuming task of balancing Soviet power. The 1990s were accordingly a decade of relatively successful multilateral cooperation,[5] defence budgetary consolidation under the banner of the so-called 'peace dividend',[6] and – most prominently – a growing appetite for humanitarian intervention to militarily oppose atrocities committed in other countries that violated Westerners' sense of acceptable conduct.[7]

Moving on from the 1990s, UK foreign and defence policy was dominated through the first decade and a half of the twenty-first century by London's participation in the coalition response to the 11 September 2001 (9/11) attacks on Britain's most important ally, the United States. The ensuing 'global war on terror' – as incensed, fearful US policymakers dubbed their expansive commitment to eradicate anti-Western Islamists – and the Iraq and Afghan campaigns that it spawned, consumed resources and attention to the exclusion of pretty much all else in British defence. Of course, other routine military commitments continued as normal; small pockets of troops, aircraft, and warships deployed hither and thither, while the Royal Navy (RN) sustained its unceasing nuclear-armed submarine patrols – the ultimate backstop of deterrence against some future re-emergent state-based threat. The 1990s' humanitarian impulse also still persisted, now under the United Nations (UN)-endorsed banner of the 'Responsibility to Protect'.[8] Nonetheless, Britain's corps-sized commitment to the Iraq invasion, divisional-sized embroilment in Afghanistan, and the bloody, intractable counter-insurgency (COIN) campaigns that each occupation descended into coloured the whole of UK defence.[9]

Nowhere was this more apparent than in the outcome of successive official defence reviews and the military force postures that they delivered. The 1998 Strategic Defence Review (SDR), conducted by the 'New' Labour government shortly after it won power following eighteen years in opposition, had promised a balanced force oriented around maritime and airborne power projection.[10] It marked a significant shift from the force posture of the Cold War, certainly, with the need to fight for control of both the North-east Atlantic and Central Europe seemingly at an end.[11] But it still promised naval, air, and mechanised ground forces of substantial scale, in line with the then-influential view – following recent experiences in the Balkans – that Britain could be a humanitarian 'force for good' around the world. Over the ensuing decade, however, the Iraq and Afghan commitments relentlessly gutted the 1998 SDR's promised force. Fighting two protracted, sizeable wars on a tight defence budget and with only narrowly bounded additional contingency funding from the Treasury saw the sorts of air, naval, and heavier ground forces best suited to defence against hostile states progressively sacrificed on the altar of a lighter, more deployable army – and supporting air-maritime logistics tail – optimised for COIN.[12] This situation was compounded by the 2010 Strategic Defence and Security Review (SDSR) – the first such full review since 1998 – conducted by the new Conservative government, which had been elected against the backdrop of the 2008–09 financial crisis and associated fiscal overstretch with a mandate for swingeing budgetary consolidation.[13] With the Army still knee-deep in Afghanistan, it was spared cuts to entire capability areas (although it still lost personnel). For the Royal Air Force (RAF) and particularly the RN, however, the 2010 SDSR bit deep. The RAF lost one of its three classes of combat jets (among many other personnel and equipment reductions), while the RN lost people and warships of all kinds, including – most iconically – its two then-remaining fixed-wing aircraft carriers.[14]

What does this potted history have to do with international-systemic polarity, a concept rarely mentioned in UK security policy at the time? The in-vogue mantras of the era – that 'war had changed', was now fought 'among the people' (rather than against state adversaries), and that COIN and terrorism would be the enduring preoccupation of British defence[15] – were in fact by-products of a particular international-systemic distribution of power. UK forces could be optimised for campaigns against weak- and non-state adversaries precisely because – as America's closest and most capable ally in an American-dominated post-Cold War unipolar system – there *were* no major powers capable of meaningfully opposing Western interests. Those actors that *did* seek to oppose US hegemony had to resort to 'asymmetric' tactics (e.g. terrorism) as a way of imposing costs on the superpower. This was seen both on 9/11 and in US-opposed 'rogue' states' particular interest in obtaining chemical, biological, or ideally nuclear means of deterrence/coercion – hence the ensuing 'global war on terror' and its conflation with armed counterproliferation. Britain's military commitment to Iraq and Afghanistan was motivated by a belief in the inherent liberal-progressive promise coupled to a more 'realist' grand-strategic heuristic – embedded in London since the Suez debacle of 1956 – that it is always in UK interests to bind American power to British security by hugging Washington close.[16] But this commitment was made *possible* by the absence of meaningful state adversaries under the most acutely unipolar concentration of power seen since the height of the Roman Empire. In such a system, there remained a clutch of second-tier major powers conceivably capable of thwarting direct US intervention in their own territory.[17] But these states were otherwise incapable of effectively opposing American foreign policy preferences,[18] with the US and its allies enjoying unprecedented command of the global 'commons'.[19] Such post-1989 systemic conditions meant that for a capable second-tier power enjoying a reliable and comprehensive US security guarantee, there was suddenly strategic 'spare capacity' for pursuing other liberal foreign policy preferences – at the barrel of a gun, where desired – rather than focusing military effort on defence against other powerful states, as had characterised Britain's strategic history prior to 1990. Such conditions also account for the growth of international law and institutions since the Cold War, advocacy of which has been another central plank of UK strategy.

The happy illusion underpinning this UK posture – that Western preponderance was so comprehensive as to ensure that there would never again be meaningful opposition from capable state adversaries[20] – was shattered for British policy elites and voters alike in 2014. Russia's operation to lop Crimea off Ukraine and subsequently freeze any further moves in Kiev towards alignment with the North Atlantic Treaty Organization (NATO) or European Union (EU) by destabilising the eastern part of the country through a combination of large-scale conventional coercion and deniable subversion proved highly effective. This series of events, along with subsequent deterrent signalling,[21] brought home to Western policymakers – in a way that even Russia's Georgian intervention of 2008 had not – that there was once again a major power in Europe with sufficiently recapitalised capabilities and ample resolve to oppose further NATO encroachment.[22] Russia's ability to frustrate Western preferences in Syria and China's increasingly capable area-denial perimeter over its maritime periphery have further emphasised this new reality, as has both powers' readiness to disregard the Western-backed international 'rules' by which UK enthusiasts had set so much store.

That new major powers would rise – or resurge, in Russia's case – and then use their new-found capabilities to protect and advance their interests, even if that meant opposing Western interests in the process, was always probable. One consequence of expanded cross-border factor flows of the kind that characterised post-1990 economic globalisation is the diffusion of productive capacity to states not yet at the leading edge of the development frontier, as capital, labour, and technology seek higher returns in environs of greater relative scarcity. As such, the very economic system that Western powers had created after 1945 and then expanded globally following the Soviet Union's demise was also the system that gave large emerging economies the scope to experience substantial 'catch-up convergence' development gains, with major implications for such powers' national capabilities.[23] Foremost among such states has been China, to the point where the United States now faces the most economically potent rising rival since its own emergence as a great power.[24] Russia, for its part, was never the same kind of 'emerging' economy. Rather than *new* industrialisation, it underwent catastrophic *de*industrialisation in the 1990s, followed by stabilisation and (partial) recovery in the 2000s. But the demand for Russian hydrocarbons and enduring technological specialisms that the post-Cold War globalisation era created has nonetheless been instrumental in restoring Moscow's capabilities to oppose Western policy.

Of course, none of this means that the United States is about to lose its overall development edge, military superiority, or associated systemic leadership – all measures on which it remains far ahead of China (a country beset by development challenges of its own), let alone Russia.[25] But one does not need to forecast the collapse of American power to still see that other major states have now acquired sufficient capability to constrain US behaviour and threaten US-aligned interests, especially in their own regions, and especially given the scale of global demands on American capabilities.[26] US unipolarity, in short, is now less concentrated and more constrained than it was in the 1990s and 2000s, and possibly even now better characterised as a variant of bi- or multipolarity, albeit still favourably skewed towards US power and interests. While this latter fault line is a subject for debate beyond the remit of this chapter, the point is that relative power is shifting as it diffuses away from the particular concentration seen in the post-Cold

War West. And UK strategy, for its part, is just about starting to recognise that fact – but still with much confusion about what the erosion and possible end of unipolarity might mean and imply.

Contemporary British invocations of 'polarity': clarity and confusion

Since the Ukraine–Russia shock of 2014, in which a major power used force to redraw European territorial boundaries and militarily coerce NATO states out of pursuing their preferences, discussions of state-based threats have returned to prominence in UK strategic discourse. The 2010 SDSR had not completely dismissed state-based threats, but it saw only a need to retain a baseline deterrent plus 'the ability to regenerate capabilities *given sufficient strategic notice*'.[27] Its quinquennial successor, by contrast, promised to 'respond robustly to the re-emergence of state-based threats'[28] – belying the fact that 2014's escalation of Russian *behaviour* prompted this assessment of a 're-emerged state threat [sic]', rather than the recovery of Russian *power* (since such capability-growth was also evident back in 2010). Likewise, whereas SDSR 2010 named Moscow as only a 'partner' for 'dialogue',[29] SDSR 2015 made Russia the main subject of a subsection on 'the resurgence of state-based threats'.[30] The military capabilities prescribed by that SDSR for the decade ahead, 'Future Force 2025', were correspondingly reoriented away from COIN and back to state-on-state defence. Still, this 2015 iteration – as is the way with high-profile public policy statements that must guard against adverse diplomatic consequences[31] – remained reticent to name *other* major powers as anything other than valued friends, despite their sometimes less-than-friendly conduct.[32] As such, while the post-Crimea SDSR reflected a reintroduction to top-line UK official security policy discourse of concern over capable state adversaries, it was still hardly a full-throated recognition of a multipolar threat environment.

Looking beyond the high-level statement of UK strategic priorities and posture provided by the SDSR, however, the 'multip…' word and its corollaries have started to appear across the British security policy landscape. Launching the Public Consultation for the Modernising Defence Programme (MDP) – an inter-SDSR mini-review of UK military needs – in March 2018, the Ministry of Defence (MOD) stated explicitly that 'the rules-based international order is under significant pressure *from emerging multipolarity*'.[33] The MDP itself, when eventually published in the December of that year, asserted that '[a]fter almost three decades of relative international stability, the world has now re-entered a period of persistent and intense state competition'[34] – not far from an official UK government concession of the end of the post-Cold War 'unipolar moment', albeit without use of the 'polar' term itself. The MDP also pledged to create a Net Assessment Unit in the MOD to look 'across all dimensions of military competition to assess how the capability choices of both friends and foes may play out', in further recognition of the need to take the relative strategic balance vis-à-vis other powerful actors seriously for the first time since the 1980s.[35] The 2017–18 National Security Capability Review (NSCR) that spawned the MDP – a broader security/intelligence review concluded just after Russia's fatal March 2018 use of a military nerve agent in Salisbury, and bearing a vociferous foreword from the prime minister reflecting that development – also featured a section on 'intensifying' state competition (although it still placed such competition behind terrorism in its list of security concerns).[36]

Moving outside the central MOD and Cabinet Office NSCR/MDP teams, further direct references and indirect allusions to multipolarity abound. The Development, Concepts, and Doctrine Centre (DCDC) – the MOD unit tasked with, among other things, conducting the Global Strategic Trends (GST) futures analysis programme to inform defence planners – has long maintained that power diffusion away from the West would eventually bring about the rise of newly capable rivals.[37] But in its 2018 version of GST (the sixth edition), unlike its fifth-edition predecessor from 2014, DCDC first invokes 'multipolarity' as an explicit characterisation of the future – albeit as only one possible future among others.[38] Turning from the executive to legislative branches of government, meanwhile, organs of parliament have also come to pay close attention to ongoing relative power shifts. The House of Lords/Commons Joint Committee on the National Security Strategy, for example, incorporated the language of both 'competitive multipolarity' and 'peer military forces' (naming Russia and China) into its 2018 report on the changing UK national security environment.[39] The House of Commons Defence Committee, for its part, did not use the 'multipolar' label explicitly in its 2018 analysis of the threat environment that the MDP would have to confront, but it did deploy the term 'peer adversaries', implying multiple powers of approximately equal capability (i.e. close to a definition of multipolarity).[40] Looking to the present day, meanwhile – with 2021's Integrated Security, Defence, Development, and Foreign Policy Review (the quinquennial successor to the 2015 SDSR) under way at the time of this book's completion – HM Government identified 'intensifying great power competition' first among its list of emergent trends.[41] The Commons' Defence Committee similarly noted 'multipolarity' and 'peer competitors' among the concerns with which the Review must grapple.[42]

With such discussion of relative power shifts and resurgent state-based threats finally permeating policy, even if a little later than certain scholars would have preferred, is the UK now well placed analytically to cope with a post-unipolar security environment? Unfortunately, despite Britain's security policy community reaching clarity on one important axis – that US-underpinned Western preponderance may not last forever and that new threats can be expected to correspondingly emerge – confusion remains along others. Tellingly, the multipolarity-invoking 2018 MDP Consultation went on to explain that '[i]ncreasingly sophisticated capabilities are being used in new domains of warfare, both by state actors ... and by non-state actors that have diffused and disaggregated'.[43] This explanation of multipolarity (the subject of the preceding sentence) with reference to new domains of warfare and diffuse, disaggregated non-state actors belies a common theme of power-diffusion discussions in UK strategic discourse: 'multi-' is often taken to mean not just a specific category of sufficiently capable states ('poles'), but new dangers of many kinds.

For structural realists, à la Kenneth Waltz or John Mearsheimer, 'polarity' is bound by a particular criterion, namely the capacity to balance independently against even the most powerful other state in the system without recourse to the charity of allies.[44] Such a specific understanding may itself be unhelpful in certain contexts, especially since nuclear weapons gave even conventionally weak states the ability to deter through the threat of unbearable punishment, but it is at least parsimonious. For the various official UK policy statements referenced above, however, 'multipolarity' is all things to all people. For DCDC's GST, 'multipolarity' is only one possible world, alongside three other posited options – 'multilateralism', 'network of actors', and 'fragmentation' – belying an understanding of multipolarity not as a distribution of capabilities but as a behavioural condition.[45] And while such GST documents over the years have indeed focused on the diffusion of power, they have covered everything from states to transnational civil society groups, terrorist franchises, lone hackers, mega-cities, and super-viruses within the scope of such diffusion; the 2018 edition, while invoking multipolarity, continues that trend. For the MDP, multipolarity was certainly associated with the resurgence of state-based conflict – but it was also implicitly associated simply with 'All Bad Things' that UK Defence will have to confront, from Russian tanks, to cyber-enabled terrorists, to the resource conflicts born of climate change.[46] Likewise, for the NSCR from which the MDP was spun off, 'resurgen[t] state-based threats' featured as one element of a laundry list, alongside terrorism, crime, natural hazards, and more besides. For the Joint Committee on the National Security Strategy and House of Commons Defence Committee, meanwhile, the strategic environment is increasingly clouded by 'peer adversaries' – but are these peers of the US, a systemic superpower, or merely the UK, a regional power with a bit of extra-regional influence? If we are talking about US peers, then that would indeed mean genuine multipolarity – but the UK should simultaneously stop calling them 'peers', since any peer of the US is significantly more than a peer to the UK. By contrast, if they are merely peers to the UK, then they are not peers to the US – and unipolarity therefore remains robust. Most likely, their 'peerness' or otherwise vis-à-vis both Britain *and* America depends on the regional context in which they are operating. Yet such caveats and qualifications diminish the clarity and utility of the overall labelling exercise.

All of this is consistent, of course, with Ben Zala's identification of the discursive power and contestation generated by invocations of polarity.[47] 'Multipolarity' meaning different things to different people is not some UK-specific trait, but a feature of linguistic efforts to stratify political actors by capability and status tiers in many national strategic contexts. What *might* be peculiar to the UK, however, is the particular tension generated between capability-centric and status-centric approaches to such thresholds. These tensions are the focus of the next section.

Britain's tortured relationship with 'great powerness'

Since 1945, Britain has remained obsessed with performing the social role – and maintaining the associated status – of 'great power'.[48] On any materially specified metric, the UK ceased to be a 'pole' at the end of the Second World War. This is not to say that Britain was suddenly trivial, but compared to the United States and Soviet Union, it no longer met the criterion of being capable of independent strategic balancing against the most powerful state(s) in the system without reliance on allies.[49] Even theorists who contended that there was more to 'great powerness' than capability alone, in the form of rights and responsibilities to uphold some conception of international order – i.e. an international-*societal* dimension – still maintained that such powers should be capable of exercising regional preponderance.[50] Again, the US and USSR could meet this criterion in their respective zones of control, but Britain – for all its commitment to the Anglo-American international order that it had done much to create – could not. Nonetheless, the desire to retain the elevated influence and standing of a 'special' role has remained strong among British elites and voters alike[51] – not unreasonably, given the esteem and other benefits that such elevation brings – with keen support from a Washington in search of allies and a Paris in a similar situation.[52] This preference manifests itself as a continued post-imperial appetite, despite seventy-plus years of post-1945 defence cuts, for acting militarily abroad to uphold Britain's conception of international order. At the same time, London has also still sought to retain enough capability in certain areas to at least make an effort at providing national security without wholesale reliance on allies – to remain a major power on 'realist' criteria, as well as role-playing ones.[53] Indeed, the 2015 SDSR promised to retain a UK 'ability to undertake war-fighting independently', even as it *also* stated that Britain 'continues to look to [America] to shape global stability'.[54]

These different kinds of pressures can pull national strategy in different directions. Consider the 2015 SDSR's three national security objectives, of which the first two – 'protect our people' and 'project our global influence' – could recommend opposite policies (i.e. if influence-motivated power projection embroils the state in some sort of conflict that jeopardises the people's protection). These are not just hypotheticals, moreover: with RN warships increasingly operating alongside US and Japanese counterparts in the Western Pacific, Britain is consciously accepting some level of risk of confrontation with the twenty-first century's rising superpower in the name of projecting influence over 'rules-based order'.[55] Indeed, the very coding of influence projection as a co-equal strategic end, as opposed to merely a *means* to *other* ends, itself tells of a country with a particular interest in international role performance. Either way, the core point stands: despite having ceased to be an international-systemic 'pole' on a material capability definition in 1945, Britain retains a preference for continued 'great power' status through discharging a particular performative role. All of this supports Zala's observation that the political discourse of polarity actually reflects and reinforces collective concern over status hierarchies more than it corresponds to political scientists' concern for measuring capability distributions.[56]

These tangled preferences further account for – and tie into – Britain's currently confused polarity debate. On the one hand, Britain has been a tremendous beneficiary of the US-led Western hegemonic system. With its own national power much diminished after 1945, the UK managed to closely align US power with its own preferences such that – occasional ructions notwithstanding – Britain has continued to enjoy expansive national security, favourable economic relations, and an elevated diplomatic position while also foregoing defence spending sufficient to afford a generous welfare state. The quid pro quo has been active UK support for US hegemony, to the point where Britain's principal grand-strategic choice has been to serve as a cog – an important and valued cog, certainly, but a cog nevertheless – in another power's grand strategy.[57] In polarity terms, this means that Britain is deeply invested in the club goods that have been supplied by a US-dominated unipolar system – a distribution of power that many have come to assume as a structural 'fact' of the international system – and is aware that the consequences of its erosion are unlikely to be favourable.

On the other hand, however, having spent seventy-plus years with a foreign superpower as the ultimate guarantor of national survival – and thirty years in a system in which that superpower ally has itself had no meaningful rivals – Britain's strategy community is not accustomed to prioritised demarcation of threats by power and proximity. In line with its role-based concern for 'great powerness' under the assumption of US-assured security, UK strategic discourse struggles to distinguish between well-armed states and weak terrorists, between proximate threats and distant concerns, between the existentially vital and the ideologically desirable. Unbounded assertions of a 'global' mission to uphold British 'values', based on a moralistic division between 'good' Britain and (implicitly) 'bad' adversaries, are preferred over recognitions of limits to UK power and interests vis-à-vis the power and interests of others. US strategic discourse displays the same moralistic traits, of course – but then, Washington still has an unprecedented concentration of national power to play with. The recent British obsession with upholding 'rules-based international order' – a term invoked no fewer than thirty times by the 2015 SDSR – without reflecting on whose interests such 'rules' are designed (not) to serve, which transgressions are most geopolitically salient, or the possible confrontations (and their costs) implied by such 'upholding' is a case in point.[58] The willingness to fit threat assessments to a predetermined defence spending threshold – NATO's much-reified 2 per cent-of-GDP target – for much of the past decade, rather than *first* assessing the threat environment and *then* deciding how much defence spending it necessitates, is another.[59] The assumption that command of the global 'commons' and associated resupply from global markets will always belong to 'the West' (read: come from the US) is one more.[60] And the belief of some that the international environment can be transformed by simply having enough faith in the British character and inherent righteousness of the UK position is yet another.[61]

Britain has thus been free to go through the performative motions of confronting perceived threats to its conception of international order, in furtherance of a social conception of its world 'role', without actually carrying the buck for its own survival – and this reflects itself in UK discourse around power and polarity. The confused invocation of 'peer adversaries', without specifying who these adversaries are 'peers' to, is particularly telling in this regard; it belies a Britain simultaneously keen to claim independent great power status while consuming the low-cost, high-quality fruits of continued US primacy. Specifying a comparator for such 'peerness' would force a choice between rejecting US hegemony (undesirable, since Britain wants to prop it up in order to continue consuming its goods if at all possible) or accepting clear subordination to another rank of powers (undesirable, since Britain wishes to retain and maximise its esteem and influence). Failing to specify whether these 'peer adversaries' are peers to the US, peers to the UK, or somehow both (depending on regional context) therefore avoids any such hard choices. But it also avoids any clarity over (a) systemic polarity in general and (b) whether Britain in particular seeks to claim any kind of great power 'polar' status for itself. The flurry of political hand-wringing in 2018 about whether the UK can remain a 'Tier 1' military power[62] – an obviously absurd idea, since no one can reasonably claim that Britain (or any other state) is currently in the same military 'tier' as the US – betrays this same obsession with hierarchical status rankings alongside collectively useful ambiguity over Britain's own claimed great-powerness (wanting the benefits of US subordination *and* the standing of US equality). Such 'tier' claims invoke some distribution of polarity, while also – by placing Britain implausibly in the 'top' one – necessarily obscuring its presumed configuration. Under such conditions of conceptual slipperiness, it is hardly surprising that many contemporary UK security policy organisations' use of 'multipolarity' slides readily from a specific distribution of relative material power, as an IR structural realist would understand it, into simply meaning 'lots of dangerous things that Britain must confront if we are to remain our kind of country'.

The impact of global power shifts on Britain

If power actually is shifting in the world – not in some vague sense, meaning social media or insurgents, but in a specific sense, to rising non-Western economies with their own foreign policy priorities – and US unipolarity is correspondingly eroding, what does that mean for UK security? In short, having discussed the various ways in which 'multipolarity' *is* being used in British strategic discourse, what are the conditions under which it *should* be invoked?

At least five potential implications of the end of unipolarity – understood as the emergence of at least one other state capable of independently balancing the most powerful state in the system – present themselves for the UK strategic environment. First, and most pressing for Britain, has been the resurgence of Russia from its post-Cold War economic nadir of the 1990s.[63] Of course, with an economy smaller than those of Italy and Canada as of 2018,[64] and facing crippling headwinds,[65] Russia is never again going to be a meaningful industrial competitor to America and will struggle to even fulfil its convergence potential vis-à-vis Western Europe. Nonetheless, years of strong economic growth through the 2000s, favourable purchasing power parity terms, and a willingness to spend a larger share of national output on defence than is seen among the welfare states of NATO have allowed Russia to reform and modernise its military forces to the point where they are the largest and (on most measures) most capable in Europe. As evidenced by Ukraine's experience, meanwhile, Moscow is capable of multiplying the strategic effects of its forces – and diminishing the strategic cohesiveness of its adversaries – through astute use of covert action, proxies, subversion, communications disruption, disinformation, financial influence, and so forth.[66] US forces remain far superior to their Russian counterparts on a global level, to be sure, but those forces are not 'automatically' available for European defence and do not preclude decisive Russian concentrations of local superiority (or Russian escalation to nuclear coercion if its subnuclear strategic options fail).

Moscow, in short, now has the coercive means to advance its regional interests once again. Foremost among these are thwarting, weakening, and ideally breaking NATO. Note that such a preference does not mark Russia as 'bad' or 'evil', since Moscow has sound and understandable strategic reasons to wish to roll back a powerful alliance that (a) was created for its containment and (b) expanded across former Soviet allies *and* territory during the post-1989 depths of Russian weakness. Nonetheless, targeting Britain – as the European NATO state that has historically displayed the greatest combination of capability and resolve to balance Russia – could prove integral to any such efforts to weaken or break the Alliance, and this would obviously harm UK security. All of this is also taking place at a time when the US is becoming less well equipped to shoulder all of its allies' defence burdens simultaneously as it focuses on balancing the rising Chinese peer-competitor in Asia (as discussed below).

In the face of these international-structural conditions, Britain faces pressing questions for its strategic posture, all of which can be traced back to the fraying of unipolarity and the waning of US preponderance. What if, as part of some limited Alliance response to a Baltic or Norwegian contingency (say), Russia faces incentives to destroy NATO's stand-off air power, including RAF stations, RN carriers, and MOD command and control facilities? How might efforts to preserve the US alliance commitment to NATO by supporting Washington's global strategy – such as deploying British forces to the Gulf or East Asia – suck Britain into commitments that are costly on their own terms, jeopardise the UK's core NATO balancing effort in Europe, and/or bring London into confrontation with Beijing and/or Moscow? What if some Russian action in Estonia/Svalbard/etc. sees NATO/Britain – with little help from a disinterested Washington, in a worst-case scenario – left choosing between acceptance of the fait accompli (i.e. the breaking of NATO), costly attempted recapture in the face of a formidable Russian anti-access/area-denial perimeter, or perilous escalation to nuclear coercion? And what would London do if, as part of an effort to weaken NATO by dissuading the Alliance's only offshore European power (i.e. the UK) from contributing to continental defence, Moscow undertook a concerted campaign of coercion against Britain itself? Patterns of Russian naval activity, bomber patrols, cyber/informational activity, and chemical/radiological weapons use in and around Britain imply that the latter scenario is already not too far away.

Second, but bound up with the previous point, the erosion of unipolarity means that the United States will be less willing – and eventually less able – to shoulder all of its allies' defence burdens simultaneously.[67] As noted above, while China has not yet reached Soviet levels of relative military spending or capability, its economy is already larger vis-à-vis its American counterpart than the USSR's ever was – and it still has the convergence potential to become even larger. East Asia will therefore be the principal theatre in which Washington must put forth its balancing effort to safeguard its allies, maritime control, and other aspects of its favoured regional order.

This presents two opposite risks for the UK, which can respectively be dubbed 'abandonment' and 'entanglement' (or 'chain-ganging'). On the one hand, while the United States is unlikely to completely forsake NATO – even Donald Trump's mercurial temperament notwithstanding, should he (or a future leader like him) return to the presidency – the consensus in Washington will only grow louder that America's rich, developed allies in Europe should carry more of the costs of their own security. For a United States that has no intention of giving up international-systemic primacy if it can be avoided,[68] even despite others' rise, getting its capable allies in regions that do not contain a true peer-competitor to US power – which applies to Europe but not Asia – to provide the bulk of their own defence makes good sense. And if the US *does* eventually give up strategic primacy, *because* of the rise of other powers, then the Europeans will be left with little choice either way. Russia's diminished strategic salience to the United States could therefore present an unpleasant paradox for America's European allies, Britain foremost among them. For despite contemporary Russia being much weaker than the Cold War USSR was, it could present just as great a challenge for European NATO powers as the Soviet Union did *if* Euro-NATO must do the lion's share of the balancing itself, with only bounded and conditional US support.

On the other hand, British efforts to prop up US hegemony carry risks of entanglement in regions of only peripheral interest to the UK, with potential for 'chain-ganging' into others' conflicts.[69] The recent British push to forward-deploy naval forces in Singapore, make defence commitments to Japan, and join US-orchestrated freedom-of-navigation operations in contested areas of the South China Sea are all motivated by a desire to demonstrate UK influence in upholding the 'rules-based' (i.e. Western-dominated) international order from which Britain has benefited.[70] Yet however much it is packaged as simply an apolitical 'upholding' of impartial 'rules', such military commitments necessarily place Britain within a US-led balancing coalition directed at China – for rules to be 'upheld', the interests of the actor 'breaking' them must necessarily be countered – with all of the escalatory risks that that relationship carries over interests that are perceivedly critical to Beijing but only peripheral for the UK.[71] This risk could even be *more* pronounced for Britain if, say, China decided that a UK warship was an appropriate proxy target against which to assert its counter-Western preferences without guaranteeing the full blowback that would follow an attack on a US vessel, aircraft, or base. Put simply, relatively modest forces deployed to far-flung regions may be big enough to get Britain into trouble but not big enough to meaningfully reduce the trouble once it starts, as UK planners faced by a similarly bleak fiscal outlook feared in the 1960s.[72] And on top of all this, any military asset deployed in East Asia to issue warm words about upholding the 'rules-based order' is necessarily a scarce asset *not* deployed on other, more pressing balancing tasks against more UK-proximate threats in Britain's home region, as per the previous point. Similar concerns apply to British embroilment in the Middle East.[73] In short, the opportunity-cost of any meaningful presence in the service of second-order Indo-Pacific interests is less consequential capability to safeguard first-order Euro-Atlantic interests.

The final three points are largely corollaries to the preceding two, and can be summarised more succinctly. Third, therefore, a multipolar world is more likely to be prone to inter-state military crises with the potential to embroil UK interests.[74] Whereas a unipolar world features one great power capable of decisively tilting the balance of any militarised inter-state dispute that it cares to join – and simultaneously, if necessary – that would no longer be true in a multipolar world. Beyond the general NATO–Russia and US–China contexts already discussed, potential flashpoints abound: in the Baltic and Black Seas, around Svalbard, in the Eastern Mediterranean and Gulf, around the India–Pakistan and India–China borders, on the Korean Peninsula, in the Taiwan Strait, in the South Atlantic, in parts of Africa, and many more. Ultimately, the point here is not to provide an exhaustive 'laundry list'; the point is to illustrate that in a multipolar world, many more potential conflict dyads in contested locations will contain at least one party that no longer feels encumbered by the potential for countervailing action by a sole superpower. And in many of these contexts, the potential exists for British interests to be affected and for London to therefore face stark choices over conceding such interests or risking potentially escalatory entanglement.

Fourth, a multipolar world is unlikely to be a world conducive to arms control or counterproliferation efforts.[75] The unipolar world was not universally conducive either, of course: in demonstrating that it would topple regimes that it opposed even if they had already relinquished weapons of mass destruction, as it did in Iraq and Libya, the superpower strengthened the case for nuclear deterrence among otherwise weak US adversaries (the fates of Saddam Hussein and Muammar Gaddafi were noticed in Pyongyang). Nonetheless, for those states that avoided enmity with the unipole, the Western hegemonic system produced relatively few pressures for either horizontal or vertical proliferation, particularly hostile bilateral contexts excepted (e.g. India–Pakistan). A multipolar world, by contrast, may produce more such incentives, insofar as more states are likely to face powerful adversaries that they are not confident they can deter through conventional arms alone. The competitive major power rivalries of a non-unipolar system may also make cooperative arms control harder to sustain; the recent unravelling of the US–Russia Intermediate-Range Nuclear Forces (INF) Treaty looked ominous in this light.[76] Of course, productive arms control measures *can* occur in multipolar and bipolar systems, as seen via the Hague Conventions of 1899 and 1907, the naval treaties of 1922–36, and the various force limitation agreements of the Cold War. Yet in all such parallels, states refused to relinquish critical means of defending their survival (or defected from treaties once there was a seemingly existential security rationale for doing so), illustrating the appeal that the ultimate means of deterrence – nuclear arms – will hold in an era of resurgent inter-state competition. And again, such developments could negatively affect UK security interests. Britain is hardly some righteous opponent of nuclear arms – indeed, if multipolarity returns with some of the consequences described here, its own nuclear deterrent will be even more valuable – but it would still face real risks from both the collapse of great power arms control and/or nuclear proliferation cascades to fragile, volatile regimes.

Fifth, albeit following from previous points, a return to competitive multipolarity could once again see contestation of the global 'commons' – air, sea, space – that America has commanded since 1990.[77] Many assumptions of UK strategy, meanwhile, have followed from the presumed structural 'fact' of such Western command. Military forces have been configured around power projection rather than gaining sea or air control against adversaries capable of contesting them, as for thirty years UK forces have operated in an environment in which the United States has supplied such control with ease.[78] Nowhere is this more apparent than the Royal Navy, which has just commissioned the two large new aircraft carriers promised by the 1998 SDR while having halved the frigate/destroyer, hunter-killer submarine, and mine-countermeasures fleets from the numbers specified by the same review. Aircraft carriers are no bad thing in themselves – indeed, well-screened and equipped carriers can themselves be valuable tools of sea/air command – but the decimation of the other sorts of naval forces necessary to escort carriers and secure sea control against adversaries' denial efforts belies a maritime posture that simply presumes a Western-dominated lake.

Beyond force composition, such assumptions are similarly pervasive.[79] For example, as 2011's Libya campaign exposed – and as an outgoing UK Joint Forces Commander recently lamented[80] – British stocks of munitions, spares, fuel, and technical expertise have been run down to unprecedentedly low levels, premised on 'just-in-time' resupply from global markets and private contractors, as if defence was a 'normal' business. Such assumptions may have maximised efficiency when engaging in expeditionary wars against minor powers, à la the 'global war on terror', but they could be cruelly exposed against a state adversary capable of (a) identifying such an obvious vulnerability and (b) targeting supply lines effectively. The same goes for the consolidation of UK forces into a few large bases, again for financial efficiency reasons, with these bases and their associated command and control nodes arguably lacking adequate air defence.[81] And looking beyond military capacity, everything from the vast majority of goods trade to fibre-optic internet cables and GPS (Global Positioning System) satellites resides in those erstwhile uncontested commons. Yet all such conditions, while often treated as some permanent new reality of international politics, have in fact been a direct benign consequence of unipolarity and – on the UK-specific dimensions – intimate alliance with that unipole. If such unipolarity erodes, therefore, then such conditions may also erode with it. Britain depends on sea lines of communication not only for its economic prosperity but also for its military capacity and indeed its population's survival. Even a modest uptick in contestation of the maritime commons could therefore bring profound consequences for Britain, especially if/when it occurs in the UK's Euro-Atlantic home region.

The way forward: polarity, prudence, and precision

Since 2014, UK strategic discourse has been replete with references to resurgent state-based competition, bringing the post-Cold War interregnum of 'abnormal' major power relations to a close. Since around 2018, moreover, the term 'multipolarity' itself has begun to appear in official policy statements. Such recognitions are not before time: the ongoing shift of economic, political, and military power from Western Europe and North America to emerging, non-Western states is the most important dynamic in contemporary international politics. This was true even during the period of Britain's self-inflicted embroilment in the Afghan and Iraq campaigns, of course – as scholars noted a decade ago[82] – but at least the drawdown from such 'global war on terror'-era commitments, coupled to the shock of Crimea, has pushed UK defence to once again contemplate concerns beyond COIN and counterterrorism.

While discussions of state-based threats, peer adversaries, and a multipolar world are back in vogue, however, such terms are not being used with clarity or consistency. Such ambiguity is both unsurprising and understandable. As Zala has demonstrated, 'polarity' in the discourse of policymakers rarely means the same thing as is meant by political scientists. Like any speech about politics, the language is itself political. British national strategy is caught between wanting to continue to consume the fruits of a US unipolar system while also wanting to claim the social role of a 'power' for itself – and all while beginning to recognise that Western hegemony is itself waning. Under such circumstances, while it is good that policymakers and the analytical community that surrounds them are beginning to contemplate the UK security implications of the return of multipolarity, it is also unremarkable that the term itself is being used to mean all things to all people. The discourse of 'multipolarity' as it exists in Britain today thus reflects enduring concerns over national standing, along with fear over a seeming multitude of threats – from terrorists to hackers, from climate change to the collapse of 'liberal order' ... *as well* as the specific meaning recognised by structural IR theory, namely growth in the capabilities of potentially hostile states to the point where they are capable of opposing the pre-existing powers' interests.

If Zala's contention is correct on a positive-explanatory level, then what normative-prescriptive recommendations follow? If 'polarity' *is* being used so expansively, how *should* it be made more precise? Of course, neither policymakers nor scholars can be expected to possess crystal balls. Efforts in the present to precisely forecast the exact future configuration of systemic polarity in, say, 2050 – or even a mere decade from now, at the start of the 2030s – are likely to be unsatisfactory. Economic growth trajectories can be approximated with at least some insight, of course. But the path between strong economic growth potential and top-tier national power is so fraught with contingency as to make definitive polarity projections circumspect. Just as this chapter has equivocated about the precise configuration of polarity now emerging, therefore – whether that be genuine multipolarity (balanced or otherwise), some form of US–China bipolarity, or simply a diluted form of unipolarity at the global level that is no longer full unipolarity within certain regions (i.e. where 'local poles' are capable of balancing the US in a way that they still cannot in the wider world) – it is perfectly acceptable for policymakers to do the same.

Nonetheless, while it is wholly forgivable to not know exactly what a post-unipolar future will look like, it is less forgivable to be imprecise about what multipolarity would even mean. Britain is not a pole and will not be again (barring some unlikely state collapse in the US and China), despite banal efforts to code it as such through nebulously defined 'soft' power resources.[83] But it remains a major power – and not simply on vague ideational grounds, but also on specific structural criteria.[84] London's suite of diplomatic, military, intelligence, financial, scientific, and cultural levers remains substantial. Such power is most concentrated in its home region, however, while it dissipates through projection – as is true for any country, of course, even the mighty United States[85] – and could yet be diminished by the unravelling of the UK itself, if Brexit and other Westminster choices drive Scotland and/or Northern Ireland to secede. The contemporary UK can thus be thought of as a regional major power with a bit of extra-regional influence, albeit with efforts to stretch that extra-regional influence serving to sap its core capability – this holds for any state, so it is not a pejorative judgement[86] – and also with non-trivial internal vulnerabilities.

For such a country, thinking rigorously about what a change in global polarity would *mean* – and adopting greater precision about what 'polarity' actually *is* as a precursor to this – will be fundamental to fashioning prudent national strategy for a post-unipolar age. So many traits of the post-Cold War international system that have been assumed to be progressive, irreversible developments by many strategists and scholars alike – the overriding preoccupation with countering terrorism, the seeming authority of international law and institutions, unchecked Western power projection in the name of liberal-humanitarian causes, a free-flowing and Western-controlled maritime 'commons', a Western-dominated internet/satellite communications infrastructure, and so forth – have in fact been products of the 'unipolar moment'. We do not know quite what configuration of polarity is coming next, but it is probably fair to say at the very least that the acuteness of post-1990 US unipolarity is now waning; China, Russia, and India too all have much less developed economies, but they also have access to new denial capabilities and, unlike Washington, are not trying to project hegemonic power into all regions of the world simultaneously.

If such unipolarity is indeed waning, meanwhile, then fundamental premises of UK strategic posture and conduct will require reappraisal. For although British policymakers are now acknowledging relative power shifts, national strategy continues to reflect unipolar habits. The reification of the NATO 2 per cent-of-GDP defence spending threshold in UK politics, following a government calculation that there was little public or parliamentary appetite to forego other areas of social spending – regardless of the deteriorating security environment – has represented a political constraint on power-balancing symptomatic of a state that has not been its own security guarantor for a very long time.[87] The enthusiasm for dispatching scarce warships and aircraft to the 'Indo-Pacific' – a 'region' spanning two-thirds of the globe, with ample scope for escalation and entanglement – to 'project influence' and 'uphold rules', even while NATO and UK national commitments alike go unfilled in the Euro-Atlantic area, similarly belies a role-obsessed state that has forgotten (but may painfully rediscover) the constraints of the balance of power. The contradictions of Britain's China policy – bandwagoning in the hope of economic gain, through the penetration of critical national infrastructure (e.g. nuclear power) by Chinese firms to the irritation of Washington, while joining the US-led counter-China balancing coalition in Asia to the annoyance of Beijing – are further symptomatic of a state rusty in the hard trade-offs of major power politics. Finally, the Brexit indulgence tells of a country deeply flippant about – and cosseted from – the dangers of an anarchic international system. For no power that was thinking seriously about the return of a multipolar threat environment would embark willingly on a project that risks diminishing its own market access and thus economic potential (along with associated capacity for both strategic spending and productive investment), damaging its own constitution, dividing its own polity, weakening its own liberty- and prosperity-promoting institutions, estranging its own proximate and powerful allies, weakening the purchasing power of its own currency, increasing its own dependence on capricious patrons (e.g. a primacist America), compromising its own EU-adjoined territories/bases (in Northern Ireland, Gibraltar, and Cyprus), undermining its own fragile internal peace (in Northern Ireland), and quite possibly breaking itself up (if Scotland and/or Northern Ireland are driven to secede).[88]

In short, if multipolarity really is returning – as HM Government's own policy statements now proclaim – then British strategy needs to become less fixated on performative identity, and more focused on defending vital interests through careful husbandry of national power while prudently eschewing unnecessary entanglements. The bleak post-COVID fiscal outlook and associated injection of additional friction in international relations only strengthens that imperative. If the UK strategy community manages this sooner rather than later, Britain may just have a chance of preserving its security, prosperity, and even its much-prized status through a multipolar twenty-first century.

Notes

1 This chapter represents a tailored version of an already published article: David Blagden, 'Power, polarity, and prudence: the ambiguities and implications of UK discourse on a multipolar international system', *Defence Studies*, 19:3 (2019), 209–34. The author thanks Manchester University Press and *Defence Studies* for permission to cross-pollinate. The chapter is dedicated to the memory of Nuno Monteiro (1971–2021), distinguished polarity theorist and this author's former MA preceptor; a brilliant scholar and wonderful mentor, gone far too soon.

2 Kori Schake, *Safe Passage: The Transition from British to American Hegemony* (Cambridge, MA: Harvard University Press, 2017).
3 On the notion and (contested) implications of such a 'moment', see Charles Krauthammer, 'The unipolar moment', *Foreign Affairs*, 70:1 (1990/91), 23–33; William C. Wohlforth, 'The stability of a unipolar world', *International Security*, 24:1 (1999), 5–41; Nuno P. Monteiro, *Theory of Unipolar Politics* (Cambridge: Cambridge University Press, 2014).
4 By 1985, the Soviet economy was only 37.7 per cent as large as its US counterpart, even measuring GDP (gross domestic product) on a Soviet-favourable purchasing power parity basis. Angus Maddison, *The World Economy: Historical Statistics* (Paris: Organisation for Economic Co-operation and Development, 2003).
5 Alvin Z. Rubinstein, 'Moscow and the Gulf War: decisions and consequences', *International Journal*, 49:2 (1994), 301–27.
6 Philip A. G. Sabin, 'British defence choices beyond "Options for Change"', *International Affairs*, 69:2 (1993), 267–87.
7 Stephen Wertheim, 'A solution from hell: the United States and the rise of humanitarian intervention, 1991–2003', *Journal of Genocide Research*, 12:3–4 (2010), 149–72.
8 The 'R2P' phrase was coined by the Canadian-instigated International Commission on Intervention and State Sovereignty in the same year as the 9/11 attacks (2001), and was subsequently endorsed by the UN at the 2005 World Summit. Of course, what was already a controversial notion – external powers giving themselves the prerogative to intervene in other states' domestic affairs if they did not like those states' chosen policies – became further tainted through its invocation by powers, Britain included, engaged on military operations in theatres such as Iraq for other, manifestly non-humanitarian reasons. Jeremy Moses, Babak Bahador, and Tessa Wright, 'The Iraq war and the responsibility to protect: uses, abuses and consequences for the future of humanitarian intervention', *Journal of Intervention and Statebuilding*, 5:4 (2011), 347–67.
9 David Blagden, 'Strategic thinking for the age of austerity', *RUSI Journal*, 154:6 (2009), 60–6.
10 HM Government, *Strategic Defence Review: Modern Forces for the Modern World* (Norwich: HM Stationery Office, 1998), https://webarchive.nationalarchives.gov.uk/20121018172816/http://www.mod.uk/NR/rdonlyres/65F3D7AC-4340-4119-93A2-20825848E50E/0/sdr1998_complete.pdf (accessed 20 August 2019).
11 Claire Taylor, *A Brief Guide to Previous British Defence Reviews*, Standard Note SN/IA/5714 (London: House of Commons Library, 2010), pp. 11–12, http://researchbriefings.files.parliament.uk/documents/SN05714/SN05714.pdf (accessed 11 February 2019); Gary Blackburn, 'UK defence policy 1957–2015: the illusion of choice', *Defence Studies*, 15:2 (2015), 85–104.
12 Paul Cornish and Andrew Dorman, 'Blair's wars and Brown's budgets: from strategic defence review to strategic decay in less than a decade', *International Affairs*, 85:2 (2009), 247–61; Blagden, 'Strategic thinking for the age of austerity'.
13 HM Government, *Securing Britain in an Age of Uncertainty: The Strategic Defence and Security Review* (Norwich: HM Stationery Office, 2010), https://

assets.publishing.service.gov.uk/government/uploads/system/uploads/attachment_data/file/62482/strategic-defence-security-review.pdf (accessed 20 August 2019); Blagden, 'Strategic thinking for the age of austerity'.

14 Illustratively, between the 1998 SDR and the 2015 SDSR, Royal Naval frigate/destroyer numbers fell from thirty-five to nineteen, while 'hunter-killer' submarine (SSN) numbers fell from twelve to six, highlighting the deep cuts to the sorts of capabilities most needed for securing control of Britain's maritime region against major state adversaries.

15 Blagden, 'Strategic thinking for the age of austerity'.

16 Patrick Porter, *Blunder: Britain's War in Iraq* (Oxford: Oxford University Press, 2018). Britain has at times sought to support US hegemony without deep military entanglement of its own, of course, most notably by eschewing a troop commitment to the Vietnam War. Yet even here, Britain still provided diplomatic support and various forms of stand-off/covert military assistance, while also providing the most important prop to the European dimension of US global strategy.

17 Monteiro, *Theory of Unipolar Politics*, pp. 43–5.

18 *Ibid.*

19 Barry R. Posen, 'Command of the commons: the military foundation of US hegemony', *International Security*, 28:1 (2003), 5–46.

20 Blagden, 'Strategic thinking for the age of austerity'.

21 For example, Darya Korsunskaya, 'Russia tests ICBM as Putin says nuclear deterrent must be maintained', *Reuters*, 10 September 2014, www.reuters.com/article/us-ukraine-crisis-defence/russia-tests-icbm-as-putin-says-nuclear-deterrent-must-be-maintained-idUSKBN0H51CJ20140910 (accessed 20 August 2019).

22 On such encroachment and Russian sentiment towards it, see Joshua R. Itzkowitz Shifrinson, 'Deal or no deal? The end of the Cold War and the US offer to limit NATO expansion', *International Security*, 40:4 (2016), 7–44.

23 David Blagden, 'Global multipolarity, European security and implications for UK grand strategy: back to the future, once again', *International Affairs*, 91:2 (2015), 333–50, at 334–7.

24 The Chinese economy is already bigger vis-à-vis its US counterpart than the Soviet Union's ever was. Of course, China also faces much more acute demands on its wealth than the US, given its relative development disadvantage – but that was also true of the USSR, which nonetheless managed to function as a systemic 'pole', not least because it avoided an ambitious US-style grand strategy of global power projection (as China has also done thus far).

25 Michael Beckley, *Unrivaled: Why America Will Remain the World's Sole Superpower* (Ithaca, NY: Cornell University Press, 2018).

26 Joshua R. Itzkowitz Shifrinson and Michael Beckley, 'Debating China's rise and US decline', *International Security*, 37:3 (2013), 172–81, at 172–7; Blagden, 'Global multipolarity'.

27 HM Government, *Securing Britain in an Age of Uncertainty*, p. 10, emphasis added.

28 HM Government, *National Security Strategy and Strategic Defence and Security Review: A Secure and Prosperous United Kingdom* (Norwich: HM Stationery Office, 2015), p. 11, https://assets.publishing.service.gov.uk/government/uploads/system/uploads/attachment_data/file/478933/52309_Cm_9161_NSS_SD_Review_web_only.pdf (accessed 20 August 2019). Note that, unlike its 2010 predecessor, the 2015 SDSR was published as a single combined document with that year's National Security Strategy.

29 HM Government, *Securing Britain in an Age of Uncertainty*, p. 61.

30 HM Government, *National Security Strategy and Strategic Defence and Security Review*, p. 18.

31 David Blagden, 'The flawed promise of national security risk assessment: nine lessons from the British approach', *Intelligence and National Security*, 33:5 (2018), 716–36, at 726–7.

32 China is mentioned only as an esteemed economic partner, for example, despite the document also featuring a subsection on foreign intelligence agencies' cyber efforts to penetrate UK government/infrastructure and steal commercial secrets – both known Chinese tactics. HM Government, *National Security Strategy and Strategic Defence and Security Review*, pp. 18–19. On UK defence/intelligence fears over Chinese leverage, particularly in cyber infrastructure, see for example: BBC, 'Huawei: "Deep concerns" over firm's role in UK 5G upgrade', 27 December 2018, www.bbc.co.uk/news/uk-46690627 (accessed 20 August 2019).

33 HM Government, *Overview: Modernising Defence Programme* (London: UK Ministry of Defence, 2018), p. 1, emphasis added, https://assets.publishing.service.gov.uk/government/uploads/system/uploads/attachment_data/file/686625/Modernising_Defence_Programme_consultation_-_overview_of_MDP.pdf (accessed 20 August 2019).

34 HM Government, *Mobilising, Modernising and Transforming Defence: A Report on the Modernising Defence Programme* (London: UK Ministry of Defence, 2018), p. 11, https://assets.publishing.service.gov.uk/government/uploads/system/uploads/attachment_data/file/765879/ModernisingDefenceProgramme_report_2018_FINAL.pdf (accessed 20 August 2019).

35 *Ibid.*, p. 17.

36 HM Government, *National Security Capability Review* (London: UK Cabinet Office, 2018), p. 6, https://assets.publishing.service.gov.uk/government/uploads/system/uploads/attachment_data/file/705347/6.4391_CO_National-Security-Review_web.pdf (accessed 20 August 2019).

37 For one such exemplar from the pre-Crimea era, see HM Government, *Global Strategic Trends – Out to 2040*, 4th edn (London: UK Ministry of Defence, 2010), https://assets.publishing.service.gov.uk/government/uploads/system/uploads/attachment_data/file/654717/GST4_v9_Feb10_archived.pdf (accessed 20 August 2019). For similar US National Intelligence Council analysis from around the same time, see US Government, *Global Trends 2025: A Transformed World* (Washington, DC: US National Intelligence Council, 2008), www.dni.gov/files/documents/Global%20Trends_2025%20Report.pdf (accessed 20 August 2019).

38 HM Government, *Global Strategic Trends: The Future Starts Today*, 6th edn (London: UK Ministry of Defence, 2018), pp. 24–5, https://assets.publishing.service.gov.uk/government/uploads/system/uploads/attachment_data/file/771309/Global_Strategic_Trends_-_The_Future_Starts_Today.pdf (accessed 20 August 2019).

39 Joint Committee on the National Security Strategy, *National Security Capability Review: A Changing Security Environment: First Report of Session 2017–19* (London: UK Parliament, 2018), pp. 13, 18, https://publications.parliament.uk/pa/jt201719/jtselect/jtnatsec/756/756.pdf (accessed 20 August 2019).

40 House of Commons Defence Committee, *Beyond 2 Per Cent: A Preliminary Report on the Modernising Defence Programme: Seventh Report of Session 2017–19* (London: UK Parliament, 2018), pp. 27, 37, 44, https://publications.parliament.uk/pa/cm201719/cmselect/cmdfence/818/818.pdf (accessed 20 August 2019).

41 HM Government, *Integrated Review: Call for Evidence* (London: UK Ministry of Defence, 2020), p. 1, https://assets.publishing.service.gov.uk/government/uploads/system/uploads/attachment_data/file/909008/Integrated_Review_call_for_evidence.pdf (accessed 29 September 2020).

42 House of Commons Defence Committee, *In Search of Strategy – The 2020 Integrated Review: First Report of Session 2019–21* (London: UK Parliament, 2020), pp. 19, 22, 28, 40, https://committees.parliament.uk/publications/2265/documents/21808/default/ (accessed 29 September 2020).

43 HM Government, *Overview*, p. 1.

44 Or some variant of this core intuition. See Kenneth N. Waltz, *Theory of International Politics* (New York: Random House, 1979), pp. 129–31; John J. Mearsheimer, *The Tragedy of Great Power Politics* (New York: Norton, 2001), p. 5; Monteiro, *Theory of Unipolar Politics*, pp. 40–7.

45 HM Government, *Global Strategic Trends: The Future Starts Today*, p. 21.

46 This tendency pervades contemporary UK security policy, owing to the post-2010 design of the National Security Risk Assessment from which all other policy plans purportedly follow. Blagden, 'The flawed promise'.

47 Benjamin Zala, 'Polarity analysis and collective perceptions of power: the need for a new approach', *Journal of Global Security Studies*, 2:1 (2017), 2–17.

48 David M. McCourt, *Britain and World Power since 1945: Constructing a Nation's Role in International Politics* (Ann Arbor, MI: University of Michigan Press, 2014).

49 Waltz, *Theory of International Politics*, p. 162; Monteiro, *Theory of Unipolar Politics*, p. 3.

50 Hedley Bull, *The Anarchical Society: A Study of Order in International Relations* (New York: Columbia University Press, 1977), pp. 13–19.

51 To be sure, voters are often less enthusiastic about military intervention than policy elites. Nonetheless, as recently as 2013 – i.e. even after the government's failed attempt to win parliamentary approval for military intervention in Syria on the back of post-Iraq/Afghanistan public war-weariness – 75 per cent of Britons thought the UK should play a major role in the world to promote its economic interests, while 65 per cent thought the same to promote national

security interests. YouGov, 'YouGov Survey Results', 23–4 April 2013, pp. 7–8, http://cdn.yougov.com/cumulus_uploads/document/dq60jrxc27/YG-Archive-Public-Administration-Select-Committee-results-240413-Trident-nuclear-weapons.pdf#page=7 (accessed 20 August 2019).

52 David M. McCourt, 'Has Britain found its role?', *Survival*, 56:2 (2014), 159–78, at 160.

53 David Blagden, 'Two visions of greatness: roleplay and *realpolitik* in UK strategic posture', *Foreign Policy Analysis*, 15:4 (2019), 470–91, at 476–84.

54 HM Government, *National Security Strategy and Strategic Defence and Security Review*, p. 51.

55 For description and enthusiastic advocacy of this behaviour, see John Hemmings and James Rogers, *The South China Sea: Why it Matters to 'Global Britain'* (London: Henry Jackson Society, 2019), https://henryjacksonsociety.org/wp-content/uploads/2019/01/HJS-South-China-Sea-Report-web-1.pdf (accessed 20 August 2019). Such risk does not mean that it is necessarily the wrong choice, of course, but neither should policymakers or analysts be deluded that such choices are costless.

56 Zala, 'Polarity analysis and collective perceptions of power', pp. 12–14.

57 Patrick Porter, 'Why Britain doesn't do grand strategy', *RUSI Journal*, 155:4 (2010), 6–12, at 9.

58 Of course, this supposedly 'rules-based liberal order' was neither liberal (hegemonic ordering is necessarily coercive work) nor rules-based (insofar as powerful states gain advantage from calling their preferences 'rules' but also break them, with little sanction, when their own interests require it). Patrick Porter, *The False Promise of Liberal Order: Nostalgia, Delusion, and the Rise of Trump* (Cambridge: Polity Press, 2020).

59 House of Commons Defence Committee, *Beyond 2 Per Cent*.

60 Blagden, 'Two visions of greatness', pp. 479–84.

61 Robert Saunders, 'Clap your hands if you believe in Brexit', *Foreign Policy*, 19 December 2018, https://foreignpolicy.com/2018/12/19/clap-your-hands-if-you-believe-in-brexit/ (accessed 20 August 2019).

62 Press Association, 'UK will remain tier-one military power, says defence secretary', *Guardian*, 7 August 2018.

63 Blagden, 'Global multipolarity', 338–9.

64 For Russia's 2018 nominal GDP in comparative perspective, see International Monetary Fund, *World Economic Outlook (October 2018)* (Washington, DC: International Monetary Fund, 2019), www.imf.org/external/datamapper/NGDPD@WEO/OEMDC/ADVEC/WEOWORLD?year=2019 (accessed 20 August 2019). That said, it is worth noting that Russian GDP on a purchasing power parity basis is much larger (close to that of Germany).

65 These include demographic decline, productivity-impeding corruption, creativity-stifling authoritarianism, Western sanctions, lack of trust from potential foreign investors, volatile global hydrocarbon demand, and the 'crowding out' of productive investment by the resource-extractive sector. Blagden, 'Global multipolarity', p. 338.

66 Such tactics are often now dubbed part of 'hybrid warfare' or a 'greyzone strategy', although such terms are banal – every strategic action in history has been 'hybrid' in some such way, just as all intercommunal politics since time immemorial has seen subversive and/or coercive actions that aim to achieve political aims without the costs of open war-initiation.
67 Blagden, 'Global multipolarity', pp. 339–41.
68 Patrick Porter, 'Why America's grand strategy has not changed: power, habit, and the foreign policy establishment', *International Security*, 42:4 (2018), 9–46.
69 This is not to say that trade (say) in East Asia is only a 'peripheral' UK interest; clearly it is one of the most economically dynamic regions of the world, and Britain will want to pursue commercial opportunities there. Nonetheless, economic engagement does not require a military presence; Germany has massive trade with East Asian states not because it sends warships to their region, but because it makes goods that they wish to buy. And East Asia *is* peripheral to UK security interests – it is geographically distant from Britain, and the UK is not a salient concern for actors in the region except insofar as it militarily positions itself in their vicinity, meaning that British security dilemmas with Asian powers are wholly avoidable.
70 Hemmings and Rogers, *The South China Sea*.
71 Avery Goldstein, 'First things first: the pressing danger of crisis instability in US–China relations', *International Security*, 37:4 (2013), 49–89.
72 Specifically, when assessing the continued viability of significant Asian military commitments – leading to what came to be known as the 'East of Suez' withdrawal – UK officials fretted that 'penny-packet' forces were already ineffective yet were also becoming dangerous liabilities. Edward Hampshire, *From East of Suez to the Eastern Atlantic: British Naval Policy 1964–70* (London: Routledge, 2013), p. 145.
73 Specifically, the Gulf *does* affect UK interests, but they are either manageable from a remove or only created by the pre-existing Western presence. David Blagden and Patrick Porter, 'Desert shield of the republic? A realist case for abandoning the Middle East', *Security Studies*, 30:1 (2021), 5–48. Britain's basing footprint in the region has also grown in the past half-decade – particularly through two new long-term naval bases in Bahrain and Oman – under the 'Global Britain' impetus (as well as Washington's urgings to facilitate the US 'pivot' to balancing China). Louisa Brooke-Holland, *UK Forces in the Middle East Region*, Briefing Paper 08794 (London: House of Commons Library, 2020), http://researchbriefings.files.parliament.uk/documents/CBP-8794/CBP-8794.pdf (accessed 29 September 2020).
74 Blagden, 'Global multipolarity', p. 341.
75 *Ibid.*, pp. 341–2.
76 Matthew Bodner, 'Russia bids farewell to INF Treaty with fresh nuclear development plans', *Defense News*, 6 February 2019, www.defensenews.com/smr/nuclear-arsenal/2019/02/06/russia-bids-farewell-to-inf-treaty-with-fresh-nuclear-development-plans/ (accessed 20 August 2019).
77 Blagden, 'Global multipolarity', p. 342.

78 Blagden, 'Two visions of greatness'.
79 *Ibid.*
80 Sam Jones, 'Britain's "withered" forces not fit to repel all-out attack', *Financial Times*, 16 September 2016.
81 David Jordan, *Britain's Air Defences: Inventing the Future?* (London: King's College London, Freeman Air and Space Institute, 2020), p. 8, www.kcl.ac.uk/security-studies/assets/david-jordan-air-defence.pdf (accessed 1 March 2021).
82 Blagden, 'Strategic thinking for the age of austerity'.
83 Marco Giannangeli, 'British culture makes us the world's only global power', *Express*, 8 November 2015, www.express.co.uk/news/uk/617807/British-culture-world-only-global-power (accessed 20 August 2019).
84 Monteiro, *Theory of Unipolar Politics*, pp. 43–5; Blagden, 'Two visions of greatness'.
85 Patrick Porter, *The Global Village Myth: Distance, War, and the Limits of Power* (Washington, DC: Georgetown University Press, 2015).
86 Kenneth E. Boulding, *Conflict and Defense: A General Theory* (New York: Harper, 1962), pp. 230–1, 245–7.
87 On the strategic limitations born of not being one's own security provider, see Porter, 'Why Britain doesn't do grand strategy', p. 9. On domestic-political constraints on adequate power-balancing, see Randall L. Schweller, *Unanswered Threats: Political Constraints on the Balance of Power* (Princeton, NJ: Princeton University Press, 2008).
88 On such potential balance-of-power implications of Britain's efforts to leave the European Union (Brexit), see David Blagden, 'Britain and the world after Brexit', *International Politics*, 54:1 (2017), 1–25, at 9–14.

Conclusion: Debating the distribution of power and status in the early twenty-first century

Benjamin Zala

'Contestability' has become a buzzword in government departments and businesses across the world. Phrases such as 'nothing is off the table' and 'everything is up for debate' bounce around boardrooms as analysts and advisors look to question the conventional wisdoms of their given fields. Yet the level and nature of the contestability that defines the debates over multipolarity found in the previous chapters of this volume raise difficult questions for the existing International Relations (IR) literature on the subject. IR scholars are quite comfortable debating the theoretical effects of changes in the polarity of the international system. Yet the theoretical polarity analysis literature provides only limited guidance on debates in policy circles over the actual distribution of power itself. It is one thing for analysts to disagree over the implications of a return to multipolarity; it is something else to disagree about whether the system is in fact returning to a multipolar configuration or not.

The previous chapters clearly demonstrate that the certitude that characterises much political and economic analysis about the new multipolar 'reality' is misplaced.[1] Whether the global order is already, is slowly becoming, or is in fact not at all multipolar, is clearly contestable in different national contexts. Not only the existence or otherwise of a multipolar order, but also the exact make-up of that particular distribution of power – exactly which states should be said to constitute the poles of power – is still subject to debate. While few would argue seriously about China's place on the list of plausible contenders for great power status, if not currently then at least in the foreseeable future, the contributions by both Luis Schenoni and Ian Hall raise serious questions about the status of Brazil and India respectively in this regard. Similarly, despite the language of 'peer competitors' in the context of a global power transition that linger in British strategic documents, David Blagden's blunt assessment that 'Britain is not a pole and will not be again' in Chapter 7 paints a very different picture of London's role in the international system. Even the chapter by Nicholas Khoo and Zhang Qingmin highlights the degree to which the Chinese advocacy of 'multipolarisation' tells us more about Beijing's aspirations for a new distribution of power than it does about its genuine assessment of the shape of the international system. The way that the structural condition of polarity actually operates at the level of national discourse appears to be fragile, malleable, open to and affected by genuine debate. Opening up polarity analysis in order to be able to account for such contestability appears to be the only way forward.

Debating the multipolar narrative

Analysts should be attuned to the degree to which polarity is subject to debate given how much the narrative of a shift to a multipolar order is used and abused for different ends. A central theme that emerges from the previous chapters is that, while the vast majority of the scholarly literature treats polarity as a purely structural phenomenon that 'shapes and shoves' agents, plenty of national decision-makers appear convinced that a transition to a post-unipolar world can be put to various political ends.

If we are to conceive of polarity simply as a particular distribution of capabilities, there is little room left to consider the purposes for which it might be used in political discourse. It is easy to see why many scholars have resisted such an inductive approach to polarity analysis. The benefit of treating polarity as an objectively measurable fact, and proceeding from that ontological position to investigate its 'system effects', is that it provides an easy basis for prediction. Kenneth Waltz made this case with characteristic clarity: '[h]ow are capabilities distributed? What are the likely results of a given distribution? These are distinct questions. The difficulty of counting poles is rooted in the failure to observe the distinction.'[2] But maintaining a sharp distinction between polarity as capabilities and the systems effects of a shift from one form to another in this way obscures the importance of the politics of polarity debates in national contexts.

Much of the literature that focuses solely on debating the effects of shifts in the distribution of capabilities also misses the extent to which, when policymakers use the concept of polarity, they are, more often than not, describing the distribution of status not capabilities. This raises the importance of the difference between the way the concept of polarity is used by practitioners (policymakers and their advisors, media commentators, and so on) and scholars.[3] For the former, polarity can be thought of as an ordering concept used to clarify the broad contours of the inter-state order. For the latter, polarity has traditionally been treated as a very specific structural phenomenon: the influence of the distribution of material capabilities possessed by states at any one time. This means that, ultimately, if scholars are interested in studying the effects of polarity (i.e. its actual influence on the decisions made by state leaders), then dealing with the issue of how power is perceived by 'real-world' practitioners is inescapable. As discussed below, if we are to think of debates about polarity as debates over the current and future distribution of status, then an engagement between what might be thought of as the 'status turn' in IR and the polarity analysis literature may offer a useful way forward.

Lessons for scholarship

A key question raised by examining contemporary debates over the polarity of the global order is whether, if perceptions appear to diverge between different actors, we can be sure that they perceive power in the same way. More pointedly, we might ask: when decision-makers and analysts look at the global order and try to characterise its polarity, do they assess the distribution of power (however defined) or instead the distribution of status? Even if there is uniformity across these different observers in terms of assessing the distribution of power alone, this still leaves open the question of how power is defined. Can the material and non-material elements of power be neatly separated and weighed? Are purely materialist conceptions of power arrived at in identical ways by different actors? Christian Reus-Smit has argued against the widely held 'fallacy that material facts have fixed meanings, amenable to singular interpretation' so that 'an actor's material preponderance – its demonstrably greater military, economic, or technological capacity – can be interpreted in only one way' by all states.[4]

For every scholarly argument in favour of measuring any one set of resources over another (and often measuring such resources in one particular way over another),[5] there are decision-makers and those who influence them making decisions based on their own understandings of power in a given historical moment. Historical contingency is impossible to escape when it comes to analysing the role of power of any sort in IR. In a previous age, the possession of overseas colonies was a clear indicator of power.[6] Such territories were gained through the use of navigational prowess and military force, and were later maintained by administrative, policing, and counter-insurgency capabilities. The ability to dispossess and subordinate a native population was an indicator of an empire's ability and will to use force against foreign populations with deadly effect. The signalling effect in terms of potential offensive force projection against that empire's competitors was obvious. Not only that, but the colony itself tended to boost the resources

– both natural and human – on which this empire could draw for the further projection of power and influence. But the transnational movement towards decolonisation which radically altered the international legitimacy and domestic worth of holding on to colonies altered some of the rules of the game of great power politics by phasing out this particular indicator. Yet it did so without ending the game itself. This was a significant change in one of the criteria used by both great and non-great powers alike for judging whether a state should be conferred with great power status. Yet for decades after the end of the major waves of decolonisation and self-determination of the twentieth century, the distinction between great and non-great powers remains as one of the primary institutions of international society.

Even major changes within one form of material capabilities can take place over time, changing the criteria used for assessing relative power, without doing away with the great and non-great power distinction (and thereby leaving polarity as a structural phenomenon intact). The invention of nuclear weaponry in 1945, by virtue of the sheer destructiveness of a single bomb or missile, completely changed not only the nature of military power but the whole likelihood of a major power war.[7] The capabilities that a state might be expected to possess in order to claim and be conferred with pole status from this time onwards had changed. The prospect of major power war – the outcome of which has been regularly identified in the IR literature as another key indicator of the polarity of the system – took on an entirely new meaning. In the nuclear age, a full-scale military conflict between the great powers raises the prospect not of victory of one side over the other, but the question of humanity's ability to exist under what scientists refer to as a 'nuclear winter' and peace campaigners describe as a 'nuclear holocaust'. Yet, as with the demise of overseas colonies, the invention of nuclear weapons changed the way in which decision-makers and scholars alike measured relative power capabilities without doing away with the notion of there being poles of power. As James Johnson's chapter in this volume highlights, new disruptive technologies are yet again challenging perceptions of what it means to be a great power today, with particular implications for polarity analysis.

The reason that the status of great/superpower has survived changes in the significance attached to certain material capabilities, is that the category itself has never been reducible to quantifiable attributes and stockpiles. Despite claims that power 'represents nothing more than specific assets or material resources that are available to a state',[8] the reality is more complex. The assertion that identifying a great power requires one to simply 'examine the distribution of capabilities and identify the states whose shares of overall resources obviously place them into their own class'[9] simply does not match up to the historical record.[10] Instead, as Hedley Bull pointed out, 'To say that a state is a great power is to say not merely that it is a member of the club of powers that are in the front rank in terms of military strength, but also that it regards itself, and is regarded by other members of the society of states, as having special rights and duties.'[11]

Yet even a more socially contingent approach to polarity that builds on the status turn in the IR literature still faces the problem raised in the chapters by Schenoni, Hall, Blagden, and Envall in this volume of the distinction between great and regional powers. Polarity analysis has traditionally struggled to clearly delineate the two categories, leading to at least some of the confusion over the different rosters of great powers at any one historical moment.

Some scholarship has attempted to provide a degree of clarity and consistency to this distinction. Barry Buzan and Ole Wæver have pointed to a relational and outcomes-focused criterion: 'what distinguishes great powers from merely regional ones is that they are responded to by others on the basis of system level calculations about the present and near-future distribution of power'.[12] Regional powers, by contrast, really only register in such calculations within their own geographic neighbourhood. Nuno Monteiro, opting for a simpler, capabilities-based definition, categorises regional powers as those states 'lacking the power-projection capabilities necessary to condition the outcomes of politico-military operations beyond their own region' while still being able to inflict heavy costs on any would-be attacker.[13] Regional powers may at certain times be dragged into superpower (in bipolar or unipolar systems) or great power (in multipolar systems) rivalry. Matters of what was often referred to during the Cold War as the 'central balance' can often lift regional powers into the limelight of great power crisis management and diplomacy (the 1970s era of US–Soviet–Chinese 'triangular diplomacy' is a good example).[14] Yet as Buzan and Wæver point out, in such circumstances regional powers are viewed by the great powers as 'the spoils in a wider competition' rather than as poles at the level of what they designate as 'global polarity'.[15]

In practice of course, the distinction is beset by ambiguity and imprecision. This means that for all the scholarly definitions that might be on offer, as with the concept of polarity itself, the use of the regional power label as an ordering concept by practitioners makes the everyday politics of the regional–great power distinction an inherently messy affair. Detlef Nolte has pointed out that this particular social status is particularly open to competing understandings given that the term itself is comprised of two essentially contested concepts: 'region' and 'power'. It is perhaps therefore not surprising that 'if you add up two ambiguous or multifaceted concepts, the semantic problems will not balance each other; instead, they will accumulate'.[16] Equally, understandings of the relationship between region and power can change over time. The polarity analysis literature that attempts to provide uniform and replicable distinctions between those states whose influence remains at the regional level and those whose regional influence is a launchpad for global-level influence often loses analytic purchase when applied to specific empirical examples. A great power's region is not always and only the building blocks of its global power projection. Regions can also be sites of local contestation over power and legitimacy, areas of economic turmoil that are hard to escape (the eurozone crisis from 2009 helped to raise questions about British, French, German, and even the European Union's (EU's) potential for great power status), and flashpoints of insecurity – or what Andrew Hurrell describes as 'snares that reduce rather than increase the projection of power'.[17]

The scholarly distinction between (global) great powers and regional powers is made even more problematic by the increasing body of work that predicts a shift towards what is referred to as a more 'regionalised' order as part of the development of multipolarity.[18] These scholarly arguments are also picked up by, and adapted in, policy-focused discourse including debates about 'multiregionalism' as Elena Chebankova's chapter on Russia highlights. These predictions rest on the assumption that the poles of power (which under this scenario are simply regional powers in a world without genuinely great powers able to exercise power and influence at a global level) are able to retreat into their own spheres of influence without meddling in each other's regions in a serious way. The artificiality of the distinction between what used to be referred to as the 'central balance' and a regional balance of power is not new. Bull, for example, drew attention to the fact that 'It was a theme of Hitler's, as of many Germans before him, that the central issue in international politics was the balance of power not in Europe, but in the world as a whole …'.[19] For Bull, it was the challenge that Germany posed to the British Empire, the United States, and the Soviet Union at the global level, not simply in Europe, that made conflict inevitable.

In a highly globalised world, it will be difficult for the great powers not to compete outside of their immediate region. If, for example, the United States was not able to keep out of China's East Asia or Brazil's Latin America, China from India's South Asia or South Africa's Sub-Saharan Africa, and Russia from the EU's European continent, then in fact we will not be in anything like a regionalised order. Instead the contours of great power politics would look much more like the kind of competitive multipolarity that we have seen in the past.

Perhaps the most important indicator of which states are and which states are not conferred with the status of 'great power' is found in the practice of great power management.[20] The unique role played by a small number of states, and accepted as a normal part of international life by the vast majority of actors in world politics, in attempting to settle crises and manage tensions is an important aspect of modern diplomacy. The level at which this practice is undertaken indicates whether a state is considered a regional or a global power. Engaging in the practice of great power management in a regional crisis in which that power is geographically located is not the same thing as being one of the select few looked to in terms of intervening in what is considered a 'global crisis'. For example, China and Japan's role in the Six Party Talks process on the North Korean nuclear issue is one thing; Russia and the United States meeting to try and find a solution to the Syrian war and refugee crisis is quite another.

The ability to shape a regional order is not the same as the ability to influence the international system as a whole, and this distinction applies to both global and regional powers. As Coral Bell warned, 'it is essential to distinguish between the management role of the dominant powers in crises of the central balance, and their power to intervene in or manipulate crises of local balances (as for instance Soviet manipulation of the early stages of the 1967 Middle East crisis)'.[21] But even if we are witnessing a rise in regional power-balancing and even regional great power management, this does not mean that system-level variables and the requirements (and established practice) of great power management disappear in tandem. Nor does it mean that a regional power's policies within its own region will necessarily be associated with practices of great power management such as crisis management, mutual restraint, and leadership on transnational issues. Sandra Destradi has pointed out, for example, that regional powers can pursue distinct imperial, hegemonic, or leadership strategies that result in very different outcomes for regional order.[22]

Lessons for policymaking

The extremely challenging lesson that this volume poses for policymakers is that government net assessments and strategic analysis of the global distribution of power must be able to anticipate and deal with ambiguity. Definitive assessments that produce clear rosters of the poles of power that can be expected to influence global politics in the medium to long term, while attractive, are ultimately of limited utility. Instead, the task for policymakers is to be clear about how they perceive the distribution of power and status while simultaneously planning for the likelihood that others will not necessarily share their judgement and will act accordingly. Therefore, the structural pressures exerted by those perceptions of polarity – the way polarity will 'shape and shove' the decisions that are made about foreign policy – will depend on the relative influence of the kinds of narratives about multipolarity discussed in the previous chapters. This does not mean that structural power is therefore 'all subjective' and that policymakers are helpless in the face of the ever changing and unreliable perceptions of others. Instead, what the analysis here suggests is that abandoning the objective of classifying the polarity of the international system on the basis of one's own preferred metrics in favour of being attuned to collective perceptions and dominant narratives is a more useful way forward.

One area where the research presented in this volume may suggest that serious attention should be focused in the years to come is the issue of alliance politics under multipolar conditions. If perceptions of multipolarity – based on the kinds of narratives discussed in the different national contexts covered in the contributions to this volume as well as other examples – persist over time, the potential for fluidity in the alliances choices of the major powers is likely to return to world politics. Much of the older literature on the balance of power in the classical realist tradition was based on assumptions about multipolar conditions being present. Writers such as Hans Morgenthau[23] and Henry Kissinger[24] pointed to the centrality of shifting alliances in the operation of the balance of power. Whether one thinks of multi-partner, anti-hegemonial alliances like those formed to face down Napoleonic France or Nazi Germany, or bilateral alliances such as the Dual Alliance of 1879 between Germany and Austria-Hungary, the potential for a major power to switch sides at any one time was fundamental to the actual operation of the balance of power. This includes examples such as: whether the Franco-Russian alliance could seriously threaten German power in the late nineteenth century; the role of the Anglo-Japanese alliance in encouraging Russia's attempts to ally with both France and Germany in the 1900s; and of course the question of whether the Soviet Union would join the Axis or Allied powers in the late 1930s.

Not only are the decisions to join or leave an alliance more important in a (perceived) multipolar world, but such shifts themselves are more likely to happen. In recent memory, alliances have been very durable with few choosing to leave an existing relationship (perhaps unsurprising given that almost all alliances have been with the world's only superpower). But as Manus Midlarsky pointed out, the growth or decline in power of junior partners has little effect on the alliance if its partner is disproportionately more powerful. Yet, 'In an alliance among equals, on the other hand, small changes in power relations could seriously disturb the coalition framework.'[25]

Not only should we expect collective perceptions of multipolarity to create greater alliance fluidity, we should also expect the return of the kind of alliances that we have not seen for many decades: alliances between the poles of power themselves. During the Cold War, alliances were important at critical junctures (the creation of NATO and the Warsaw Pact, the Berlin and Cuban crises, the Soviet-Sino split, and so on),[26] but in general became so fixed as to be less relevant in changing the general trajectory of major power relationships. Major power alliances (i.e. alliances between the poles of power themselves) were completely absent from world politics. The post-Cold War era continued this trend as only the United States maintained serious alliances as the singular pole in a unipolar order. Now with the perception of a return to a multipolar order, diplomatic and military partnerships between the poles themselves become a possibility once more.

The two most likely possibilities, and the two that have attracted the most attention so far, are a Sino-Russian alliance[27] and a US–Indian alliance.[28] Both would face serious hurdles, but neither can be discounted. Nor should policy-focused analysis only concentrate on these two possibilities. Perceptions of multipolarity – particularly when they diverge across different actors – are likely to create a much more varied and dynamic environment for alliance choices in the decades to come. Also, alliances need not be thought of in traditional terms. Perceptions and narratives of a multipolar future may yet blur the already indistinct lines between alliances, alignments, and 'strategic partnerships'.[29] In addition, a return to older concepts, hardly discussed in policy circles for some time, such as non-aggression pacts, is likely to accompany this broadening of thinking and debate on the politics of alliances.[30]

Even in situations where historical animosities and recent memories of conflict would seem to preclude any sort of alliance between two states, history shows that multipolar systems open up a much wider range of cost–benefit calculations for decision-makers navigating a more complex environment. For example, in the two centuries leading up to 1878, Russia and Turkey fought each other no less than ten times (with the longest stretch of peace lasting for less than thirty years). Yet Napoleon's invasion of Egypt in 1798 produced a brief alliance, described by Geoffrey Blainey as a 'miracle of miracles', in which 'the sultan permitted a Russian naval squadron to leave the Black Sea and sail the narrow torrent past Constantinople, sail through the guarded Dardanelles, and so enter the Mediterranean'.[31] Their alliance, enshrined in a treaty signed at the end of that year, was reaffirmed (and even included the promise of mutual armed assistance in the event of an attack) in 1805, but less than a year later, the alliance was broken and the two were once more at war with each other.

While alliances can be central to a state's long-term survival, they can also be useful diplomatic tools for other means. As states rise up the global hierarchy they look to project power in different ways. What is referred to as 'status signalling' can take a variety of forms including the signing of formal alliances with other states that are widely recognised as major powers.

For example, the signing of the 1902 Anglo-Japanese Treaty of Alliance was important for Japan's strategy of great power projection, particularly as it faced the barrier of being geographically and historically outside the great power 'club' of continental Europe.[32] Such a strategy is also available to declining as well as rising powers. The diplomatic history of the late nineteenth century in Europe is littered with similar examples of states using alliances to project status, but in contrast with Japan, the likes of the Austro-Hungarian, Prussian, and Ottoman empires used alliances to make up for a lack of material prowess instead. Looking towards a post-unipolar order today, Barry Posen has argued that 'states will look for ways to "measure power" without war. The diplomacy of making and breaking coalitions, and counting allies, will present itself as an attractive, if complex alternative.'[33] In an age in which the narrative of multipolarity is outrunning the material realities of the distribution of economic and military capabilities in the international system, the link between major power alliances and status seeking is likely to be renewed once more.

The difficulty is that everything that we have learned from the practice of alliance relationships over the last seventy years comes from a context in which there were so few major powers that alliances between them (as opposed to between them and lesser powers) were non-existent (under bipolarity) or impossible (under unipolarity). So if we raise the prospect of a return to major power alliances, then we have to look at least seven decades back (and before the advent of nuclear weapons) to be able to apply the lessons of history. Yet the political, economic, and security contexts in which world politics plays out have obviously changed over that time. Mark Beeson has argued that '[i]f alliance theory – or practice, for that matter – is to have any continuing relevance, it ought to be able to tell both scholars and policy makers something useful about the world we currently inhabit'.[34] Learning the lessons of the past in order to understand the present and make judgements about the future always presents us with an enormous intellectual challenge. Meeting this challenge will require grappling with the everyday realities of managing alliances, rivalries, and crisis management under conditions of much greater complexity than we have been used to for some time.[35]

Conclusion

The introductory chapter to this volume noted that polarity analysis has had many critics in the IR literature, but few serious rivals. The contributions to this volume confirm the importance of continuing to engage with the concept of polarity in theory, and the use and abuse of the concept in practice, as part of any attempt to make sense of the changes under way in the global order. Collectively, the chapters paint a complex picture of an inter-state order in flux in which perceptions of power and status diverge across different national contexts. Therefore contestability must be something that the polarity analysis literature can both account for and make sense of if it is to connect with the everyday practice of power politics. This requires a broader engagement with the subject than can be achieved through any one theoretical lens. This echoes the arguments made by Stacie Goddard and Daniel Nexon for a pluralist and multifaceted approach to power politics as a whole: 'Treating power politics as an object of analysis subject to multiple theoretical perspectives – and focusing those theoretical perspectives on the causes, processes, conditions of possibility, and mechanisms of collective mobilization – provides a way forward.'[36]

For scholars and policymakers alike, understanding the current politics of the global power transition requires an appreciation of the contingent and contestable nature of perceptions of power. This includes being finely attuned to the kinds of criteria used by actual practitioners to measure power – even if they do not align easily with whichever criteria are favoured by scholars at a particular moment. It also requires being cognisant of changes in the exercise of power at both the regional and global levels over time. The markers of a great power today may not remain relevant tomorrow. Even the practical task of distinguishing between regional and great powers may not be as analytically straightforward as it might seem at first. Yet difficulties notwithstanding, for policymakers charged with responding to an ambiguous power shift, making judgements about relative power and status under conditions of uncertainty is unavoidable. Striking a balance between reflecting critically on the lessons of previous multipolar periods, such as those relating to alliance management discussed above, on the one hand, and avoiding the pitfalls of the analytic rigidity and structural determinism associated with traditional polarity analysis, on the other, will be increasingly important in the years to come.

Multipolarity is variously used as a description of the current distribution of power, of the likely shape of a future global order, or even as a prescription for how power 'should' be distributed in the international system. More often than not, what might seem to be an objective description of a structural condition is better thought of as a 'strategic narrative' about power and order. As one account puts it, strategic narratives are 'about both states and the system itself, both about who we are and what kind of order we want'.[37] To truly understand the power of the different – and sometimes competing – narratives on offer today about a new multipolar order we must interrogate the different national contexts in which they play out. The hope of the editor and contributors to this volume is that the preceding pages will act as an invitation to further work in this vein from different perspectives.

Notes

1 For recent examples that specifically use the language of a 'multipolar reality' in both scholarly and policy-focused contexts, see Robert Muggah and Yves Tiberghien, '5 facts you need to understand the new global order', *World Economic Forum* [website], 30 January 2018, www.weforum.org/agenda/2018/01/five-facts-you-need-to-understand-the-new-global-order/ (accessed 18 February 2020); Michael Rubin, 'There's nothing progressive about a multipolar world', *The National Interest* [website], 5 January 2019, https://nationalinterest.org/feature/there%E2%80%99s-nothing-progressive-about-multipolar-world-40587 (accessed 18 February 2020); Thomas G. Weiss, 'Turkey, global governance, and the UN', in Emel Parlar Dal (ed.), *Middle Powers in Global Governance: The Rise of Turkey* (Basingstoke: Palgrave Macmillan, 2018), p. 103; Luba von Hauff, 'Towards a new quality of cooperation? The EU, China, and Central Asian security in a multipolar age', *Asia Europe Journal*, 17:2 (2019), 195–210, at 208.

2 Kenneth Waltz, *Theory of International Politics* (New York: Random House, 1979), pp. 130–1. For further elaboration of this line of argument, see Nuno P. Monteiro, *Theory of Unipolar Politics* (New York: Cambridge University Press, 2014), pp. 42–7.

3 Benjamin Zala, 'Polarity analysis and collective perceptions of power: the need for a new approach', *Journal of Global Security Studies*, 2:1 (2017), 2–17.

4 Christian Reus Smit, 'Power, legitimacy, and order', *Chinese Journal of International Politics*, 7:3 (2014), 341–59, at 348.

5 Michael Beckley, 'The power of nations: measuring what matters', *International Security*, 43:2 (2018), 7–44.

6 See Barry Buzan and George Lawson, *The Global Transformation: History, Modernity and the Making of International Relations* (Cambridge: Cambridge University Press, 2015), pp. 240–70; Ellen J. Ravndal, 'Colonies, semi-sovereigns, and great powers: IGO membership debates and the transition of the international system', *Review of International Studies*, 46:2 (2020), 278–98.

7 Robert Jervis, *The Meaning of the Nuclear Revolution: Statecraft and the Prospect of Armageddon* (Ithaca, NY: Cornell University Press, 1989); John H. Herz, *International Politics in the Atomic Age* (New York: Columbia University Press, 1959).

8 John J. Mearsheimer, *The Tragedy of Great Power Politics* (New York: W. W. Norton, 2001), p. 57.

9 G. John Ikenberry, Michael Mastanduno, and William C. Wohlforth, 'Introduction: unipolarity, state behavior, and systemic consequences', in G. John Ikenberry, Michael Mastanduno, and William C. Wohlforth (eds), *International Relations*

Theory and the Consequences of Unipolarity (Cambridge: Cambridge University Press, 2011), pp. 1–32, at p. 6.

10 Martha Finnemore, *The Purpose of Intervention: Changing Beliefs about the Use of Force* (Ithaca, NY: Cornell University Press, 2003), pp. 102–37; Barry Buzan, *The United States and the Great Powers: World Politics in the Twenty-First Century* (Cambridge: Polity, 2004), pp. 58–73; Zala, 'Polarity analysis'.

11 Hedley Bull, 'The great irresponsibles? The United States, the Soviet Union, and world order', *International Journal*, 35:3 (1980), 437–47, at 437. Such an approach is echoed by Jack Levy who includes the criterion of 'treatment as a relative equal by other Great Powers, in terms of protocol, alliances, and so on' in measurement of great power status. Jack S. Levy, 'Alliance formation and war behavior: an analysis of the great powers, 1495–1975', *Journal of Conflict Resolution*, 25:4 (1981), 581–613, at 585.

12 Barry Buzan and Ole Wæver, *Regions and Powers: The Structure of International Security* (Cambridge: Cambridge University Press, 2003), p. 35.

13 Monteiro, *Theory of Unipolar Politics*, p. 46.

14 On the 'triangular diplomacy' of this period, with specific reference to its effect on the perceived bipolar structure of the time, see Carsten Holbraad, *Superpowers and International Conflict* (Basingstoke: Macmillan, 1979), pp. 118–20; Lowell Dittmer, 'The strategic triangle: an elementary game-theoretical analysis', *World Politics*, 33:4 (1981), 485–515.

15 Buzan and Wæver, *Regions and Powers*, p. 37.

16 Detlef Nolte, 'How to compare regional powers: analytical concepts and research topics', *Review of International* Studies, 36:4 (2010), 881–901, at 883.

17 Andrew Hurrell, *On Global Order: Power, Values, and the Constitution of International Society* (Oxford: Oxford University Press, 2007), p. 251.

18 For overviews, see Amitav Acharya, 'The emerging regional architecture of world politics', *World Politics*, 59:4 (2007), 629–52; Barry Buzan, 'The inaugural Kenneth N. Waltz annual lecture: a world order without superpowers: decentred globalism', *International Relations*, 25:1 (2011), 3–25.

19 Hedley Bull, 'Introduction: the challenge of the Third Reich', in Hedley Bull (ed.), *The Challenge of the Third Reich: The Adam von Trott Memorial Lectures* (Oxford: Clarendon Press, 1986), p. 12.

20 Shunji Cui and Barry Buzan, 'Great power management in international society', *Chinese Journal of International Politics*, 9:2 (2016), 181–210.

21 Coral Bell, *The Conventions of Crisis: A Study in Diplomatic Management* (London: Oxford University Press for the Royal Institute of International Affairs, 1971), p. 8.

22 Sandra Destradi, 'Regional powers and their strategies: empire, hegemony, and leadership', *Review of International Studies*, 36:4 (2010), 903–30.

23 Richard Little goes so far as to say that 'In fact, Morgenthau effectively reduces the balance of power to a game of alliances.' Richard Little, *The Balance of Power in International Relations: Metaphors, Myths and Models* (Cambridge: Cambridge University Press, 2007), p. 105.

24 See Henry Kissinger, *Diplomacy* (New York: Simon & Schuster, 1994), pp. 181–2; Henry Kissinger, *World Order: Reflections on the Character of Nations and the Course of History* (London: Allen Lane, 2014), p. 233.

25 Manus I. Midlarsky, *The Onset of World War*, 2nd edn (Abingdon: Routledge, 2014), p. 159.

26 Although some have questioned just how important alliances were to actually causing some of these crises. See Dale C. Copeland, *The Origins of Major War* (Ithaca, NY: Cornell University Press, 2000), p. 48.

27 See Douglas E. Schoen and Melik Kaylan, *The Russia–China Axis: The New Cold War and America's Crisis of Leadership* (New York: Encounter Books, 2014); Elizabeth Wishnick, 'In search of the "other" in Asia: Russia–China relations revisited', *Pacific Review*, 30:1 (2017), 114–32; Alexander Korolev, 'On the verge of an alliance: contemporary China–Russia military cooperation', *Asian Security*, 15:3 (2019), 233–52. For the (largely) sceptical view, see Bobo Lo, *Axis of Convenience: Moscow, Beijing, and the New Geopolitics* (London: Chatham House and Brookings Institution Press, 2008). It should be noted that Lo's scepticism about a Sino-Russian political-military alliance in 2008 was largely based on both Moscow and Beijing calculating that their respective relations with Washington could continue to improve (and that an alliance would jeopardise this) – a prospect that has significantly eroded in the years since in both cases. See Lo, *Axis of Convenience*, pp. 186–7.

28 See Richard L. Armitage, R. Nicholas Burns, and Richard Fontaine, *Natural Allies: A Blueprint for the Future of US–India Relations* (Washington, DC: Center for a New American Security, 2010); Evan Braden Montgomery, 'Competitive strategies against continental powers: the geopolitics of Sino-Indian-American relations', *Journal of Strategic Studies*, 36:1 (2013), 76–100; Paul Smith and Tara Kartha, 'Strategic partners or an emerging alliance? India and the United States in an era of global power transition', *Comparative Strategy*, 37:5 (2018), 442–59.

29 Thomas S. Wilkins, '"*Alignment*", not "*alliance*" – the shifting paradigm of international security cooperation: toward a conceptual taxonomy of alignment', *Review of International Studies*, 38:1 (2012), 53–76.

30 Yonatan Lupu and Paul Poast, 'Team of former rivals: a multilateral theory of non-aggression pacts', *Journal of Peace Research*, 53:3 (2016), 344–58.

31 Geoffrey Blainey, *The Causes of War*, 3rd edn (South Melbourne: Sun Books, 1988), p. 177.

32 Benjamin Zala, 'Great power management and ambiguous order in nineteenth-century international society', *Review of International Studies*, 43:2 (2017), 367–88, at 378–9.

33 Barry R. Posen, 'From unipolarity to multipolarity: transition in sight?', in G. John Ikenberry, Michael Mastanduno, and William C. Wohlforth (eds), *International Relations Theory and the Consequences of Unipolarity*, p. 340.

34 Mark Beeson, 'Invasion by invitation: the role of alliances in the Asia-Pacific', *Australian Journal of International Affairs*, 69:3 (2015), 305–20, at 309.

35 For a useful discussion of the management of inter-state rivalry beyond a simple dyadic approach, see Brandon Valeriano and Matthew Powers, 'Complex interstate rivals', *Foreign Policy Analysis*, 12:4 (2016), 552–70.

36 Stacie E. Goddard and Daniel H. Nexon, 'The dynamics of global power politics: a framework for analysis', *Journal of Global Security Studies*, 1:1 (2016), 4–18, at 14.

37 Alister Miskimmon, Ben O'Loughlin, and Laura Roselle, *Strategic Narratives: Communication Power and the New World Order* (Abingdon: Routledge, 2013), p. 2.

Index

Note: 'n.' after a page reference indicates the number of a note on that page

Abe, Shinzō 155, 156, 157, 158, 159
Afghanistan 51, 124, 125, 155, 170, 171, 172, 185, 192n.51
Africa 22, 27, 45, 69, 75, 80, 111, 201
alliances 13, 31, 79, 105, 108–9, 110, 112, 124, 150, 170, 176, 177, 203–5
  military 45, 52, 108, 112, 170, 182, 204
  see also under individual country
arms control 49, 96, 183, 184
artificial intelligence (AI) 12, 121–3, 126–43
  commercial drivers 123, 132, 133, 135, 136n.8
  decentralisation/rise of the rest 122, 124, 136n.12
  definition 136n.10
  innovation arms race 123, 126, 132, 134
  military use 122, 127–34
Asia 22, 27, 45, 104, 111, 145, 151, 156, 157
  Central 51, 104, 125
  East 31, 33, 50, 55, 148, 156, 182, 194n.69, 201
  Northeast 10, 154
  South 43, 49, 55, 201
  South East 31, 147
Asia-Pacific 30–1, 54, 145, 147, 148, 149, 150, 151, 157, 159, 160
Association of Southeast Asian Nations (ASEAN) 111, 157
Australia 133, 157

Belt and Road Initiative (BRI) 56–7, 112, 131, 140–1n.72, 156
Biden, Joe 13, 131, 159, 160
Bolsonaro, Jair 66, 69, 87
Brazil 8, 65–93, 196, 201
  economy 7, 67, 68, 69, 70, 78
  foreign policy 10–11, 65–93
  military power 70, 71, 83, 85
  politics 67, 69, 74, 75, 79–81, 86
  seat on UN Security Council 68, 88n.15
  see also BRICS
BRICS (Brazil, Russia, India, China and South Africa) 6, 8, 11, 27, 66, 68, 78, 80, 81, 83, 86, 88n.15, 110
  BRICS+ 110–12
  Chinese finance/influence 75, 79
  Contingent Reserve Arrangement (CRA) 75, 81
  GDP 70
  military expenditure 71
Bush, George H. W. 96, 123, 124, 148, 155

capabilities *see* resources/capabilities
China 6, 8, 9, 21–41, 52, 85, 99, 125, 201, 202

China (cont.)
artificial intelligence (AI)/ technologies 123, 128, 129, 130–2, 134–5, 138n.44
assertiveness 10, 53, 55, 56, 57, 148–9, 151, 173
Belt and Road Initiative (BRI) 56–7, 112, 131, 140–1n.72, 156
bipolarity with the US 12, 30, 33, 86, 123, 124, 186
economy 24, 33, 51, 54, 56, 70, 78, 112, 151, 173, 182, 187, 190n.24
foreign policy 9, 24, 26, 27, 28, 31
India relations 46, 47, 48, 53, 54–5, 56, 57
Japan relations 148–9, 150–2, 156, 158
military power 33, 53, 54, 56, 70–1, 83, 125, 127, 128, 129, 130, 131, 138n.44, 182
nuclear tests 47
Pakistan relations 49
politics 25–6, 31, 131
Russia relations 26, 112, 204
Soviet alignment 149, 150, 151
UK relations 182–3, 188
seat on UN Security Council 47
US relations 24, 26, 121, 126, 134, 147, 150, 151
see also BRICS
Cold War, end 25, 29, 45, 48, 50, 51, 54, 70, 96, 152
coronavirus/COVID 126, 188
corruption 69, 75, 132, 193n.65
Crimea 172, 174, 185
Cuban Missile Crisis 47, 204

da Silva, Luiz Inácio Lula 68, 76, 79, 80
definitions/different perceptions of polarity/multipolarity 4, 5, 11, 12, 94, 175, 197–205
Brazilian academic debate 81–6
Brazilian discourse 66, 67, 72–93
Chinese scholars' views 28–31
Chinese state views 23, 24–8
conceptual stretching 72–5, 83
Japanese scholars' views 146–9, 151, 157–8
Japanese state views 158–9
Russian interpretations 98–113
UK interpretations 174–5, 185–6
US view on multipolarity 123–6
Deng Xiaoping 22, 23, 151–2
developing countries 6, 23, 24, 26, 27, 79, 111

economy/economies
economic alliances 108, 110
economic development 3, 45, 50, 54, 55, 106, 111, 173
economic power 24, 47, 54, 125, 152
free trade agreements 109, 110, 111
GDP international comparisons 69–70, 78, 83
see also under individual country
Eurasian Economic Union (EAEU) 11, 107, 108–10, 111
Euro-Atlantic region 170, 183, 185, 187
Europe 7, 22, 23, 27, 47, 51, 52, 78, 95, 96, 99, 101, 102
Eastern 70, 104
European Union (EU) 6, 7, 8, 27, 106, 109, 110, 201
potential pole of power 6–7, 76, 78, 85

foreign policies 4, 5, 11, 109, 180, 202
see also under individual country
France 32, 47, 85, 133, 142n.89, 203
nuclear tests 47

G7/8 6, 8, 149
G20 8, 80
Germany 22, 23, 32, 85, 193n.64, 194n.69, 201, 203
global financial crisis 8, 155, 171
globalisation 28, 54, 55, 107, 109, 111, 147, 173
Gorbachev, Mikhail 22, 96, 170
Great Britain *see* United Kingdom
Gulf War 3, 51, 152, 153, 158

Hatoyama, Yukio 155–6, 158
humanitarianism 49, 52, 155, 170, 171, 187

India 8, 9, 23, 24, 26–7, 42–64, 70, 80, 99, 111, 133, 157, 183, 196, 201
  China relations 46, 47, 48, 53, 54–5, 56, 57
  economy 43, 46, 48, 50, 54, 69, 78, 187
  foreign policy 9–10, 42–5, 52, 55, 57, 59n.36
  military power 44, 45, 47, 48, 49, 50, 55, 70, 71
  multialignment 54–6
  nonalignment 10, 43, 45–8, 52, 55
  nuclear capacity/tests 49, 50, 51, 53, 55, 154
  politics 44, 47, 48, 50, 53, 69
  polycentrism 48, 52, 54
  Soviet Union treaty 49, 50, 51
  US relations 49, 53, 54, 55, 204
  see also BRICS
Indo-Pacific 10, 56, 57, 157, 158, 159, 160, 183, 187
International Monetary Fund 50, 111
Iran 88n.15, 110, 111, 112
Iraq 50, 68, 124, 125, 152, 155, 171, 183, 185, 189n.8
Islamism, radical 51, 170

Japan 9, 12–13, 144–68, 202, 205
  China relations 148–9, 150–2, 156
  economy 27, 152
  foreign policy 144, 145, 149–57
  military 153, 155
  nuclear capacity 160
  pole of international politics 27
  politics 46, 152, 153, 155, 158
  Soviet relations 150
  UK relations 150, 182
  US alliance 150, 151, 152–3, 154, 155, 156, 157, 158
  US military bases 150, 155

Kashmir 48, 51, 53, 57
Koizumi, Jun'ichirō 154–5
Korean War 150, 151
Kosovo 29, 52
Kuwait 50, 51, 152

Latin America 22, 28, 75, 201

Middle East 70, 112, 183, 202
military
  arms race 51, 123, 129, 183
  expenditure 71, 83
  naval 33, 104, 171, 173, 182, 184, 185, 187, 190n.14
  power 3–4, 24, 30, 51, 52, 69–70, 71, 84, 97, 98, 104–5, 112, 121, 125, 129, 130, 132, 133, 134, 142n.89, 175, 185, 198, 199–200, 205
  technology 49, 51, 122, 127–34, 142n.92
  see also under individual country
Modi, Narendra 10, 55, 56, 57
multilateral groupings 6, 7, 8, 11, 24, 95
multilateralism 11, 55, 66, 81, 95, 99, 102, 104, 154
multipolarisation 9, 23–34, 36n.30, 146–7, 157–60, 197
  see also definitions/perceptions of polarity/multipolarity

Nehru, Jawaharlal 10, 43–5, 46, 47, 59n.19
New Development Bank (NDB) 75, 81, 111, 112
Non-Aligned Movement (NAM) 27, 47, 60n.31
North Atlantic Treaty Organization (NATO) 49, 52, 172–3, 174, 179, 180, 181, 182, 187, 203
North Korea 142n.89, 154, 155, 202
Nuclear Non-Proliferation Treaty 49, 53
nuclear tests *see* under individual country
nuclear weapons 47, 49, 50, 51, 53, 55, 96, 154, 160, 171, 172, 181, 183, 184, 199, 202

Obama, Barack 26, 123, 125, 145

Pakistan 47, 48, 49, 51, 53, 57, 154
polarity *see* definitions/different perceptions of polarity/multipolarity
  see also multipolarisation; power(s)
politics *see* under individual country

power(s)
balancing 3, 7, 28, 29, 42, 44, 46, 49, 53, 54, 85, 98–9, 103, 104–5, 125, 133, 135, 146, 157, 182, 188, 201, 203
concert of 98–9, 104
defining 5, 198–202
non-state entities as poles 6, 8, 76–8, 81, 97, 122, 133
regional 25, 72, 76, 98, 200–2
relations 1, 3, 26, 32, 185, 203, 204
soft 3, 4, 55, 97, 98, 104, 106, 186
status 5, 7, 8, 9, 10, 13, 68, 71, 78, 84, 178, 179, 196, 199, 201, 208n.11
see also military, power
Putin, Vladimir 26, 31, 56, 94, 102, 105

racism 44, 46, 52, 99
realism 44, 48, 55, 66, 69, 72–4, 80, 84, 86, 93n.75, 126, 158
regionalisation 11, 98, 99, 108–12
resources/capabilities 5, 15n.13, 24, 43, 45, 48, 83, 86, 108, 131, 133, 134, 136n.7, 173, 177–8, 186, 197, 198–200, 205
Rousseff, Dilma 69, 75, 80
Russia 8, 11, 23, 24, 25, 29, 32, 56, 94–118, 193n.65, 201
artificial intelligence (AI)/technologies 127, 128, 129, 132, 138n.44
China relations 26, 112, 204
currency zones proposal 111–12
economy 69, 70, 173, 180, 187
foreign policy 11, 54, 70, 94, 102, 105, 108, 109, 112, 172
military power 70, 71, 104–5, 108, 127, 128, 138n.44, 180–2
nuclear issues 71
politics 69, 103, 107–8, 110
state sovereignty 105–8, 109
trading partners 110, 111
Turkey relations 204
US relations 126, 127
see also BRICS; Soviet Union

Second World War 94, 95, 124, 146, 149, 151
security, national/international 44, 46, 48, 51, 53, 55, 104, 106, 112, 121–43, 149, 150, 153, 154–7, 170, 171, 174–6, 177, 178–9, 181, 182, 186, 205
cybersecurity 71, 129, 130
Munich Security Conference 94
Quadrilateral Security Dialogue (Quad) 157, 160
role of AI 127–9
Shanghai Cooperation Organisation (SCO) 11, 25, 112
Singapore 133, 142n.89, 182
South Africa 8, 27, 46, 66, 69, 70, 75, 80, 110, 201
see also BRICS
South China Sea 31, 70, 112, 127, 156, 182
South Korea 133, 142n.89, 156
Soviet Union 2, 22, 23, 42, 46, 49, 96, 202
China relations 149, 150, 151
collapse/dissolution 51, 97, 103, 154, 170, 173
economy 170, 189n.4, 190n.24
Japan relations 150
military power 51, 96, 170
treaty with India 49, 50, 51
US relations 150
see also Russia
Sputnik moment 123, 128, 129–32
superpowers 23, 32, 46, 47, 48, 52, 67, 128, 134, 152, 158, 169, 172, 176, 178, 183, 199, 200, 203
Syria 112, 173

Taiwan Straits 127, 148, 154, 183
technology 24, 48, 49, 50, 51, 53, 108, 173, 198, 199
artificial intelligence (AI) 12, 121–43
emerging 122, 131, 137n.14
robotics 122, 128, 131, 133, 142n.90
terrorism 53, 68, 155, 172, 175, 176
Trump, Donald 13, 104, 124, 126, 131, 145, 158–9, 182

Ukraine 109, 127, 172, 174, 180
United Kingdom 46, 169–95
  Brexit 7, 24, 186, 188
  China relations 182–3, 188
  counter-insurgency (COIN) campaigns 171, 172, 174, 185
  economy 169, 185, 188
  foreign policy 170, 174, 175, 188
  Japan relations 150, 182
  military power 142n.89, 169, 170–2, 174–5, 177–8, 180, 182, 184–5, 187, 190n.14
  Modernising Defence Programme (MDP) 174–5, 176
  obsession with greatness/power status 13, 169, 177–80, 186, 187–8, 192–3n.51
  politics 169, 180, 187
  Russian use of nerve agent in Salisbury 175
  strategic defence and security reviews (SDSRs) 171, 174, 175, 178, 179, 190n.14
  US alliance 170, 171, 172, 177, 178–9, 181, 182, 185, 190n.16
United Nations 44, 45, 46, 47, 49, 52, 107, 153, 154, 171, 189n.8
United Nations General Assembly (UNGA) 10, 22, 65, 76, 77, 79
United Nations Security Council (UNSC) 29, 47, 50, 68, 80, 88n.15, 96, 153, 157
United States 23, 46, 107
  9/11 (11 September 2001) 29, 68, 170, 172, 189n.8
  allies 9, 48, 51, 170, 172, 177
  artificial intelligence technologies 121–43
  bipolarity with China 12, 30, 33, 86, 123, 124, 186
  China relations 24, 26, 121, 126, 134, 147, 150, 151
  Chinese investment in Silicon Valley 130, 140n.65
  economy 70, 78
  foreign policy 3, 10, 13, 49, 104, 124, 125, 126, 170, 172
  India relations 46, 53, 54, 55, 204
  Japan alliance 150, 151, 152–3, 154, 155, 156, 157, 158
  military aid 48, 49
  military power 3, 22, 51, 70, 71, 83, 85, 104–5, 112, 123, 124, 125, 127–9, 131, 150, 173, 180, 183, 184
  politics 30, 49, 126
  power decline 12, 23, 31, 56, 113, 122, 123–6, 133, 137n.28, 145, 155, 159, 173, 181, 187
  Russia relations 126, 127
  Soviet relations 150
  technological leadership 126, 128, 130, 140n.62
  UK alliance 170, 171, 172, 177, 178–9, 181, 182, 185, 190n.16
  unipolarity 3, 9, 12, 26, 28, 31, 32, 42, 51, 52, 56, 67, 76, 85, 96, 97, 112, 121, 123–6, 127, 144, 147–8, 154, 156, 158, 169, 173, 177, 178, 180, 181, 182, 183–4, 185, 187
  war on terror 68, 124, 154, 155, 170, 185

Vietnam 49, 110, 190n.16

world order
  models 95–9
  rules-based international order 12, 56, 157, 174, 178, 179, 182–3, 193n.58
World Trade Organization (WTO) 80, 111
  Doha Round 53, 68, 88n.15

Xi Jinping 26, 31, 33, 56, 126, 130, 131

Yoshida, Shigeru 149–50, 151, 152, 153

EU authorised representative for GPSR:
Easy Access System Europe, Mustamäe tee 50,
10621 Tallinn, Estonia
gpsr.requests@easproject.com

www.ingramcontent.com/pod-product-compliance
Ingram Content Group UK Ltd.
Pitfield, Milton Keynes, MK11 3LW, UK
UKHW021010120926
8556IPUK00029B/451
9781526159373